Representing Women

INTERPLAY

THEORY ARTS HISTORY

Representing Women

Linda Nochlin

With 170 illustrations Thames and Hudson

To Dick, in loving memory

ACKNOWLEDGMENTS

Among the many people who have assisted me, both
intellectually and materially, in the course of writing this
book are Tamar Garb, Marni Kessler, Elizabeth Marcus,
Ellen McBreen, Edward Powers, Maura Reilly, Robert Simon,
and Abigail Solomon-Godeau.

First published in paperback in the United States of America
in 1999 by Thames and Hudson Inc., 500 Fifth Avenue,
New York, New York 10110

Library of Congress Catalog Card Number 98-61187
ISBN 0-500-28098-3

Printed and bound in Singapore

Contents

Part One: Against Methodology

Putting "woman" in her place

The essays in this volume consider a variety of subjects, ranging over a fairly long period–the late eighteenth century to the early twentieth– and represent a variety of approaches to art and art history. What brings them together is their subject matter: each is concerned with the representation of women in artworks from this period. As I state in the first essay, "woman...cannot be seen as a fixed, pre-existing entity or frozen 'image,' transformed by this or that historical circumstance, but as a complex, mercurial and problematic signifier, mixed in its messages, resisting fixed interpretation or positioning despite the numerous attempts made in visual representation literally to put 'woman' in her place. Like the woman warrior, the term 'woman' fights back, and resists attempts to subdue its meaning or reduce it to some simple essence, universal, natural, and above all, unproblematic." So the fact that each chapter deals with the representation of women says very little about the specificity of each essay. In some, the concern is for a specific issue involving such representation, and includes a wide range of artists and works; in others, a single artist–in one case, a woman artist– is considered; in other essays, a single work comes under scrutiny, and in at least two cases, very different in date, subject and structure, I examine a rhetorical device, allegory, insofar as it concerns the representation of women. Despite the feminist position that underlies all the texts in this book, it cannot be said that they demonstrate a single methodological approach. But, paradoxically, nor would I describe my work as eclectic.

I should like to clarify, or at least attempt to unpack, the implications of the rather provocative titles of this introduction by explaining what I mean by being "against methodology" and an "ad hoc art historian." I will begin, out of honesty, not self-indulgence, with a little

1 EDGAR DEGAS Woman with a Lorgnette (detail), c. 1865

personal intellectual history. I will then examine some relevant theoretical issues, and try to fix the genesis and the specificity of my approach in each chapter of this book in terms of inspiration, date, circumstance and so forth.

Methodology: Aesthetics and Experience

In my first undergraduate year at Vassar College in 1947–48, I was introduced to a rudimentary methodology in a history class; it has stood me in good stead ever since. The practical aspect of "doing" history was subsumed under a research procedure called the "note-topic." You decided on the topic of your research—or it was assigned to you—and then you went out and bought note-topic cards, dividers and a box. As you did your research, you consigned each of your notes to the appropriate section of your box, first identifying it with a specifying title. At the end of this process, you wrote an introduction, which set up a hypothesis or at least a founding generalization of some sort, and then, on the basis of the information duly gathered and collated, a conclusion. I do not wish to denigrate the "note-topic" approach, especially its central part, the research: I freely admit that my heart still beats faster when I enter an archive and my hand touches a page that was touched by Courbet or a piece of the creamy vellum on which Valenciennes inscribed his thoughts on landscape and perspective, or, best of all, when I come upon a painting I have only known before through reproduction but can now scrutinize face to face. As a methodology, the "note-topic" was nearly flawless, and practically foolproof, at least in the highly empirical terms which its practice inscribed. By means of it—and by dint of getting up at six o'clock every morning for a month and working until eight in the evening—I produced a prize-winning paper, a study of Beatrice Webb and Fabian socialism. My essay asked, "Why would a woman, born to every privilege, dedicate her life to socialism and eventually become a convinced communist?" and aimed to answer this question, on the basis of a great deal of historical and biographical evidence, arranged in a logical sequence and contextualized within the matrix of British social history. Although perhaps I didn't realize at the time, it was what one might call a feminist, or at least a proto-feminist, essay, predicting a much later but major direction of my scholarly work. Elegant, certain to produce effective results, fixed in its form yet flexible and commodious in its structure, allaying natural feelings of anxiety with its lovely, shapely certitude, the "note-topic" procedure was certainly aesthetic in the broadest sense of the term. It glowed with a certain down-to-earth, common-sense intellectual beauty.

With the prize money I received for the essay under the note-topics' benign tutelage, I bought a bicycle and took a summer trip to England where I encountered the other member of the dyad which determined the course of my academic career: experience.

By "experience" I do not mean being groped on a crowded railway car by some sailors with whom my friend and I had to share a compartment (this was 1948 and the services were much in evidence); nor do I mean barking at flocks of sheep to see them run as I pedalled up hills in South Wales in the rain, although the beautiful, wave-like pattern of their retreat should in any case be chalked up to aesthetics rather than experience; nor do I mean the romance of staying in a room made roofless by a bombing raid, so that I could look up at the stars from my bed in the heart of London and ponder eternity. No, what I mean by "experience" was the growing sense at once of alienation and difference, that realization of identity which one gets only when one has left the shelter of familiar scenes and ways and is cast out into the wilderness of an uncaring world. I could only discover who I was away from home. Far from the comfort of my native New York and the support of friends and family, I gradually realized who and what I was, if only by negation: I was not English, despite my immersion in Anglo-American culture; I was a Jew from Brooklyn. Out of this experience came aesthetics: a poem—not bad for a seventeen year old, published by the then quite liberal *Commentary Magazine*—entitled "At Merton College, Oxford." It began: "By Merton's darkening walls I sat/Brushed by the fall of summer's rain/Feeling the Eternal Jew/Homunculus, starting in my veins..."; it ended, rather pessimistically, by decrying the hope of unity raised by the end of the war, perhaps, among Jews, particularly by the founding of the State of Israel: "Destruction's sheltering touch at last/In passive union binds all men/Still the deceptive tongue of brass/Jerusalem shall not rise again." Here was another topic that has haunted my later work: the issue of identity, of ethnicity, and of their representation, be it of women, of "Orientals" or of blacks. My awakening to these issues found various outlets: an article entitled "The Imaginary Orient"; two lectures in 1987, one on late nineteenth-century North-African anthropological photographs in the Budgett Meakin Collection of the Royal Anthropological Society, the other on the visual and verbal representation of the Sepoy Mutiny presented at a meeting of the College Art Association; and an interest in the Jews, starting with a long article on Degas and the Dreyfus Affair in 1987 and culminating in a book of commissioned essays, *The Jew in the Text*, edited by Tamar Garb and myself, with introductory essays by us both, in 1995.

In professing myself to be against methodology I am neither taking an anti-theoretical stance nor advocating an unthinking empiricism, neither decrying bold speculation nor advocating the benefits of a naive lack of self-consciousness about what one is doing and the position from which one is doing it—what I would call the "just go ahead and do it" school of art history. What I am questioning is the possibility of a single methodology—empirical, theoretical, or both, or neither—which is guaranteed to work in every case, a kind of methodological Vaseline which lubricates an entry into the problem and ensures a smooth, perfect outcome every time. Nor, in declaring myself to be an "ad hoc" art historian, am I advocating a user-friendly eclecticism. In my experience, which has shaped this strongly held opinion, each concrete art-historical issue, problem or situation demands a different set of strategies. Some of these develop out of working on the issues themselves, a constant process or dialectic between object and method; and certainly, in my case, commitment, be it political or aesthetic, is not only not identical with narrowly defined methodology but, on the contrary, demands flexibility.

For someone who holds this view, what underlies and binds each instance of my work is a sense of moral and ethical commitment, combined, perhaps surprisingly, with a highly developed sense of play and a deep, and often contradictory, love of the sheer visual seductiveness of some kinds of art and the adventurous refusal of conventional formal value of others: the undeniable pleasures of the visual text. What single methodology could ever cope with such disparate elements? I like Claude Lévi-Strauss's concept of "bricolage"—constructing your method as you go along to suit the needs of the material and the evolving argument and, in turn, examining the material in the light of the argument so constructed; or what Clifford Geertz, another anthropologist, has called "zigging and zagging" between alternatives. The Greek locution Τὰ μέν δέ...Τὰ ἄλλα δέ (roughly translated "on the one hand...on the other hand" but more indicative of a process of movement between seeming opposites, a locution much used by Plato in the Socratic dialogues) conveys something of my argumentative spirit, but it may also come from an atavistic memory of generations of disputatious rabbis. Although I subscribe to the dialectic between object and method of investigation, I do not pretend to anything as complex as dialectical thought, much less dialectical materialism, despite my deep admiration for the work of Walter Benjamin, Theodor Adorno and Ernst Bloch from all of whom I have learned a great deal.

Such an ad hoc "methodology," if I may contradict myself and call it that, came in very handy in the challenging enterprise of constructing a feminist art history in the early 1970s, as I describe it, through personal experience, in the second part of this Introduction. This enterprise involved combining conventional art-historical methods—i.e. formal analysis and iconography—with social history, Marxist critique and critical theory; existentialism, mainly via Simone de Beauvoir; phenomenology; and sociology, as well as the linguistic philosophy on which I had teethed as a philosophy major at college. Original work (and thought), is invariably attained in dialogue with already existing work. If, in this sense, painting is about painting and writing about writing, so scholarship and interpretation are about previous scholarship and interpretation—as paradigm, critique, or perhaps most potently as causes for an "anxiety of influence." Work that I dislike or find antipathetic, if it is intelligent, is often extremely useful. Working up an argument against a forcefully articulated antithetical position builds up intellectual muscle, forces one to think harder, to look further afield for supporting evidence. Rage, although it can be blinding, can also illuminate. "The tigers of wrath are wiser than the horses of instruction," wrote Blake, and he is right, sometimes.

Not only social history, linguistic analysis and literary criticism, but psychoanalytic theory as well, in all its varieties, mainly the French ones—often filtered through the perspective of sophisticated British feminists like Jacqueline Rose and Juliet Mitchell, or film theorists like Laura Mulvey—came into play in my career as an ad hoc art historian, most overtly in my analysis of Courbet's *The Painter's Studio* in the form of a catalogue essay for the "Courbet Reconsidered" exhibition (curated by Sarah Faunce and myself at the Brooklyn Museum in 1988). The first half of this long piece is devoted to a reinterpretation of the "real" allegory in the light of Walter Benjamin's early *The Origin of German Tragic Drama*, while in the second I attempt to "read" the painting as a woman, and to reverse the pictorial power relations of the vast canvas with the help of some textual appropriations from Julia Kristeva, among others. Psychoanalytic theory seems to me invaluable in revealing the ever-present work of the unconscious in the business of both representation and interpretation, as well as accounting for the persistence of stereotypical gender roles, power and position within the discursive and social frameworks in which art is produced.

Issues and Approaches

I should now like to turn briefly to some of the issues and subjects with which I deal in this book, and to explain something of the circumstances of their birth. In many cases, they were children of circumstance: someone asked me to participate in a particular symposium, to contribute to a catalogue or to write an article for a journal on the occasion of a particular exhibition. I have never thought any the less of J. S. Bach, my favorite composer, because almost his entire output was commissioned! Some of these essays, like "Géricault: The Absence of Women" (originally presented as a lecture at the symposium on the artist at the Louvre in 1991), came to me quickly: in fact, I thought of the title in the course of a long-distance phone-call from Paris; others, like "Courbet's Real Allegory: Rereading *The Painter's Studio*," developed over the course of many years, descending ultimately indeed from the initial work on my doctoral dissertation in the mid-1950s. This ongoing work on Courbet was revised and critically rethought during a stay at the Institute for Advanced Studies at Princeton in 1985. Most of these chapters were written after the publication of a previous volume of essays, *Women, Art, and Power and Other Essays* but some predate this volume and some are contemporary with it. I rarely revise or "correct" previous essays. It makes better sense to write something new if one has new ways of thinking about a subject and to preserve an old text's integrity as a testimony to what one thought, and above all, how one articulated one's thoughts, at the time it was written.

A certain consistency of thematic engagement—identity, absence, marginality, opposition—recurs throughout the seven essays contained in this volume. If my methodology is ad hoc, my approaches to the problems I tackle are anything but random. It sometimes seems to me that fate, as much as free choice, determines what I am going to think about—and a good thing, too, in the end. Often, the most unlikely subject will stimulate the most interesting ways of thinking.

In the first essay in this volume, "The Myth of the Woman Warrior" (first presented as a lecture at the Courtauld Institute of Art in London in 1989) the emphasis was quite literally on "'the *case* of the woman warrior'—the most extreme exemplar of a feminine being as independent agent of her own destiny—conceived of as a problem rather than an image, a visual oxymoron in need of analysis." The subject is constructed and the essay itself is synthetic rather than analytic: a putting-together of various instances, and in some cases counter-instances, of the visual representation of the powerful, fighting, active woman in various historical circumstances. Indeed, I recycled an essay dealing with Delacroix's and Daumier's images of Liberty and the Republic, "Gender Advertisements in Nineteenth-Century Political Allegory" (originally presented at the College Art Association in 1981, and then, in a different format, at the International Association of Art Historians meeting in Strasbourg in 1989) as an appropriate final section for this investigation of the representation of the powerful woman. I was just as interested in how the terms "woman" and "women" were to be understood under certain historical conditions as I was in collecting instances of the woman warrior throughout the ages; how the unlikely conjunction of female sex and fighting spirit is rationalized or, more usually, made to appear perverse or villainous through a variety of visual strategies, often re-created with variations over time. The emphasis is on the thematization of this relatively rare trope rather than on content: the way in which the physical evidence sets up its own tension with a given hypothesis.

The second essay in the collection demands a rather different approach, since it deals with a single artist rather than a series of "case studies" on a single theme, and with an issue of absence rather than presence. In this case, I found my path prepared for me by Géricault's earliest biographer, Charles Clément. It is hard to think of women, or a place for women, in Géricault's work, and when we do, we come up with a model of abjection and marginalization: a child, a cripple, two madwomen, a corpse, and perhaps a portrait or two. Even in cases where the representation of woman might originally have figured, or, even more, occupied a central place in the signifying structure of a painting, it is ultimately omitted. I take as my major example Géricault's most ambitious painting, *The Raft of the Medusa*, which bears witness to this striking occlusion of the feminine in the earliest stages of Géricault's development of his subject. Despite the absence of women in his *œuvre*, the *signs* of femininity and the feminine—in the form of the castrated (or otherwise marginalized or disempowered) male body—abound in Géricault's work. It is simply that these signs of the feminine have been detached from the representation of the actual bodies of women. To paraphrase the title of a recent, important book by the cultural critic, Tania Modleski, what we have here is "femininity without women." By restricting the representation of the female nude to the realm of the private and by investing his erotica with such palpitating directness and energy, Géricault left himself with no place to go in terms of public exhibition: hence his strangely reduced, marginal production of this subject. Yet this nineteenth-century artist who most overtly occluded "woman" from his production was also the one to body her forth without pretext as an active, sexual being.

Paradox—the establishment of a seeming contradiction between works or situations—is one of my preferred strategies in constructing an argument or deconstructing an art historical "given." In the sixth essay, concerning Cassatt (originally presented as the Rubin Memorial Lecture at the Metropolitan Museum of Art in 1995), I start with a lengthy formal and iconographic analysis, comparing Cassatt's portrait of Mrs. Riddle (*Lady at a Tea Table* [fig. 107]) with portraits by Sargent, Van Gogh, Degas and Cézanne, while at the same time attempting to place the subject within the conflicted context of "women's greatest art as the creation of atmospheres," a context provided by the great and little-known novelist, Dorothy Richardson, a contemporary of Virginia Woolf. Cassatt's portraits, and indeed her whole *œuvre*, at once demonstrate the prevalence of the notion of women's "separate spheres" of activity at the same time as problematizing the woman artist as the "authentic" voice of women. Both Cassatt's life and her art bring out the complex inter-action which existed historically between woman as ideal construction (particularly the way in which the maternal role was seen as essential and predestined), and the way women were themselves "constructed" and constructed femininities as social and psychological beings. In "Mary Cassatt's Modernity," I have tried to show how Cassatt the artist went far beyond the restrictions placed on both ambition and achieve-ment in the construction of the ideal woman of her time.

Paradox is again the framing strategy in the essay on Degas, "A House is not a Home: Degas and the Subversion of the Family" (orig-inally written for the Liverpool conference on Degas organized in 1989 by Richard Kendall and Griselda Pollock around an exhibition of Degas's representations of women curated by Richard Kendall). I had noticed, as have many art historians before and since, that Degas's family portraits, starting with the great *Bellelli Family* (fig. 88), often represented the members of the family isolated from each other pictorially, physically and psychologically. (This sense of tension and isolation was, of course, true not only of family portraits, but of other group compositions of Degas's early period, including *Young Spartans* [fig. 89], *Sulking*, and *Interior* [fig. 90].) How striking it was then to find that it is mainly in his brothel scenes that Degas, in a work like *The Name Day of the Madam* (fig. 96), creates an image of family "warmth" and "togetherness," which, it is true, is parodic—ironic certainly, but warm nevertheless. "The whole brothel setting", I argue, "with the naked girls pressed together, proffering both their sexual charms and their congratulatory bouquet, creates a sense of family values displaced: the house is certainly a home in terms of warmth, of the pressing together of bodies in a fleshly intimacy impossible to the chilly decorum governing the behavior of a 'real' bourgeois family like the Bellellis..." The concept of the family itself was of course in considerable disarray, beset with paradox, and far from being a fixed, known entity in the mid-nineteenth century. Rather, like woman, it was a social and cultural formation in the process of construction. What had begun as a surprising visual discovery—the hindquarters of a small dog at the right-hand margin of *The Bellelli Family*—ended up by becoming a substantial investigation of the problematic situation of the French family in the middle of the last century.

The range of the essays itself exemplifies the multiplicity of the category "woman" and strives to de-essentialize it. The rural and urban worker in "The Image of the Working Woman" (a lecture prepared for the Minneapolis Art Institute in 1978); the upper-class lady in the Cassatt essay; the female nude, a category which can itself be subdivided into categories, such as the bather, the prostitute, the goddess, or, in the case of Seurat's *Poseuses* or Courbet's admiring nude female, the studio model: all these representational types exemplify the multiplicity of the category "woman" itself.

In the two-part essay on Courbet, originally published in the catalogue of the Brooklyn Museum exhibition of 1988, "Courbet Reconsidered," I deliberately appropriate the artist's great allegorical statement of purpose and identity, *The Painter's Studio*, for polemical purposes. I make my strategy in this text explicit from the beginning, and my "methodology" here is hardly that of traditional art history, whether formalist or iconographic. Both parts of this essay, "Courbet's Real Allegory: Rereading *The Painter's Studio*," concern themselves with the issue of gender in nineteenth-century painting, Part Two more particularly. My "methodology" in both—in the first part, in which I am engaged with allegory and its strategies, and in the second, where I zoom in on gender and its representation more explicitly—is extremely free-wheeling. "Je fais penser les pierres," Courbet is said to have declared on one occasion. In these *Studio* essays, I in turn attempt to "make the painting think," as it were, making my position of authorial authority clear from the outset, or, to put it another way, citing the epigraph I borrowed from Jane Gallup, speaking from "the position of authority, in a way that exposes the illusions of that position without renouncing it..." Although the "methodology" of these pieces might be described as ad hoc in the extreme, the political nature of the project is far from ad hoc because there is a pre-existing ethical issue at stake which lies at the heart of the undertaking: the issue of women and their representation in visual art. I use what I need, and construct what will make my case: painting at the service of polemics, polemics in the service of revealing what was hitherto invisible within the structure of the painting. I try to make the painting speak for good cause, in full awareness of the tension that these approaches create around the category of "woman" itself.

"And will you never finish that Great Book?" my father used to ask me: the complete volume, preferably a monograph in hard cover, authoritative, authoritarian, magisterial, with a clear beginning, middle and end, methodologically consistent, the final word. Well frankly, no; thanks a lot, but no thanks. Even when I finish *the* book—*Bathtime*, for instance, a study of bathing practice and representation in the later nineteenth century, or a projected volume on the modern portrait—it will still be a collection of essays rather than a continuous narrative. I don't feel at ease with closure, with establishing connections, with setting down the truth with methodological consistency: it's too phallic, too redolent of the old man with the beard giving us the word from the mountain top, engraved in stone. I prefer, or feel compelled, to teeter around on the high heels of ad hoc-istry, bricolaging my arguments, appropriating my paradigms, stumbling blithely from intellectual flower to flower. I find depth, or the pretention to it, suspect. Give me surfaces and lots of them: facets, not deep pools of profound meaning. Rather than apologizing for my inconsistencies, such as they are, I see them as a major source of strength, as is my lack of a single methodology. Indeed, when I am tempted to make some broad generalization—about my work or anything else—I take a deep breath and wait until the temptation passes. And with just such a (metaphorical) deep breath, I will end this first part of the introduction, thereby avoiding the grand finale and remaining unabashedly ad hoc to the end.

Part Two: Starting from Scratch

In 1969, three major events occurred in my life: I had a baby, I became a feminist, and I organized the first class in Women and Art at Vassar College. All these events were in some way interconnected. Having the baby—my second daughter—at the beginning of the Women's Liberation Movement gave me a very different view of motherhood from the one I had had back in the mid-1950s when my first child was born; feminism created a momentous change in both my personal life and my intellectual outlook; and organizing that first class in feminist art history irrevocably altered my view of the discipline and my place in it, so that all my future work was touched by this first moment of insight and revision.

It is hard to recapture the sheer exhilaration of that historical moment, harder, perhaps, to remember the concrete details of a conversion experience which, for many women of my age and position, was rather like the conversion of St. Paul on the road to Damascus: a conviction that before, I had been blind; now I had seen the light. In my case, the light had been provided by an acquaintance who, shortly after my return from a year in Italy with husband and baby to my familiar job in Vassar's art history department, showed up in my apartment with a briefcase full of polemical literature. "Have you heard about Women's Liberation?" she asked me. I admitted that I hadn't—political activity in Italy, although vigorous, had not been noteworthy for its feminist component—but that in my case it was unnecessary. I already was, I said, a liberated woman and I knew enough about feminism—suffragettes and such—to realize that, in 1969, we were beyond such things. "Read these," she said brusquely, "and you'll change your mind." So saying, she thrust her hand into her bulging briefcase and brought forth a heap of roughly printed, crudely illustrated journals on coarse paper. The pile included, I remember, *Redstockings Newsletter*, *Off Our Backs*, *Everywoman* and many others, including special editions of radical newsheets run by men which angry women had taken over for the explicit purpose of examining the conditions of their exploitation. I started reading and couldn't stop: this had nothing to do with old-fashioned ideas about getting the vote for women and getting men out of the Saloons. This was brilliant, furious, polemical stuff, written from the guts and the heart, questioning not just the entire position of women in the contemporary New Left and anti-Vietnam movements (subordinate, exploited, sexually objectified) but the position of women within society in general. And these articles— which touched on every area in which women were involved, from repression in the workplace to oppression at home, from art-production to housework—were above all striking in their assertion that the personal was political, and that politics, where sex-roles and gender were concerned, began with the personal. That night, reading until 2 A.M., making discovery after discovery, with cartoonish lightbulbs going off in my head at a frantic pace, my consciousness was indeed raised, as it was to be over and over again within the course of the next year or so. Or perhaps the best figure of speech would be a spatial one: it was as though I kept opening doors in an endless series of bright rooms, each opening off from the next, each promising a new revelation, each moving me forward from a known space to a larger, lighter, unknown one.

Some time later, after a certain amount of thought but not much specific research apart from a thorough rereading of Simone de Beauvoir, I posted the following notice on the bulletin board of the art history office at Vassar:

Art 364b

25 November 1969

I am changing the subject of the Art 364b seminar to:
The Image of Women in the Nineteenth and Twentieth Centuries.
I have become more and more involved in the problem of the
position of women during the course of this year and think it
would make a most interesting and innovative seminar topic,
involving materials from a variety of fields not generally included
in art-historical research. This would be a pioneering study in an
untouched field. Among areas to be included might be:
1. Woman as angel and devil in nineteenth-century art.
2. The concept of the nude through history with special
    emphasis on the nineteenth and twentieth centuries.
    (Anatomy; must a nude be a female? What is shown
    and what is not shown.)
3. Pornography and sexual imagery.
4. The social significance of costume.
5. Social realities and artistic myths (i.e. women working
    in factories and the *Birth of Venus* in the Salons).
6. Advertising imagery of women.
7. The theme of the prostitute.
8. The Holy Family and the joys of domesticity (imagery of
    the secular family as nexus of value in bourgeois art in the
    nineteenth century).
9. Socially conscious representations of lower-class women
    (almost always in "low" art rather than "high").
10. Freudian mythology in modern art; Picasso and Surrealism.
11. Matisse and the "harem" concept of women.
12. Women as artists.
13. The Vampire woman in art and literature (in relation to
    social, psychological and economic factors).
14. Women in Pre-Raphaelite painting and Victorian literature.

Most of this territory—and a great deal more—has never been touched. It would involve work in history, sociology, psychology, literature, etc.

Linda Nochlin Pommer

Looking back over a quarter of a century, I am struck by the remarkable combination of ambition and naiveté characterizing that project. Did I really think we could cover all those topics in the course of a single semester? Why did I confine "women as artists" to a single class? (Actually, there were several sessions on women artists in the class as it was taught.) And why was I so fixated on the Vampire woman? Alas, since I have never kept a diary and only minimal documentation of that first seminar remains in my keeping, I cannot answer specific questions about what I had in mind. My fuzziness about these issues is a poignant reminder to historians about the unreliability of witness accounts, especially when the witness is the historian in question. Nevertheless, I am struck by the fact that many of these topics have continued to be of major importance to feminist art historians and critics, and, equally, that they have served as the basis for much of my own work in the years since. Even more amazingly, we did, as a class, "cover" all these issues and more, admittedly not with the nuance and wealth of information which have marked subsequent efforts in these areas, but with a lot of passion, a sense of discovery and with the knowledge that whatever we did counted; for everything, quite literally, remained to be done. We were doing the spadework of feminist art history, and we knew it.

I say "we" because, in this undergraduate seminar, we were "we": a committed group of proto-feminist researchers tracking down the basic materials of our embryonic discipline. Although as teacher of the group I was responsible for directing the inquiry, I was in many ways as ignorant as my students: everything had to be constructed from the beginning. We were both inventors and explorers: inventors of hypotheses and concepts, navigating the vast sea of undiscovered bibliographical material, the underground rivers and streams of women's art and the representation of women. As far as bibliography was concerned, the reading list had to be constructed as we went along. There were no textbooks, no histories of women artists, no brilliantly theorized examinations of the representation of prostitution, no well-illustrated analyses of pornography from a feminist point of view. The concept of the gaze insofar as it related to the visual representation of women had yet to be articulated. Yes, to be sure, there were some outdated and rather patronizing "histories" of women artists like Walter Shaw

Sparrow's *Women Painters of the World* (1905); interesting because of its sheer anachronism, it served as raw material for analysis rather than as valid documentation. For raw information, not always accurate, about the nineteenth century and earlier, there were Mrs. Elizabeth Ellet's *Women Artists in All Ages and Countries* (1858); Clara Erskine Clement's *Women in the Fine Arts* (1904); and Ellen C. Clayton's two-volume *English Female Artists* (1867). None of these was illustrated. And luckily for us, since Vassar had been a women's college, there was a rich repository of materials on individual women and their achievements in the arts as well as in other areas, and a great deal of material about the social position and the problems of women historically. Vassar had had a feminist, as well as a purely feminine history, although this aspect of its past was decidedly low-key during the 1950s and 1960s, especially since, at the very moment when the Women's Liberation Movement was getting off the ground, the college itself was switching from being a single-sex institution to a co-educational one.

Yet in a certain sense, given the specific nature of my own experience of Vassar, where I had been a student (class of '51) and teacher for many years by the time I taught my first class in women and art, I had always been a feminist, albeit a partly subconscious and often confused one. Certainly, I believed that I was as intelligent and capable as most of the men I knew, although I was constantly riven by the self-doubts and pangs of guilt that afflicted smart and ambitious women in those days. Like most intellectual women in the 1950s and 1960s, I thought my problems were my own, unique, the products of neurosis or disorganization, not social problems afflicting all women of my sort. Neurosis, not the double message of high achievement coupled with sacrifice of self for husband and family conveyed to intelligent women by the ideological structures controlling gendered behavior, was the reason we were so mixed up, I thought, so often incapable of focussing on intellectual work without pain and conflict. I was exhausted so often, I believed, because I wasn't well organized enough to juggle housework (admittedly only rudimentary, but necessary nevertheless), childcare, husband, teaching and graduate studies while also commuting from Poughkeepsie to New York, part-time. My graduate "program" consisted of whatever was given at the Institute of Fine Arts on Wednesday afternoons and Saturday mornings. If I couldn't manage such a full life (which also included poetry-writing, parties, taking in vanguard dance and theater in New York and playing the recorder with an ancient music group) with sufficient calm and expertise, I felt it was because I somehow hadn't figured things out properly, not because I was doing so many things without a support system to give me a sense that I was entitled to do them. Organized childcare was non-existent and women were supposed to run the household single-handed even if they were professionals. If I had to correct papers, I felt guilty about not doing research for a seminar report in graduate school; if I worked on the seminar report, I felt haunted by neglected shopping; if I shopped, I felt I wasn't paying enough attention to my child.

Yet, at the same time, my Vassar education and my years of teaching gifted women there had given me a profound sense of what women could do, even if they weren't encouraged to do much but charitable work and childcare after graduation. My own work was respected and rewarded, my energy and passionate commitment admired. And in some ways, I had always been interested in the achievements, and problems, of talented women. After all, the first paper I had written in freshman history in 1948 had been about the Fabian socialist, Beatrice Webb. In my social psychology class, I had produced a "content analysis" of women's magazines, demonstrating their contradictory message about women's roles. I discovered after months of reading *Ladies' Home Journal* and *Good Housekeeping* that despite the fact that achieving women like Mrs. Roosevelt and Dorothy Thompson were featured in their high-minded articles, the fiction section told a different tale: in these emotionally charged stories, professional women were invariably punished for their ambition, and wives and mothers who dedicated themselves to husband and family were always rewarded for their sacrifice as well as winning the readers' sympathy. Then again, the head of the Vassar art history department, Agnes Rindge Claflin, had always encouraged women artists. I remember visits and gallery talks from Lauren MacIver, Irene Rice Pereira, and Grace Hartigan in the early 1950s. They were unforgettable: I thrust a poem into the hands of MacIver as a sophomore, and as a young teacher, I remember being bowled over not just by Hartigan's work, but by her tough, bohemian, unconventional persona. Work by Georgia O'Keeffe, Kay Sage, Florine Stettheimer, Veira da Silva, Agnes Martin and Joan Mitchell hung in the gallery; a lively woman sculptor, Concetta Scaravaglione, taught sculpture in the studio. Even earlier, in my teens, my mother had shared with me her enthusiasm for women writers such as Virginia Woolf, Katherine Mansfield, Rebecca West and Elinor Wylie. At Vassar, women were my teachers, respected scholars and intellectuals in their own right. While most of them were a little too tweedy and unglamorous to serve as exempla in any sphere but the academic, some, like Agnes Claflin, were elegant, worldly, sophisticated, and a bit wicked as well as brilliant—all characteristics which charmed me, and continue to do so today. All in all, I might have been called a "premature feminist" in many ways before 1969 and my discovery of Women's Liberation. And now my time had come: what I had felt, confusedly, partially, individually, had become a mass movement, passionately articulated in speeches, articles, books and meetings by ever-increasing groups of women, taking inspiration and gaining power from each other, sharing their feelings, their ideas, and their indignation.

By the time the Art 364b class got underway in January 1970, there were a few changes and additions to the course: topics became more specific and a rudimentary bibliography had come into being. The reading list was decidedly interdisciplinary and included not only Ironside and Geer's *Pre-Raphaelite Painters* (1948); Lister's *Victorian Narrative Paintings* (1966); Theodore Reff's "The Meaning of Manet's *Olympia*" (*Gazette des Beaux-Arts*, 1964); Barr's *Matisse: His Art and His Public* (1951); and Françoise Gilot's *Life with Picasso* (1964), but Gertrude Himmelfarb's *Victorian Minds* (1968); Havelock Ellis's *Studies in the Psychology of Sex* (1942); Mary Wollstonecraft's *A Vindication of the Rights of Women* (1792); and Mrs. Sarah Ellis's *The Education of Character with Hints on Moral Training* (1856). The seminar included a crash course on nineteenth- and twentieth-century cultural history, sexual ideologies and feminist, as well as feminine, notions of what constituted women's place and identity. Nor was "low" art neglected: the bibliography included C. Gibbs-Smith's *The Fashionable Lady in the Nineteenth Century* (1960); James Laver's *English Costume of the Nineteenth Century* (1958); and Emily Burbank's *Woman as Decoration* (1917), as well as several books devoted to advertising and film:

2 MERET OPPENHEIM Objet (Le Déjeuner en fourrure), 1936

3 FRIDA KAHLO The Two Fridas, 1939

E. Jones's *Those Were the Good Old Days: A Happy Look at American Advertising* (1959); L. De Vries's *Victorian Advertisements* (1969); and Alexandra Walker's pioneering *Sex in the Movies* (1966).

Although it is hard to recall the specific features of the class, much less specific students, after the passage of time and the repetition of the seminar in various forms in subsequent years, I do remember with great clarity the general air of excitement and enthusiasm that characterized each of its sessions. Students literally fought to give not merely one or two but as many as three class presentations. Discoveries were rife, especially when it came to class presentations on women artists: Frida Kahlo, then relatively little known to all but a small group of *cognoscenti*, came to light, as did Meret Oppenheim, known only as the author of the notorious *Objet* (a fur-lined teacup), but not recognized as a *woman* artist by most of the class. I remember that Donna Hunter, now an art historian at the University of California at Santa Cruz, sent away to Sweden for a recent but obscure exhibition catalogue of Oppenheim's work and revealed to us the richness, variety and marvelous nature—in the Surrealist sense—of her production. Donna has since taught courses on

4 BERTHE MORISOT The Cradle, 1872

5 PIERRE–AUGUSTE RENOIR Portrait of Mme Renoir Nursing Pierre (Maternity), 1885

art history and feminism and is now working on a project involving a gendered reading of the visual and verbal imagery of the Terror, and the martyrs of the French Revolution in particular.

Susan Casteras, one of the stars of the class, the former Curator of Paintings at the Yale Center for British Art, remembers that the "tremendous sense of intellectual excitement and expectation that was generated was quite palpable, and those in the class...all shared this unspoken and heightened awareness." This was Donna's impression, too: "What I remember most about the seminar was the atmosphere in the room, the high level of energy and enthusiasm—a buzz. Everyone was aware that this was a first: that we as women were working with a woman professor on women artists..." "In retrospect," Susan explained, "it was a feeling of vicarious empowerment and pride that particularly enthralled us—the idea that women mattered as creators of art and that their efforts, whether frustrated, failed, or successful, were worthy topics to study..." She recalls in the same letter "that several undergraduate presentations were outstanding, and the list of areas covered—demonic and angelic images of women, the concept of the nude, pornography, women workers, prostitution, harems, women artists, the vampire/ *femme fatale* and Pre-Raphaelite feminine prototypes—now reads like a prophetic list of some of the central concerns of scholars of nineteenth-century art in the last twenty years." In the case of her own work in the class, Susan Casteras, author of several important books and organizer of at least two major exhibitions about the representation of Victorian womanhood, remembers that one of her reports, "a focus on Victorian courtship imagery, proved to be the germ of my doctoral dissertation and much subsequent iconological research and writing..." Another of her presentations "concentrated on Mary Cassatt and her *Modern Woman* mural (the pendant to Mary MacMonnies's *Primitive Woman*) for the Woman's Building at the World's Columbian Exposition of 1893" (figs. 141, 142), and resulted in a long senior essay and, later, an important article. The essay, which I still have on my shelf as a reference work, is an outstanding piece of research about what was then a little-known yet major achievement of Cassatt's, lost after the exhibition.

But it was not merely the discovery of women artists and their achievements that was exciting. Looking at old themes in new ways was equally revealing. The imagery of the family, especially of mothers and children, was seen in a new light: a comparison of Mary Cassatt's *The Bath* (fig. 125) and Berthe Morisot's *The Cradle* with Renoir's *Portrait of Mme Renoir Nursing Pierre (Maternity)* revealed that it was the male

6 DOROTHEA TANNING Self-Portrait (Maternity), 1946

artist's image that was more sentimental, traditional and clichéd, the women's more emotionally distanced and avant-garde. And Dorothea Tanning's hallucinatory image of twentieth-century motherhood, *Self-Portrait (Maternity)* (fig. 6)—bleak, isolated, preternaturally silent— shredded the myth of essentialist nurture entirely, leaving it in Surrealist tatters. Work by such modernist masters as Picasso and Matisse was examined in ways that called into question the whole formalist appara- tus of art criticism and demanded a more critical view of what had formerly been seen as relatively gender-neutral territory. It was not just the iconography of works like *Les Demoiselles d'Avignon* or Matisse's harem women that was called into question, but the whole position of the female nude within Western pictorial culture itself. Why were there so few male nudes by women artists and so many female nudes by males? What did that say about power relations between the sexes, about who was permitted to look at whom? And about who was objecti- fied for whose pleasure?

These issues were pursued at greater length in the introduction I gave to a session on "Eroticism and the Image of Woman in Nineteenth- Century Art" at the College Art Association meeting in San Francisco in 1972. It was subsequently published as "Eroticism and Female Imagery in Nineteenth-Century Art" in *Woman as Sex Object*, edited by Thomas Hess and myself in the same year. It was illustrated with a now- notorious photograph of a bearded male nude coyly holding a tray of fruit at penis level, entitled *Buy My Bananas*, created as a pendant to a nineteenth-century female version of the topos called *Buy My Apples*. Today, such critiques might seem obvious, but in 1969 and 1972, when whole lectures or classes could go by without any reference to the specifically sexual qualities of nudes like Manet's *Olympia* or Goya's voluptuous *Naked Maja*, discussions of the sexual politics of paintings were anything but self-evident.

I gave the course again in the spring term of 1970, this time in con- junction with one given by Professor Elizabeth Daniels of the English Department on women in Victorian literature, incorporating three joint sessions, one on women in Pre-Raphaelite painting and Victorian litera- ture, which again bore fruit (not bananas this time!) in my own work. When I was asked to give the Walter Cook Alumni Lecture at my gradu- ate-school Alma Mater, The Institute of Fine Arts, New York, I decided on a feminist theme, incorporating both French art, which had always been my field of interest, and Victorian painting, with which I had recently become involved. The lecture, "Holman Hunt's *Awakening Conscience*: The Theme of the Fallen Woman in Nineteenth-Century

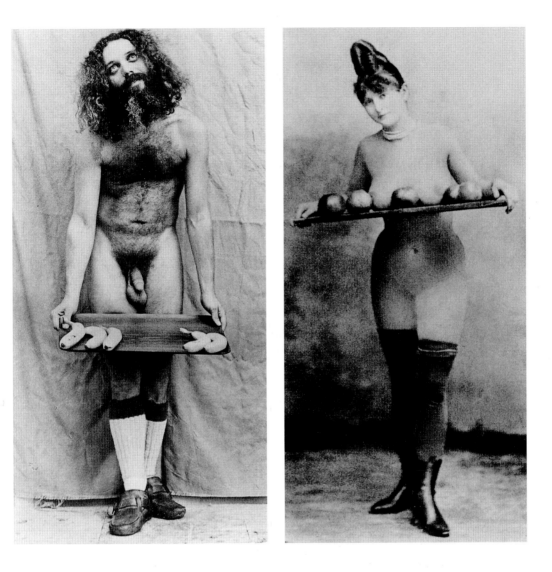

7 LINDA NOCHLIN Buy My Bananas, 1972

8 ANONYMOUS Buy My Apples, nineteenth century

9 WILLIAM HOLMAN HUNT Awakening Conscience, 1853

Realism," attempted, perhaps for the first time, to read sexual ideologies through a critical analysis of formal structure as well as iconography, and in that it was unequivocally feminist in its viewpoint. It included not only images of "fallen women" from the works of Degas and Hogarth, Augustus Egg and Cézanne, as well as the two featured paintings of the lecture, Holman Hunt's *Awakening Conscience* and Manet's *Nana*, but also juxtapositions of misogynist texts by those prolific, mid-nineteenth-century diarists, essayists and novelists the Goncourt brothers with feminist ones by John Stewart Mill, and took Realism as seriously as it did the representation of women. I ended with a stirring address to the audience, calling on them to see the two paintings as "two poles of a single dimension of perception and feeling, establishing the validity of Realism, but at the same time, revealing its inner contradictions and limits. Both make a claim to record direct experience...yet both fall back on artistic schemata and social and moral stereotypes as

10 EDOUARD MANET Nana, 1877

essential to the Realist style and outlook as to any other in the history of
art...Manet's view of the situation", I continued, "may be more sympathetic to the modern sensibility: it is hardly a more authentic view of the
situation itself. In fact, to today's liberated woman, Holman Hunt's
version of the Fallen Woman theme may be infinitely more meaningful:
woman, gazing beyond the spectator towards transcendent possibilities,
chooses to reject objecthood in a single existential gesture; really, much
more contemporary than Nana staring brazenly out at us, accepting her
status as an object with an inviting wink of complicity, the pictorial
embodiment of the male chauvinist dreams of Second Empire Paris."

I am not sure that I would agree with this estimation today, but for
mainstream art history in 1970, it was heady stuff. The lecture was published eight years later, in a very different form and with considerably
more polish and sophistication as "Lost and *Found*: Once More the
Fallen Woman" in the *Art Bulletin*, without the comparison between

French and English art and with its main focus on Dante Gabriel Rossetti's unfinished painting on the theme of prostitution, *Found* (fig. 46), as its centerpiece.

My "Woman and Art" class surfaced again in a new incarnation at Stanford University during the summer term of 1971. By now the course outline was more complex in its material and more rationalized in its organization, and the reading list grouped texts thematically for each class session. There were, in fact, the beginnings of a feminist literature in art history and criticism, as well as in many other fields. Looking back, one can see that a discipline, a discourse, and a field of scholarly inquiry were in the making, and watch ideas in the process of formulation. Among the texts, some of which were fairly standard art-historical ones, were included such specifically feminist works as Naomi Weisstein's "Psychology Constructs the Female" from *Women's Liberation and Literature* (1971); my own "Why Have There Been No Great Women Artists?" published that January in *Art News* and simultaneously in *Women in Sexist Society* (1971); interviews with Judy Chicago, Miriam Schapiro and Faith Wilding in *Everywoman*; *The Victorian Woman*, a special issue of *Victorian Studies*; Lucy Komisar's "The Image of Woman in Advertising," also from *Women in Sexist Society*; and Alex Shulman's "Organs and Orgasms," from the same volume. Students, of course, contributed additional bibliography to the reading list as they prepared their presentations.

The two introductory sessions were devoted to a discussion based on the reading and slides of the interrelated issues of women in art and women as artists; the third class dealt with the theme of woman in twentieth-century high art: Matisse and the harem conception of women; Picasso, Surrealism and Freudian mythologies of woman; De Kooning's brutal tactics in his *Women*; and women in Pop art—pornokitsch. The fourth class was dedicated to nineteenth-century imagery of women. The fifth class, however, struck out into relatively new territory, or at least considerably expanded on what had previously been a minor issue: women in "low" or popular art—advertising, TV, movies, costume, women's magazines—and the relation of such imagery to high art. One woman in the class, I remember, brought her grandmother's lacy bloomers and petticoat as objects worthy of art-historical scrutiny and social analysis. For the next session, "Women as Sex," which included pornography and sexual imagery, class members went down to the famous porn shops of San Francisco, where the *habitués* were shocked speechless by the spectacle of proper young female students avidly thumbing through the most explosive merchandise. The final reports

were on women artists: such nineteenth-century heroines as Rosa
Bonheur, Mary Cassatt, Berthe Morisot, the women sculptors of Rome
(the so-called White Marmorean Flock), and twentieth-century ones:
Georgia O'Keeffe, Romaine Brooks, Helen Frankenthaler, Lee Bontecou,
and, as a bow to local talent, Julia Morgan, a San Francisco architectural
pioneer who had created William Randolph Hearst's fantasy castle, San
Simeon, among other achievements.

But perhaps most interesting of all was a final session with Miriam
Schapiro and Judy Chicago, up from Womanhouse in Los Angeles and
full of ideas and recent innovations in the making of art and the empowerment of women artists. While I strongly disagreed with their assertion
that there was an innate feminine style, signified by centralized imagery
or circular forms and existing apart from history and the historically
conditioned institutions of art, I agreed just as strongly with their ideas
about supporting the work and the working lives of contemporary
women artists. The students were enthralled and participated very
actively in the discussion that followed Schapiro and Chicago's presentation. Among those attending the class was a Stanford graduate
student, Paula Harper, who was herself to take a leading role in the early
development of feminist art history. In 1971, Paula taught a course on
the pioneering Feminist Art Program of the California Institute of the
Arts—a seminar on the history of women artists—and then went on to
participate in the organization of the Women's Caucus at the College Art
Association and to chair the first CAA session devoted entirely to
women's art history in 1973 in New York. That session included memorable presentations by Eunice Lipton on Manet; Susan Casteras on Susan
Eakins; and June Wayne on the "feminized" position of artists in general
in American society.

Needless to say, I later made a trip to Womanhouse and found it
exciting and provocative, inspiring and controversial. In the works on
view in the rackety "domestic" setting, the aggressive emphasis on the
representation of women's bodies as well as the sense of the unrelenting
oppressiveness of women's lives was novel and disturbing: the unforgettable *Menstruation Bathroom* with its wall-to-wall Kotex and vivid
red-and-white decor was an outstanding case in point. Yet as a Vassar
woman and a seasoned professional, I was surprised at the unremitting
fascination with domesticity and sexuality that marked the work on
view and surprised too to find that women art students actually needed
so much support and encouragement simply to do their work: we, as
students, after all, had taken it for granted that we could produce plays,
do the lighting, paint sets, make frescoes and be articulate, independent

and feisty. My one-day experience at Womanhouse made it clear that this was hardly the case universally. Then too, I had always had interesting and brilliant women professors as mentors, in art as well as more scholarly realms, and assumed that other women had had the same opportunity. Womanhouse made it obvious that for many women, authority figures were masculine by definition and having teachers of one's own sex who were openly conscious of their femininity was indeed a radical innovation. At that point in the Women's Art Movement, contemporary art-making and the history of art, insofar as they concerned women and their representation, were mutually stimulating and interrelated. Once again, excitement was in the air, and time seemed too short for all we wanted to investigate, to argue about, to critique and discuss. The class's attitude was decidedly *engagé*, and yes, I think that California made a difference.

It was shortly after that Californian summer that Ann Sutherland Harris and I embarked on a major enterprise in the early history of women's art history: the preparation of the exhibition "Women Artists: 1550–1950" and its accompanying catalogue. The exhibition came into existence at least in part through the persistent activism of women artists and the progressive spirit of the Los Angeles County Museum of Art. During the course of preparing the show, Ann and I traveled extensively in Europe and the United States, encountering every possible attitude on the part of museum curators, ranging from bemused curiosity to patronizing contempt to genuine and enthusiastic support for our project. Open-minded and knowledgeable curators, like the Tate Gallery's Richard Morphet, were rare and greatly appreciated. One museum official actually went so far as to ask me why there had never been any great women artists! Needless to say, some of the same curators who had sneered or begrudgingly made us a few meager loans were themselves showing women artists a few years later. Working on "Women Artists" was one of the most difficult, and yet ultimately one of the most rewarding, tasks of my life. On the one hand, I knew I was taking a position that directly contradicted my stance in my article "Why Have There Been No Great Women Artists?" Yet it seemed to me, after digging around in the basements and reserves of great European museums and provincial art galleries, that there had indeed been many wonderfully inventive, extremely competent, and, above all unquestionably interesting, women artists; some of these had been cherished and admired on their own native turf, even if they could not be considered international superstars. Their work and its historical import deserved to be shown and, even more importantly, deserved to be thought about and seriously analyzed within the discourse of high art. The show had other effects as well, both simpler and more direct. Even today, women artists or art historians come up to me and say things like: "That show changed my life. I never knew before that I, as a woman artist or art-worker, had a history. After that show, I knew I was part of a long tradition and it gave me the courage to go on."

Nothing, I think, is more interesting, more poignant, and more difficult to seize, than the intersection of the self and history. Where does biography end and history begin? How do one's own memories and experiences relate to what is written in the history books? Can one complain of "distortion" in historical writing when, inevitably, with the passage of time, our own memories of events and experiences become confused, filmy or uncertain? I have been drawn to the topos of self and history since the age of twelve, when I wrote a long blank-verse poem called "The Ghosts of the Museum," inspired by my spiritual home-from-home, the Brooklyn Museum. In that poem, I attempted to communicate with an Egyptian princess; I brought museum objects, like mummies and cherry-wood cradles, to articulate life in terms of my own, unique, present-day experience of them, and predicted dolefully that our own cigarette lighters and coffee-pots, our radios and necklaces would soon find their place "in the vast, dusty halls of the museum." Later, when I was considerably older and more sophisticated, I wrote a poem entitled "Matisse/Swan/Self" in which I contemplated a photograph of Matisse sketching a swan in the Bois de Boulogne in 1931, the very year I was born, and meditated on the coincidence of totally unrelated events which nevertheless could be interpreted as meaningfully integrated on some transcendent level. Yet in 1969 and the years that followed, the intersection of myself and history was of a different order: it was no mere passive conjunction of events that united me to the history of that year and those that followed, but rather an active engagement and participation, a sense that I, along with many other politicized, and yes, liberated, women, was actually intervening in the historical process and changing history itself: the history of art, of culture, of institutions and of consciousness. And this knowledge even today, more than twenty-five years later, gives us an ongoing sense of achievement and purpose like no other.

In this essay I will examine some unusual pictures: the woman warrior as a historical subject, and then, more generally, fighting and powerful women. The emphasis will be quite literally on "the *case* of the woman warrior"—the most extreme examplar of a feminine being as independent agent of her own destiny—conceived of as a problem rather than an image, a visual oxymoron in need of analysis.

Although one of my case studies involves a work from the seventeenth century, I will for the most part be focussing on issues in the eighteenth and nineteenth centuries. In my analyses, I shall be as interested in how the terms "woman" and "women" are to be understood as in the issue of the woman warrior *per se.* For woman, in my examination of the various cases, cannot be seen as a fixed, pre-existing entity or "image," transformed by this or that historical circumstance, but as a complex, mercurial and problematic signifier, mixed in its messages, resisting fixed interpretation or positioning despite the numerous attempts made in visual representation literally to put "woman" in her place. Like the woman warrior, the term "woman" fights back, and resists attempts to subdue its meaning or reduce it to some simple essence, universal, natural, and above all, unproblematic.

My first case study comes from seventeenth-century French art: Claude Deruet's *Mme de Saint-Balmont* (c. 1643), an image which exists in two versions, the larger in the Musée Lorrain in Nancy, the smaller, with minor variations, in the Musée des Beaux-Arts in the same city.

Two major misconceptions marked my efforts to understand these paintings, the first technical, the second iconographic. Both the slides I took of these works were flawed by the confusing reflections created by flash-bulb illumination. But these defective slides were records of a bigger and more interesting mistake: my initial, hasty impression that this was an equestrian portrait of some local, *male* military dignitary of the seventeenth century and of only passing interest. Yet even my first glance revealed that something was wrong with this initial reading of the work, despite the fact that the figure was completely dressed in male attire, riding astride and in a position of considerable authority. Some disturbingly contradictory visual signals given by the softness of the face of the sitter, a lack of beard and moustache, the presence of Athena in the clouds to the left in the smaller version, even a certain knowing look in the eyes of the horse led me to believe that this might in fact be something interestingly Other. This intuition was confirmed both by the placard in the Musée Lorrain identifying the image as "Madame de Saint-Balmont, Dame de Neuville-en-Verdunois, 'l'Amazone Chrétienne'" and subsequent research: the figure I had thought was a man was actually a woman, Alberte d'Ernecourt, Dame de Neuville, better known as Mme de Saint-Balmont. My "mis-taken" slides with their shiny surfaces, then, in some sense might be said to constitute a visual allegory of Freud's punning introduction to his essay on fetishism, in which the author equates the German word *Glanz* or "shine" with the English word "glance."[1]

The subject of the portrait, Mme de Saint-Balmont, wife of Jean-Jacques de Haraucourt, Seigneur de Saint-Balmont, was evidently a heroic woman who protected La Woëvre against Croatian incursions while her husband was occupied by military duties elsewhere. Deruet, who specialized in the equestrian portrait, has represented her as a heroine of the Thirty Years War. Dressed as a man and controlling her steed in the levade, she occupies the center of the painting. Behind her, a vast landscape, animated by tiny figures—eight hundred of them, in the large version—gathers together in an imaginary but visually precise topography all the land-holdings of the family, dominated by the castle of Neuville-en-Verdunois. The upper part of the painting is devoted to allegorical references to the achievements of the woman warrior: winged genies announce the fame of the heroine on trumpets ornamented with her family coats of arms to the right; to the left, putti bear crowns of laurels, and of flowers—in subtle deference to her femininity, perhaps—while a third putto points to a book with the words poetry and music inscribed in it, references to her talents. To the far left is Athena, female goddess of wisdom and the arts, but also of war, dressed in armor, holding the attributes of victory: the palm and the laurel wreath.[2] Taken as a whole, this is an image in which the oxymoron "woman warrior" is erased as a descriptive term, so completely have the categories of class (aristocratic, of course), possessions, role and conventions of representation overwhelmed or indeed occulted the signifiers of femininity. "Warrior" fits "woman" here like a second skin and obscures the feminine presence it clothes. In other words, at least for the non-expert in the field of earlier seventeenth-century French painting, rather than appearing to be a woman warrior, this image seems to represent a warrior *tout*

12 CLAUDE DERUET Mme de Saint-Balmont, c. 1643

court, a perfect case of transvestism. If there are hints of feminine identity, they are subtle—a certain roundness of face, perhaps and absence of
masculine facial hair—or else displaced to the allegorical accouterments.
But certainly, the woman warrior is not problematized in visual terms:
the signs of her masculine power—as a military leader and member of
the ruling classes—are far more overt, and those of her femininity far
more discreet, than in such later equestrian versions of the topos as
Thorvald Erichsen's portrait of Empress Catherine II of Russia, where the
horse is less active and the figure, despite its astride position and masculine clothing, is more conventionally feminine; or the contemporary
photograph of Queen Elizabeth II at the Trooping of the Colour, where

13 JACQUES-FRANCOIS LE BARBIER Jeanne Hachette at the Siege
of Beauvais, 1781 (photographed before its destruction in 1940)

the military severity of the monarch's costume is contradicted by the
femininity of her hair and the fact that she is mounted not astride, but on
an archaic and indisputably feminine side-saddle.

My second case of the woman warrior is a very different one: *Jeanne
Hachette at the Siege of Beauvais*, a painting by Jacques-François Le
Barbier exhibited in the Salon of 1781, where it was remarked upon at
some length by Diderot and several less renowned critics. It was eventually installed in the Town Hall of Beauvais, where, with a period of
interruption during and after the Revolution, it remained until it was
destroyed during the course of World War II, in 1940.[3] Figure 13 is taken
from the only, rather blurred, existing photograph of the original *Jeanne
Hachette*; a preliminary sketch for the painting exists, with rather
striking differences, notably the absence of the half-nude corpse in the
foreground; and finally, there is a somewhat inaccurate, much hardened
but more legible lithograph (fig. 14) by Maggi after a drawing of the
painting by Laduré, probably from about 1826, the year of Le Barbier's
death.[4] An interesting and innovative work for its time, if not
a completely successful one, Le Barbier's *Jeanne Hachette* confronts us
squarely with issues of class, of national definition, and of pictorial
genre, as well as with the obvious ones of feminine identity versus
masculine agency and physical force inscribed by the women warriors
in the painting.

Although Le Barbier's *Jeanne Hachette* can be seen as simply one of
a number of paintings of themes taken from French national history

encouraged during the 1770s and 1780s by the Comte d'Angiviller, Louis XVI's Directeur des Bâtiments,[5] it is unique among them in having both a feminine protagonist *and* a modern, non-aristocratic, lower-class one in addition.[6] Since the subject was not a commissioned one, we can only conclude that this unusual choice was Le Barbier's own.

Who was Jeanne Hachette? Or, more importantly, who was Jeanne Hachette for Jacques-François Le Barbier, because her myth or her reality, like that of Joan of Arc, has had many often contradictory constructions. Indeed, by the end of the nineteenth century, there was even a current of scholarly opinion which asserted that Jeanne Hachette had never existed, that she was simply a mythic construction based on the heroic actions of the women of Beauvais as a group during the famous Siege of Beauvais by the Burgundians in 1472.[7]

In Le Barbier's painting, Jeanne Hachette, far from being non-existent, holds the eponymous hatchet in her right hand, and leads a vigorous, even Amazonian, band of women warriors wielding a large assortment of improvised weapons, including rocks, burning brands, and axes, against their hapless, male enemies, whose half-nude corpses litter the foreground. In effect, Le Barbier (like his near contemporary Watteau de Lille in whose painting of Jeanne Hachette of the later

14 JACQUES–FRANCOIS LE BARBIER Jeanne Hachette at the Siege of Beauvais, 1781. Lithograph by Maggi after a drawing by Laduré, c. 1826

eighteenth century the Amazonian overtones are much stronger and the composition far less focussed and unified) has actually combined *two* incidents involving women from two separate days during the Siege of Beauvais: Jeanne Hachette's seizure of the banner on 27 June and an incident of 9 July, during which, according to the earliest chronicler:

> The women and girls...carried to the said warriors on the wall a great abundance of great dressed stones, clay pots full of live coals, barrel-hoops and big tuns and other barrels, linked one to the other, with spiked clubs, cinders, boiling hot oil and grease to throw on the said Burgundians, so that they would not be able to climb the wall.[8]

Various literary sources from Le Barbier's own time were available to the artist, most notably in dramatic form. There were plays featuring Jeanne Hachette by Voltaire and by Lemierre, for instance, and the Marquis de Sade wrote a five-act tragedy on the subject which was read at the Comédie Française in 1791. Published with considerable stir, the now-forgotten poet Jean-Antoine Roucher's long and sensational epic poem, *Les Mois*, is the work closest in date (1779–80) to the inception of the painting itself; several pages of Chant V of are dedicated to the warrior-woman of Beauvais.[9]

Both the poem and the poet bear some examination in relation not only to Le Barbier's interpretation of the Jeanne Hachette legend, but to the myth of the woman warrior and to gender issues at the end of the eighteenth century more generally. Roucher emphasizes Hachette's unusual and indeed manly courage by giving the story several twists not present in the chronicler's version—twists, it seems to me, that are reflected in Le Barbier's painting. In the first place, Hachette has a weapon in her hand, despite the chronicler's insistence that she was unarmed; and in the second place, she is not a single actress in the drama, but rather the leader of an equally ferocious band of women; and, perhaps most important of all, the women in Roucher's version are temporary warriors not because of the absence of their husbands fighting for France elsewhere, but because of their husbands' cowardice. At a high point in the epic, after the cowardly flight of the men of the city from the Burgundians' onslaught, Jeanne Hachette harangues her fellow women as follows: "What! You can fight and you cry instead!/Leave to your husbands such fear and such dread./Let us march and compel them to blush through and through,/Be men for them, if they are women for you."[10] The women form up in a battalion behind Hachette, who leads them with spear in hand and seizes the Burgundian standard directly from Duke Charles. Women are here represented as more manly—more courageous and militant—than their absent men.

If I have gone into considerable detail over the presumed literary source of Le Barbier's painting, it is not for the sake of gratuitous erudition, nor simply because in some way it delights me, but rather because the image represents a high point in the positive and unqualified—non-oxymoronic—representation of the woman-as-warrior, fighting women who fight and prevail over a masculine enemy not simply because it is their nature, like the Amazons, but consciously, out of choice, for a larger cause, and who tread with considerable aplomb over the fallen bodies of their male victims. The main figure of Jeanne is somewhat idealized and classicized, not represented as a simple *bourgeoise* at all, as one critic has pointed out, but rather, allegorized as a kind of Nike (Victory) of the battlements. Idealizing, classicizing and allegorizing a subject taken from modern history, with a non-aristocratic cast of characters, was of course a way of bestowing elevation and dignity upon it. But Le Barbier insisted on the gender of his cast of characters as a major selling point in his admittedly unsuccessful efforts to convince d'Angiviller to buy the painting for the king. In a letter to the Directeur des Bâtiments of 1782, Le Barbier emphasizes the innovations of his *Jeanne Hachette* by saying: "It is perhaps in all of French history the one subject where women play such a brilliant role. And no one has ever thought of it."[11] Certainly, this novelty was noted and remarked on by several critics of the time, including Diderot, who wrote about the work in their accounts of the Salon of 1781.[12] At this moment in history, one might say, if the topos of the woman warrior constituted a conscious novelty in terms of history painting, it did not yet give rise to undue anxiety or outright terror: on the contrary, in 1781, it is seen as a plausible *exemplum virtutis* for inspiring moral fervor and patriotic emotion on behalf of the nation in the hearts and minds of its viewers, both male and female. The woman warrior, fighting on behalf of French nationhood, could stand as an emblem of patriotism for both men and women at this pre-Revolutionary moment.

Indeed, I would say that there is no visual representation from the entire period of the French Revolution in which women are represented positively in as forceful a way as they are in Le Barbier's painting. Scholars like Lynn Hunt and Joan Landes have pointed out that the masculine anxiety caused by women's political struggle to participate in Revolutionary public life as citizens and club-members tended to suppress the theme of the woman warrior in official Revolutionary imagery and in unoffical art as well.[13] For instance, a drawing of a Revolutionary heroine, the so-called Citoyenne de Saint-Milhier for the Competition of the Year II, now attributed to François-André Vincent, is far more subdued than Le Barbier's image of a decade earlier. And the heroic "citoyenne," a Vendenne farm-woman who threatened to blow up her own home rather than let it fall into counter-Revolutionary hands, is hardly a warrior-woman. The setting and the deed are properly domesticated, and the composition itself represents a rather half-hearted attempt to impose a Davidean neoclassical dignity on what is essentially a genre subject. In this case, the "woman warrior," if she can even be defined as such, is a dry, morose, austere, self-sacrificing creature, whose aggressiveness is considerably hampered by a fainting daughter.

Nor is feminist activism looked on with any greater favor in the watercolor attributed to Therieux, *Le Club des femmes patriotes* (c. 1792–93), a representation in which women's struggle for self-determination is inscribed by hysteria and grotesquery in roughly equal proportions—a strategy that was to be continued and exaggerated by caricaturists like Daumier in the following century.

The female figures allegorizing Revolutionary virtues in the official art of the Revolution, are, like Jean-François Janinet's *Liberty* (1792) and Philibert-Louis Debucourt's *Republican Calendar with Figure of Liberty* (1792), on the whole, a rather feeble, definitely placid, and often domesticated lot. What is striking, in fact, is the lack of strong vigorous female figures actively embodying Revolutionary ideals.[14] Female figures representing the Republic or Liberty tend to be static and remote, ill at ease even when they have considerable youthful charm, as does a "hockey captain" version by Jean-Antoine Gros of 1794–95. In Jean-Baptiste Regnault's memorable *Liberty or Death*, exhibited in the Salon of 1795, it is not the female figure of Liberty that makes the active appeal to the spectator, either in terms of rhetorical gesture or in terms of the seductive beauty of the flesh, but rather the male embodiment of "Le Génie de la France," the enlivening flame of *l'esprit* springing from his brow. Paradoxically, on the very eve, as it were, of what the German costume historian, J. C. Flugel, has denominated the "great masculine renunciation" (the time when men were despecularized and abandoned their "right to all the brighter and more elaborate forms of ornamentation," leaving these entirely to the use of women) when men begin to abandon their claim to be considered beautiful and transform their tailoring into the most austere and ascetic of arts, it is a beautiful—and naked—young male, representing the French nation, who actively offers himself to the spectator.[15] The Revolution assumed an ambiguous and increasingly negative attitude towards women's calls for equality, the rights of

15 JEAN-ANTOINE GROS Liberty, 1794–95

16 JEAN-BAPTISTE REGNAULT Liberty or Death, 1795

17 THOMAS ROWLANDSON (after Lord
George Murray) The Contrast, 1792

18 ANONYMOUS The Emancipated
Woman, 1871

citizenship, and independent identity; the feminist agenda, and the
women who supported it, were squelched and executed, stripped of their
powers and their public identities.

It is no accident, therefore, that the woman warrior is transformed
into a negative rather than a positive signifier during the Revolutionary
period, transvalued by the forces of counter-Revolution, perhaps most
spectacularly in England rather than France. Liberty—or rather the *sans-
culottes* version of Revolutionary Liberty—is savagely caricatured in a
debased and abject version of the woman-warrior topos, a female figure
now unequivocally proletarian, aged, and sporting the pendulous
breasts and streaming hair of the traditional Invidia or Discordia or the
Wild Woman of popular imagery. In Thomas Rowlandson's version
(fig. 17), a grotesque recycling of Le Barbier's *Jeanne Hachette*, Liberty
strides vigorously over the fallen body of a naked man whose head is
impaled on her pike. This is not an image of heroism but a castration
nightmare incarnate.

In Johann Zoffany's painting, *The Women of Paris Dancing on the
Bodies of the Swiss Guards After the Assault on the Tuileries, 10 August
1792* (1794–95), one of a series of three commemorating the *sans-
culottes* atrocities of the Revolution,[16] British terror of the destructive
power of the Revolutionary mob, a terror specifically associated with
beheading, is displaced onto the castrating powers of the sexualized,

lower-class female. Zoffany embodies class fears in a gendered and classed signifier, which might be called the "negative woman warrior." He opposes this menacing hag to the pitiful victim of Revolutionary savagery, the white-clad fallen mother in the left foreground of the painting.

The figure of the proletarian "negative woman warrior"—malevolent, hysterical, destructive, witch-like, often bare-breasted and always dissolute—assumes a central role in counter-Revolutionary iconography from this time forward. One memorable example is the anti-Commune image from 1871, *The Emancipated Woman*. This crude caricature of one of the working-class women accused of setting fire to Paris under the Commune allegorizes the upper-class nightmare of a world upside down: the *pétroleuse*, a fantasmic figure combining sexual with social anarchy, stands for that reversal of the natural order which is understood to result from the destruction of the traditional political establishment.

No wonder, then, that when *bien-pensant* nineteenth-century French artists chose to present the proletarian woman warrior *par excellence*—Joan of Arc, the Maid of Orleans—they chose to emphasize the

19 JOHANN ZOFFANY The Women of Paris Dancing on the Bodies of the Swiss Guards After the Assault on the Tuileries, 10 August 1792, 1794–95

20 HONORE DAUMIER The Republic, 1848

religious aspect of her performance. Jules Bastien-Lepage, in his *Joan of Arc Hearing the Voices* (1879), shows her as a goofy farm girl listening to the spectral voices in her orchard. Ingres's *Joan of Arc at the Crowning of the Dauphin at Reims Cathedral* (1854) depicts Joan as a stalwart matron, well-corseted, looking heavenward in thanks in Reims Cathedral. Only Emmanuel Fremiet in his 1872–74 sculpture *Joan of Arc*, under the immediate pressure of the Franco-Prussian War and Lorraine's humiliation by the Prussians, musters up a calm equestrian figure in armor. Joan is never shown in the same fighting postures as male figures in command of armies.

For my next case study, I would like to discuss two allegorical female figures from the Revolutions of 1830 and 1848 respectively, which bear strikingly different relations to the woman-warrior topos: a positive one, in the case of Delacroix's *Liberty Leading the People* (1830) which both looks back to Le Barbier's *Jeanne Hachette* for inspiration, and, at the same time, I believe, makes use of the vivid energies of the counter-Revolutionary "negative" woman-warrior image; and Daumier's *The Republic* (1848), which draws more on the Revolutionary repertory of static, placid, domesticated and above all, maternal visual

21 EUGENE DELACROIX Liberty Leading the People, 1830

vehicles. To analyze these works, we need first to address allegory and
how it works, or doesn't.

The late, great sociologist Erving Goffman demonstrated how much
we can learn about expectations about sex-roles by looking, not *through*
the visual signifiers of advertising to the products they are designed to
sell, but rather *at* the signifiers themselves.[17] Variables like dominance
versus subordination, energy versus passivity, childishness versus maturity can be associated within specified contexts with appropriate
indicators of masculinity or femininity to sell to the public the virtues of
a given product. Goffman's analytic strategies seem eminently applica-
ble to the political art of France in the late eighteenth and the nineteenth
centuries, an art in which the representation of woman plays a dominant
role. The setting forth of a political message to a large and varied public

through a feminine allegory is, after all, not such a different enterprise from selling a product to the public with an alluring female image. In both cases, the feminine vehicle must both communicate clearly with, and engage the sympathies of, the potential audience.

In the case of the two works under discussion—Delacroix's *Liberty Leading the People* and Daumier's *The Republic*—the tasks of the artists raise a particular kind of difficulty specifically associated with the creation of a female allegorical figure suitable for conveying a Revolutionary political meaning. How do you get across that sense of highly charged, often open-ended political energy and militancy associated with Revolutionary ideology without creating an image of woman which seems threatening and inimical rather than positive and emotionally engaging to an audience which is understood to be primarily masculine? Too strong a reversal of customary roles—even customary fantasy roles—for women can easily work to negate, or at the very least weaken, the positive impact of even the most engaging political cause by making men uneasy. Yet too weak a feminine image—one more in conformity, that is, with conventional notions of a female role—is unsatisfactory in conveying that primary sense of missionary *élan*, force and dynamism which is, after all, at the heart of Revolutionary conviction.

Jacques-Louis David, to return to the period of the French Revolution in 1789, with the intuitive simplicity of a propagandist of genius, assumed an absolute difference between men and women in a work like the *Oath of the Horatii* (1785). Avoiding traditional allegory completely in his best political paintings, he instead conveyed his messages through the unequivocal opposition between masculine and feminine. One might almost say that the self-evident antithesis of masculinity versus femininity exists as a sort of *langue* for David of which the *Horatii*, the *Brutus* or the *Sabine Women* are individual speech-acts. It is precisely the self-evidence of the male–female opposition in these paintings which guarantees the clarity of the political message.[18]

Even David's later and more complex *Sabine Women Attempting to Make Peace Between Their Warring Husbands and Brothers* (1799) maintains this effect of sexually polarized clarity, despite the fact that there is now an opposition between two groups of active men, Sabines to the left, Romans to the right, whose bellicose action is viewed as negative, and an equally active group of women, their sisters and wives respectively, the positive force attempting to reconcile the two groups, in the center.

Delacroix, in his *Liberty Leading the People*, took over David's sexually differentiated structure in the *Sabine Women*—active female in the

22 JACQUES-LOUIS DAVID Oath of the Horatii, 1785

center, active groups of men to either side—but rejected both its meaning and the nature of the activity itself. For Delacroix's female figure is not a conciliatory peacemaker but a bellicose leader, a descendant not merely of the woman warrior of traditional high art, but, even more significantly, of those threatening slatterns who strutted atop the bodies of fallen aristocrats in popular counter-Revolutionary imagery. Delacroix's Liberty is not engaged in bringing two opposing groups of men together, but rather in leading a differentiated, but unified, masculine group forward with her dramatic energy and conviction. True, in Delacroix's picture, woman is permitted such force, such a position of active and aggressive leadership of men, only by virtue of the fact that she is neither a historical personage nor a contemporary member of the crowd she leads but rather, an allegorical figure. Nevertheless, she is only partially so: she does not fly, she strides; if her profile is classical and idealized, her bare breasts are concrete and sensual; if there is an attempt to distance her from her audience by giving her the semi-nudity

23 J. H. EGENBERGER and B. WIJNVELD Kenau Hasselaar on the Walls of Harlem, 1854

of sculpture, the lower part of her drapery is of rough proletarian cloth
and resembles a working-class skirt; if she holds the symbolic tricolor
in one hand, she holds a businesslike musket in the other. Indeed, one
might say that a large part of the power of the painting arises from
the ambiguous status of the feminine figure which dominates it. Art
historians have tended to defuse the issue of her realism by assimilating
the figure of Liberty to the norms of the discipline, calling attention to
classical prototypes like the *Aphrodite of Melos* or the Louvre *Nike* to
account for her pose and figure-type. Non-specialists, sympathetic with
the political cause with which she is associated, see the figure primarily
as a stalwart "femme du peuple."

Indeed, the energy and aggression of Delacroix's figure of Liberty
and the compositional structure in which she exists seem to be derived
directly from the rare history painting dedicated to all-female heroism
and militancy that we have already considered: Le Barbier's *Jeanne
Hachette at the Siege of Beauvais.*[19]

Under what circumstances could women be represented as fierce,
aggressive and powerful, militantly engaged in physical victory over

male opponents yet still capable of conveying positive rather than negative, threatening implications? After all, looked at from the historical perspective of post-Revolution visual representation, and looking "through" rather than "at" the manifest iconography of Le Barbier's painting, what we arrive at is just that situation which the historian Natalie Zemon Davis has denominated "woman on top," that most potent of all topoi of the early modern period signifying the reversal of the natural order, the loosing of chaos and anarchy.[20] What then justifies such a reversal of the normal order of things? One such exceptional circumstance is the one represented in Le Barbier's painting: the women are understood to be substituting for missing male warriors.

The same subject—women substituting for absent males in defense of nation and native city—is represented by the Dutch artists J. H. Egenberger and B. Wijnveld in their *Kenau Hasselaar on the Walls of Harlem* (1854) in which heroic middle-class wives, under the leadership of a local woman, are depicted giving hell to Spanish invaders in the late sixteenth century. The ferocity of these women, quite disturbing in certain cases in which the physical violence is extremely explicit, like the pouring of boiling oil on the enemy to the right, is here, as in the case of the related Le Barbier painting, justified by the fact that these women are filling in for men. Yet even more, it is suggested that these women are defending their homes, that the walled city for which they fight so fiercely is in some way identified with that domestic sphere appropriate

24 FRANCISCO GOYA They Are Like Wild Beasts, from the Disasters of War series, c. 1810

to women. Ultimately these Dutchwomen are to be interpreted not as threatening Amazons but rather as stalwart matrons defending their natural territory. Like all such female personae, from the Maid of Saragossa to Rosie the Riveter, their masculine behavior is justified by the fact that they are replacing men on the home front in defense of their nation.

Still another situation in which women are permitted a degree of triumphant ferocity in the art of the period is in defense of the young, as in Goya's *Disasters of War* series: once more, an exceptional situation in which women are permitted to deviate from customary gentleness without blame. *They Are Like Wild Beasts*, declares Goya in the title to his memorable aquatint from the *Disasters* (fig. 24). The suggestion is that war forces women to behave like tigresses or lionesses in defense of their young. Such aggressive behavior, natural to the animal kingdom, is something women—peasants, to be sure, and therefore closer to the animal realm of instinct—are reduced to only under the most dire circumstances. These are not, in other words, cases of the warrior-woman as much as cases of women forced by war to behave like something *other* than women: men or animals.

Something of the same notion lies behind Horace Vernet's *Scene of the French Campaign of 1814*, a work which refers interestingly back to Le Barbier's *Jeanne Hachette* and forward to Delacroix's *Liberty*. Painted in 1826, the year Vernet was named officer of the Légion d'honneur and took over Le Barbier's seat in the Académie des Beaux-Arts, the *Scene* may both have constituted a subtle homage to the painter of Jeanne Hachette whose place Vernet was taking among the Immortals, and possibly have provided inspiration for Delacroix's *Liberty*. Once more it is the defense of child and dying husband that justifies this farmer's wife's heroic and militant behavior: a kind of domestic virtue no matter how exaggerated.

If Delacroix turned to a tradition of feminine aggressiveness and activism for his allegory of the Revolution of 1830, Daumier turned to a prototype of feminine self-abnegation, the Christian Charity—no doubt, Andrea del Sarto's painting in the Louvre—and the iconography of motherhood, that most conventionally acceptable of all feminine roles, for his commemoration of the ideals of 1848. Subtitled "The Republic Nourishes Her Children and Instructs Them" by Champfleury, this painted sketch was submitted by Daumier to the contest for an image of the Republic announced by the Provisional Government in March 1848. Although praised at the time for being a bold and heart-warming invention ("a strong and sober sketch," as Champfleury called it[21]), shining out among the mediocre and chilly allegories against which it competed, Daumier's *The Republic* (fig. 20), looked at, not through, by a woman, not a man, is a disturbing image. A pin-headed, huge-breasted female figure, Michelangelesque in its pose, braces herself with the tricolor against the twin assaults of two lunging youths—no sucklings, these!— while a third boy reads a book in the foreground. From a distance the two dark heads look startlingly like wounds, their fervor like a brutal aggression against the body of their nurturer-mother.

Daumier's choice of a maternal, nurturing image rather than a militant, active one for his female political allegory may indeed have something to do with the change in political ideology which had taken place between February 1830 and March 1848, a greater emphasis on tolerance and goodwill requiring, in the words of Albert Boime, "a more temperate and low-pitched symbol."[22] I think, however, that Daumier's ideas about the proper role of *women* have even more to do with his choice of allegorical vehicle than his political beliefs. By this I don't mean to suggest that a motherly image of feminine excellence was a purely personal choice of Daumier's but rather, that by the middle of the nineteenth century, antagonism to any sort of female self-determination—to any role but the domestic, nurturing, subordinate one for

25 HORACE VERNET Scene of the French Campaign of 1814, 1826

women—was widespread among the working class as well as the bourgeoisie, and vigorously promulgated by some of the leading spokesmen of the left, like P.-J. Proudhon. It was, after all, Proudhon who articulated the working-class outlook most successfully and who also happened to be the most phallocratic of all nineteenth-century thinkers. "For women," he declared in 1849, "liberty can only consist in the right to housework."[23] Proudhon, who explicitly valued feminine submissiveness and treasured women's ignorance of learning or public affairs, who believed that feminine influence in 1848 had been "one of the plagues of the Republic" in his posthumous *La Pornocratie, ou Les Femmes dans les temps modernes*, states in no uncertain terms that a woman must either be an obedient wife and mother or a whore: there were no alternatives.[24]

Daumier, a man of the left in his time, lower middle class in his origins, basically shared these views, without even having to think them through. He took great pains to ridicule the odious females who participate in politics, or write books or have independent opinions instead of staying at home and taking care of children and housework where they belong. In other words, women's demands for basic human agency were perceived as a "natural" joke, like slipping on a banana peel; for a woman to aspire to belong to a political club or to write a book counted as pretentiousness, and deserved the most severe and graphic deflation. His caricatures of the feminists of the day, many of whom were active in the cause of the working classes as well as that of women, are scathing and merciless.

Daumier's three series of anti-feminist lithographs—the *Bluestockings* (1844), the *Divorcees* (1848) and the *Socialist Women* (1849)—originated precisely in the years around the 1848 Revolution, the very time he created his allegory of the Republic.

In many of these caricatures, such as *Man with Baby* or *Trousers*, it is the awful effects of dereliction of domestic duty that are stressed: husbands forced to take care of babies, made to sew on their own trouser buttons, relegated to household duties—a substitution which is represented as demeaning, against the natural order. At other times, it is the neglect of children that is made paramount: women who involve themselves in politics or in good works outside the home—like Dickens's Mrs. Jellyby in *Bleak House*, the classic example—condemn their own children to a life of recurrent disaster.

Daumier's strongest anti-feminist images, however, are precisely those in which he ironically contrasts the selfishness and ugliness of women who strive for independence or the right to participate in public affairs with the self-evident virtue of the charming little mother who

26 HONORE DAUMIER There's a Woman Who, in These Momentous Times, Is Content Merely to Play Stupidly with Her Children, from the Divorcees series, 1848

27 HONORE DAUMIER As Mother Is in the Throes of Creative Fervor, Baby Tumbles Head First into the Bathtub, from the Bluestockings series, 1844

knows her place, or rather, does not need to know it, simply exists like a flower or a plant in the sunshine of the natural order, for example, *There's a Woman Who...* And we, of course, are invited to share in the joke, as right-thinking people—men or women. Then as now, brilliant ridicule was a potent weapon against feminine aspiration.[25]

If, in his lithographs, Daumier consistently pilloried feminist activism in favor of domestic tranquillity, in his more serious paintings and drawings he constantly presents us with a maternal image of feminine virtue. Motherhood is envisioned as the only redeeming role for women, poor women particularly. In one of Daumier's best-known paintings, *The Laundress* (c. 1863, fig. 28), working-class motherhood is idealized by a romantic heightening of composition and monumentalization of the figure. The protective gesture of the laundress and the self-effacing bend of her pose as she turns to help her child are "accidentally" silhouetted by the irregular urban halo behind her, and the double burden of the mother's laundry and her maternal task are emphasized by the slant rime of the composition. Indeed, one of Daumier's most popular works, usually considered a realistic image of the *anomie* of the modern city, is in effect a consciously constructed hymn to the redemptive role of motherhood and the family. What we are confronted with on the front bench of the *Third-Class Carriage* (1856) is not social fragmentation, but on the contrary, a secularized, contemporary working-class version of the Holy Family in the form of stalwart grandmother, tender mother, infant, and child. It is the pyramidal force of this maternal relationship that holds the chaos and impersonality of the city at bay: the founding image of human warmth, dignity, and interrelatedness makes the painting at once memorable and sentimental.

No wonder then that Daumier chose the maternal image over all other possibilities for his allegory of the good Republic of 1848! Motherhood for him, as for most of his contemporaries, was the most positive feminine image available, and by the same token, the least threatening. What better vehicle for setting forth the virtues of the new Republic? I would not maintain that attitudes towards women played an absolute and decisive role in the invention of female political allegories in the nineteenth century—obviously, many other factors intervene—but rather, I am asserting that such attitudes should not be neglected in an attempt to give an adequate reading of these works or in trying to understand their creators' choices or rejections. I have also attempted to suggest a certain irony in this discussion. It is Delacroix, the dandyish élitist and a lifelong bachelor, the creator of scenes of female torture and victimization, an artist who satisfied his sexual urges impersonally with his models, who creates an allegorical figure of outright feminine activism, Liberty, the prototypical woman-warrior figure of all time. Indeed it was Delacroix, the friend and portraitist of George Sand rather than the satirist of her accomplishments, who had had the temerity to transform the same Charity image that had inspired Daumier's maternal *The Republic* (Andrea del Sarto's in the Louvre) into the ferocious but dramatically vivid image of *Medea* (1838), murderer of her own children, brilliantly reversing all the implications of his conventional model. Domesticity, a salvation at once personal and universal for Daumier, was either contemptible or irrelevant for Delacroix, maternity only interesting in its perversion. Delacroix's imagination ranged more freely among the possibilities: Enlightenment liberty and romantic enslavement and savagery could be brought to life with the same sensual vividness in his feminine representations.

For those of us who tend to see women's independence and self-determination as inextricably connected to the ideas of the political left since the nineteenth century, or who optimistically view women's freedom and self-determination as a kind of inevitable

28 HONORE DAUMIER The Laundress, c. 1863

historical evolution, this examination of two political allegories, and of the case of the woman warrior in general, should be instructive if not particularly cheering. At the same time, it should be clear that both Delacroix's *Liberty Leading the People* and Daumier's *The Republic*, as well as the earlier works considered above, offered their contemporaries messages about women as well as convincing political ones. Or, to put it another way, this analysis may have helped to reveal that the apparently public political beliefs and the presumably private feeling people have about gender roles at any given moment in history are more closely intertwined than has previously been suspected.

It was Charles Clément, Géricault's first biographer, who said it, in the context of a discussion of the young woman observer in the artist's lithograph, *A Pareleytic Woman* (fig. 45): "The figure of the young girl is lovely, and it is almost an exception in the great master's work. As a matter of fact, Géricault never, so to speak, represented women..."[1] When one considers the plethora of women in the work of David or Delacroix, their absence in Géricault's output is particularly striking.

Women are, indeed, relatively rare in Géricault's production. In this, his output differs from David's, in which gender opposition plays a central role in the creation of meaning; nor does it resemble that of his younger contemporary, Delacroix, where woman, allegorized as Liberty, represents the very aspiration—the unified and exalted project—of the variegated male figures following behind her in the artist's painting of 1830. It is hard to think of women, or a place for women, in Géricault's work, and when we do, we come up with a model of abjection and marginalization: a child, a cripple, two madwomen, a corpse, and perhaps a portrait or two.[2] Even in cases where the representation of women might originally have figured, or, even more, occupied a central place in the signifying structure of a painting, it is ultimately omitted. I take as my major example, Géricault's most ambitious painting, *The Raft of the Medusa* (ex. 1819), which bears witness to this striking occlusion of the feminine in the earliest stages of Géricault's development of his subject.

In a preliminary study for a different moment in the tragedy, the *Scene of Mutiny* (fig. 30),[3] a family group occupies the center stage, and was obviously of considerable importance to the intentions of the artist as he carefully experimented with the pose and expression of this woman-centered group in at least two detailed drawings (fig. 31).[4] But this emotionally charged group, consisting of a dying or exhausted mother, a meditative father and a heroically nude child quickly disappears; it is absent from the most finished preliminary study for the *Mutiny*, and is certainly no longer present in the next stage of the development of the subject, the *Scene of Cannibalism*,[5] never to appear again in any of the sketches or the final version.

30 THEODORE
GERICAULT Scene of
Mutiny, 1818

31 THEODORE
GERICAULT Family
Group, study for Scene
of Mutiny, 1818

32 THEODORE
GERICAULT The Raft of
the Medusa, 1819

In the final version of the *Raft*, the family group has been replaced by the "father–son" dyad, a paternal topos replete with pathetic evocations of the Ugolino legend. Age difference has been substituted for the original gender opposition; or one might say that the father–son couple now takes over the emotionally charged position previously occupied by the family triad, mother–child–father, in an earlier stage of conception.

One might, of course, insist that Géricault altered his cast of characters in the interests of accuracy: that is, he was merely following the all-male scenario offered him by the classic account of the shipwreck by two of its survivors, J. B. Henri Savigny and Alexandre Corréard. But did the same witnesses, in fact, supply information justifying the presence of a family group in the *Mutiny*? Now that I have gone back and read with extreme care Savigny and Corréard's hair-raising, highly detailed account of the fate of the raft,[6] a narrative which includes the events preceding, following and synchronous with that tragedy, I must answer "no" to both questions of empirical evidence. The Savigny-Corréard raft scenario did *not* stipulate an all-male cast of characters, but in fact included, with considerable prominence, a woman; on the other hand, there is no mention in their account of a family group among the ship-wrecked survivors on the raft. Géricault is usually held to have stuck closely to this best-selling description of the raft's vicissitudes: to have examined the drawing of the raft which served as the frontispiece of the French edition; to have followed the account's information about the presence of blacks among the survivors; to have noted the presence of water-casks on the deck; and of course, apart from his printed source, he is reported to have made a miniature mock-up of the raft which he floated on the waves of the Atlantic, and to have studied corpses in his studio in order to achieve a greater degree of horrific accuracy.[7]

On the other hand, Géricault, like most artists, even those held to be most "accurate" in reporting the facts of an event, was at once highly selective in terms of exactly which episode in the account to choose for his final version, and in his choice of a cast of characters. At the same time he was quite flexible in terms of temporality, putting together fragments of reality that did not necessarily co-exist all at one time in his textual source. This is, after all, a painting and not a film, although the Savigny and Corréard story could provide the basis of a superb script for a melodramatic and violent blockbuster.

Let us consider, in greater detail, both the presence of the family group in the preliminary drawings and the absence of women in the final version in relation to Savigny and Corréard's account. The family group, explicitly missing from the textual source, was Géricault's own pictorial invention at an early stage of his construction of the composition, a conventional enough figure of contrast, an island of normal life and feeling, isolated in the midst of hellish brutality and referring back to prototypes in traditional plague scenes and battle paintings. Géricault must quickly have realized that such a conventional representation, with no factual support from his well-known text, had no place in his picture, and removed it.[8]

Yet a woman—not a family group—played a considerable part in the Savigny narrative. This woman first appears as part of a couple, thrown overboard by drunken mutineers early in the ordeal. The account of her rescue figures heavily in the Savigny and Corréard text. It seems that after the rescue, she tried to reward Corréard with a little snuff, her last possession. "A more affecting scene, which it is impossible for us to describe, is the joy which this unfortunate couple displayed when they had sufficiently recovered their senses to see that they were saved," declare the authors.[9] The woman, unlike most of those on the raft, is given a full biography: she turns out to be, in the authors' pro-

Napoleonic, anti-Restoration construction, a kind of middle-aged Marianne, or Republican Mother Courage, who had served as a sutler—a *vivandière*—during the campaigns in Italy. She declared, in Savigny and Corréard's account "that she had never quitted our armies. 'Therefore', said she, 'preserve my life, you see that I am a useful woman...I also have braved death on the field of battle to carry assistance to our brave men.'" [10] True, she was not present at the end of the journey, having been thrown overboard after terrible suffering, but the authors give her a stirring eulogy, a eulogy heavy with political and nationalist overtones: "This French woman, to whom soldiers and Frenchmen gave the sea for a tomb, had partaken for twenty years in the glorious fatigues of our armies; for twenty years she had afforded to the brave on the field of battle, either the assistance which they needed, or soothing consolations..." [11] In brief, there was definitely a vividly characterized and even heroic woman on board the raft, available to Géricault's imaginative reconstruction of the narrative if he had wished to include her. On the other hand, while black soldiers are discussed—not very positively, to be sure—in accounts of the earlier portion of the raft's vicissitudes, there is no detailed description of black survivors at the end of the ordeal, much less any stipulation that it was a black man who waved the white rag at the top of the barrel.

The decision about which sections of Savigny and Corréard's account Géricault chose to illustrate and which details and players he included in his scenario is crucial to our reading of the work. Therefore, the elimination of the single woman from the cast of characters constitutes a significant choice within Géricault's larger patterns of decision, as does the inclusion of black males. Indeed, within the single-sex structure of oppositions creating meaning and expressive tension in the *Raft*, racial difference plays a major role, despite the facts that only a single black man seems to have survived to the end of the voyage, and that there is no documentary evidence whatever to indicate that a black man was at the pinnacle of those sighting the rescue-ship. [12] Racial difference nevertheless constitutes an important element in the construction of meaning in the *Raft*: like age difference, it takes the place so often inscribed by gender in major paintings.

To put it another way, the *Raft* as we know it, in its urgently unified yet interestingly variegated straining for the beyond, the unattainable, is premised, indeed depends upon, an all-male cast of characters. Homosociality—or even homoeroticism—is the conscious as well as the unconscious underpinning of the almost unbearable build-up of visual and psychic tension here. There is no room, no place for women in this carefully orchestrated symphony of masculine desire embodied in a crescendo of muscular urgency in which only the effectively dispersed corpses, pitiful, a little feminized, like rest notes in a musical composition, provide a measure of relief. One might even go so far as to say that the object of desire hovering so tantalizingly on the horizon is the ever (in Lacanian terms) absent phallus: that which is missing and appears, delusionally, in the unattainable distance.

This mounting toward nothingness, the perpetually doomed and frustrated chase after the missing phallus, is as far from the psychic (and

33 THEODORE GERICAULT The Wounded Cuirassier, 1814

34 THEODORE GERICAULT The Swiss Guard at the Louvre, 1819

formal) structure of Davidian balance as it is from that of Delacroix's allegory, in both of which women must be present to figure the opposing term, the closure of the trope, as it were. Géricault's figuration remains—painfully, dramatically, romantically—open.[13]

Still another strategy of displacement of the feminine in Géricault's production is constituted by the artist's frequent positioning of the male as victim. In his various military paintings and drawings, like *The Wounded Cuirassier* (1814) or *Wounded Soldiers in a Cart* (c. 1817), men are usually relegated to this time-honored "feminine" position. Or, to put it another way, one might say that in the whole series of memorable works dealing with wounded soldiers and veterans of the Napoleonic Wars, masculine vulnerability functions as a sign of the feminine. But even more provocatively, the wounded man, as in *The Swiss Guard at the Louvre*, a lithograph of 1819,[14] may covertly suggest castration rather than mere victimization.

One might maintain, of course, that femininity and castration are mirror images of each other, interchangeable within any given system of

35 THEODORE GERICAULT Decapitated Heads, 1818

representation. And castration imagery, in the form of executions and decapitations, haunts Géricault's imagination, from the time of the artist's days in Italy to those of his voyage to England[15] and in between, in his preparatory studies for the *Raft*. The series of uncanny still lifes of *Decapitated Heads* constitutes the ultimate post-Revolutionary castration theme in Géricault's work. But even more important, the meaning they construct, read in its historical context and bearing in mind Géricault's position within that context, is political as well as sexual, or, more accurately, political and sexual at the same time.

To summarize my argument so far: I would say that despite the absence of women in Géricault's *œuvre*, the signs of femininity and the feminine (in the form of the castrated or otherwise marginalized or disempowered male body) abound in his work. It is simply that these signs of the feminine have been detached from the representation of the actual bodies of women. To paraphrase the title of an important book by the cultural critic Tania Modleski, what we have here is "femininity without women."[16]

Nor are these the only strategies of substitution. Despite the dangers of parlor Freudianism, I must make a few observations about the central place occupied by the horse in Géricault's production of the sensual body, a place more usually occupied by the human female. The equine body is lovingly explored from front to rear throughout his career, from forelock to fetlock, as it were.[17] Can a horse be the object of the gaze, in

36 THEODORE GERICAULT Head of a
White Horse, c. 1816

37 THEODORE GERICAULT Horses' Rumps
and One Head, 1813

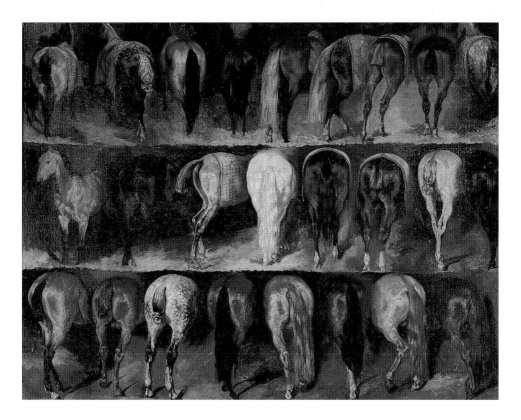

38 THEODORE GERICAULT Portrait of Louise Vernet as a Child, c. 1818

Lacanian terms? If so, the animal portrayed in *Head of a White Horse* (fig. 36) certainly is that object: soft-muzzled, hot-blooded and seductively coiffed.[18] The object of desire may have four legs and a tail, and indeed, be the object of a different kind of desire, but the analogue to a certain kind of erotica makes itself felt in terms of the sheer investment of libidinal energy in these and many other horse-images. The animal sensuality at play certainly raises these pictures from the banality of the sporting print to something more spine-tingling.

There are, of course, representations of actual women in Géricault's *œuvre*, representations which, if marginalized in every sense of the word—constituted by female subjects who are immature, crippled, mad or black—are nevertheless profoundly engaging and significant: marginal for good reason. The marginality of women is so conspicuous in Géricault's visual production that it may be said to constitute a central issue in the critical discourse surrounding his work.

First of all, we need to consider the question of origins. If the early work features the customary male *académies* (academic nudes) it is nevertheless clear that the young artist is capable of confronting the female nude with a certain amount of relish when required to do so. A comparison of his version of *Oenone Refusing to Heal Paris* (1816), a Prix de Rome drawing, with the prize-winning painting of the subject by J. B. A. Thomas reveals a much lustier, more assertive nude from Géricault than the bland, draped heroine in Thomas's offering.

But more to the point, in the mature work, if Géricault represents a female child, as in *Portrait of Louise Vernet as a Child* (c. 1818, also known as *L'Enfant au chat*), rather than a grown woman, it is hardly the conventional image of childish innocence—a good little girl—that confronts the bemused viewer.[19] Indeed, in the immortal words of Mae West, "goodness has nothing to do with it." This is a little girl with a

39 GUSTAVE COURBET Portrait of Béatrice Bouvet, 1864

40 BALTHUS Young Girl with a Cat, 1937

difference: an unforgettable, almost monstrous Lolita, comparable only with Courbet's rather similar though much later *Portrait of Béatrice Bouvet* (1864, fig. 39). The same coy, primitivizing quality is present in both works, perhaps attributable to the impress of popular imagery. In Géricault's portrait, the effect of uncanniness is heightened by a sort of gigantism: the swollen child overwhelms the surrounding, storm-tossed space, and uneasily masters the equally over-scaled cat on her knee.

Fetishism of the body of the female child and her accouterments has a small but significant place in nineteenth-century art history, often supplemented by the presence of an accompanying animal. There are perverse implications in the furry toy lamb Béatrice Bouvet clutches in Courbet's portrait. But it is the cat that is generally figured as the sinister portent of potential evil in child portraiture, especially when juxtaposed with childrens' "natural" innocence, as it is in Goya's portrait of *Manuel Osorio de Zúñiga* (1788) or, more explicitly, if unconsciously, in the case of the young girl in Thomas Eakins's *Young Girl with a Cat* (1872), as an evocation of latent feminine sexuality. In Géricault's *Portrait of Louise Vernet as a Child*, the roguish or seductive glance, the lifted skirt, and the falling shoulder of the dress seem like a foreshadowing of that odd sense of constraint, that hypersophisticated primitivism, above all, that atmosphere of the uncanny often associated with Balthus's twentieth-century renditions of the young girl, in at least one case, *Young Girl with a Cat* (1937, fig. 40), also accompanied by a feline. How different this is from the virginal delicacy and middle-distance remoteness of Géricault's more conventional *Portrait of Louise Bro* (n.d.), a mature woman, and, one would have thought, a subject more suitable for close-up delectation.[20]

Géricault's representation of the figure of the madwoman is in many ways as unconventional as that of the female child, both in its subtle mapping of the human geography of disarray and, at the same time, in the relative restraint of its representation of "monomanias," as they were then called.[21] Despite, or perhaps because of, Géricault's strict adherence to the project of his friend, Etienne-Jean Georget, head of the Salpetrière asylum, in cataloguing recognizable types of madness, it is remarkable that the artist avoided those stigmata of grotesquery or sexual excess so often inscribed on the figure of the mentally ill woman, and often considered identical with female insanity.[22] Indeed, Géricault's *Monomania of Gambling* (c. 1822) and his *Monomania of Envy* (1822–23) are remarkably gender-neutral: these are not represented as explicitly sex-related mental diseases like "hysteria" or "nymphomania," the female afflictions which were typically staged—and photographed—by Jean Martin Charcot later in the century.[23]

41 THEODORE GERICAULT Monomania of Envy, 1822–23

Géricault's is a very different kind of representation of madness in the feminine than that set forth at the end of the century by André Brouillet in his histrionic *Charcot at the Salpêtrière* (1888), marked by a beguilingly sexualized inscription of that specifically female symptom, hysteria. Indeed, one might say that difference is suppressed in Géricault's series: there is more that unites the male and female exemplars—a wandering, unfocussed gaze, red-rimmed eyes, a general sense of dislocation and inner tension—than anything that distinguishes Géricault's male from his female maniacs.

42 THEODORE GERICAULT Slave Trade (sketch), 1823

Equally interesting from the perspective of muting the representation of sexual difference (or maintaining a certain level of human dignity, if I may use the phrase), is Géricault's sympathetic *Head of a Black Woman* (1822–23),[24] where the artist has avoided the inclusion of the "natural" or "primitive" woman's exposed breasts as part of her portrait. Delacroix included them in his *Aspasie la Mauresque* (1826), as did several other artists of the period, among them a woman artist, Marie-Guillemine Benoist, who depicted the elegant black woman in her *Portrait of a Negress* (1800), with a bare bosom.[25] And certainly, as Géricault's first biographer, Charles Clément, points out, Géricault intended several women to figure in the great *Slave Trade* painting he planned: Clément makes specific mention of a "young girl who hides her face with both hands" to the right, a figure which adds much to the poignancy of the scene by suggesting the terrible rupture of family life and intimate feeling wrought by the trade in human beings, a theme explored more directly by the central group.[26]

43 MARIE-GUILLEMINE BENOIST
Portrait of a Negress, 1800

44 THEODORE GERICAULT Head
of a Black Woman, 1822–23

45 THEODORE GERICAULT A Pareleytic Woman, 1821

Equally responsive to the depredations of oppression embodied in the feminine persona, and again, a representation of personal suffering that inscribes a larger social malaise, is Géricault's lithograph, part of a series of prints inspired by a visit to England of 1821, *A Pareleytic Woman*.[27] How does one go about interpreting this painful yet relatively opaque vignette of backstreet misery? It does not tell its story clearly. Clément was drawn to the work and describes the daintiness of the younger woman onlooker and the contrasting bestiality of the chair-puller-attendant in considerable detail. He also contrasts the poverty of the bricolaged barrow of the paralyzed woman with the richness of the coach in the background.[28] Yet it is also possible (as the art historian Lorenz Eitner has suggested) that the dimly adumbrated vehicle to the right is a splendid funeral coach, decorated with a coat of arms, suggest-ing the impending doom of the victim in the foreground as well as offering a meaningful contrast to her state of impoverishment. The

46 DANTE GABRIEL ROSSETTI Found, 1854

paper tacked up on the wall above her seems to be an advertisement "For all sickness and the...", although it is tantalizingly unclear, like the meaning of the image as a whole.[29] I believe that there is a gendered subtext at work here. Paresis or general paralysis, the ultimate stage of syphilitic infection, was viewed, in the eighteenth century as well as the nineteenth, as the natural punishment for sexual infraction. In Hogarth's series of engravings, *The Harlot's Progress* (1732), it was represented as the final stage of the harlot's ironically titled "progress."[30] Could Géricault, thinking back to Hogarth, be representing a prostitute fallen on evil days? Would this account for the exaggerated reaction of the younger woman? Does this implicate the bestiality of the male assistant? Is the barred structure in the background a graveyard? It is very reminiscent of what appears to be a graveyard in the background of Rossetti's *Found* (begun 1854) which, though much later, also figures an urban, specifically London, setting and a fallen woman. One can also speculate, in considering this pictorial meditation on poverty, misery, social inequity and the modern city of London, that Géricault might well have read Blake's most apposite *Song of Experience: London* which begins: "I wander thru' each charter'd street,/Near where the charter'd Thames does flow,/And mark in every face I meet/Marks of weakness, marks of woe" and ends, "But Most thro' midnight streets I hear/How the youthful Harlot's curse/Blasts the new born Infant's tear,/And blights with plagues the Marriage hearse."[31] Although they are not an exact equivalent, Blake's lines, like Géricault's print, are a potent evocation of the dark side of urban modernity, using figures of prostitution, commodification and death to make their point.

Clément expresses regret about his hero's lack of appreciation of the more refined type of feminine beauty: "It does not seem that the audacious and learned painter was aware of feminine beauty in all its delicacy and distinction," he asserted. Nevertheless, Clément was well aware of the extraordinary quality of the group of erotic drawings that he then went on to discuss, prefacing his comments with a brief anecdote illustrating Géricault's lusty—even coarse—appetites for women: "He himself said 'I begin a woman and it becomes a lion.'" And even more revealingly: "and also, with great familiarity, tapping the shoulder of one of his friends: 'the two of us, X…, we like big b...s.'"[32] This anecdote reveals Géricault's directness in sexual matters, but, at the same time, the private nature of his expression of such feelings. Drawings like

47 THEODORE GERICAULT The Embrace, c. 1817

48 THEODORE GERICAULT Nymph and Satyr, 1817

Nymph and Satyr (1817) or *The Embrace* (c. 1817) were intended for private pleasure and restricted consumption—for sharing with a few friends, perhaps; they were not meant as studies for vast Salon productions or public exhibition. There are few graphic equivalents to Géricault's vividly articulated *agones* of sexual engagement. There is nothing coy or cozy, nothing vulgar, and no formal pyrotechnics—I'm thinking of Picasso's erotica specifically in making this exclusion—about these wash drawings: this is, if it is possible to say so, real sex. What is surprising is the figuration of women as sexual beings, active participants in the contest of passion, not merely passive objects of the gaze—poor little rich girls of the harem or poor little girls of the studio.[33] These women—mythic, for the most part, it is true, and creatures of fantasy—are strong and active, not passive victims. The male figures, interestingly enough (bringing to mind Géricault's involvement with the horse) are often partly or wholly—as in *Leda and the Swan* (1816–17)—animal. Again, to borrow the words of Clément: "He needed ample and robust forms, exaggerated, violent movements, expressions full of energy: always drama and passion with an overtone of heat, of sensuality, even of brutality, such as we find in his *Women Carried Off by Centaurs*, in the bacchantes of *Silenus...*"[34]

Clément regrets, or is at least "astonished by this disposition"; all the more astonished in that Géricault has indicated "by means of a hundred proofs the elevation of his character, the sensitivity, the excellence, the tenderness of his heart."[35] Yet we may count ourselves lucky, perhaps, that Géricault kept his elevated character and his tender heart to himself insofar as the representation of women was concerned. The issue, of course, goes far beyond the psycho-biographical one of a single artist's feelings or "attitudes" towards women, as it is often put. Géricault, the artist, produced his work at a specific moment in the social history of women as well as the history of representation. Social and cultural historians studying the late eighteenth and early nineteenth centuries like Lynn Hunt, Joan Landes, Dorinda Outram and Chantal Thomas have "made us aware of the peculiarly relentless exclusion of women from the radical renovation that ought logically to have furthered their liberation."[36] To borrow the words of Dorinda Outram, "The same arena which created public man made woman into *fille publique*."[37] The exclusion of women from public life which began during the French Revolution continued apace in its aftermath. In order to constitute a suitable public iconographic context for the representation of women, Géricault could, like Ingres, have resorted to Madonnas, Odalisques, and conventional portraits. To none of these practices would he lend himself. Instead, his rapport with women is established only in a small number of private representations, in the form of fantasized sexual images in which self-determined women engage in *agones* with often incompletely human male creatures, like centaurs. It would seem that Géricault gave himself permission in private images to fantasize about what was not possible, even thinkable, in his public images. By restricting the representation of the female nude to the realm of the private and by investing his erotica with such palpitating directness and energy, Géricault left himself with no place to go in terms of public exhibition: hence his strangely reduced, marginal production of this subject.[38]

I seem to have arrived at the paradoxical position of asserting that only those who, in the conventional terms set forth by Clément, are misogynists are capable of representing women fairly—an odd position for a feminist, but then again, not really. Degas, Seurat and, finally, Géricault, in their different ways, seem to have made out the most interesting cases for feminine representation in the nineteenth century, not those apparent admirers and idealizers of them, Ingres and Renoir. In the nineteenth century, with its increasingly commodified system of representation of the female body, a body disempowered, objectified, pacified, prettified, exaggeratedly sexualized or purified, Géricault's absenting or marginalization of women, like his representation of other oppressed groups—the poor or blacks or the insane—assumes the position of a positive intervention within the dominant discourse. Or one might say that, living as he did, briefly, before the conventional modes of both conservative and vanguard objectification of women's bodies had definitively been put in place, at the very time of what the costume historian Flugel has called the "great masculine renunciation," the boundaries of gender representation were still relatively fluid, more flexible and open to exploration than they were to become later in the century.[39]

Géricault was working at the beginning of a long trajectory: the hardening up and rationalization, through science, through recourse to the realm of the "natural," through the commodification of visual imagery, of clearly defined "separate spheres" for the two sexes, in social practice as well as in representation. Géricault was in fact, to borrow Clément's terms, but with quite different implications, too refined, too sensitive to indulge in this commodified kind of representation, or to create a sexualized image of woman at all, it would seem, except for his private pleasure and that of his close friends. Within the complex, but generally oppressive discursive construction of femininity during the early years of the nineteenth century, I understand Géricault's absenting of women from his *œuvre* as a relatively positive gesture: an absence which is, in fact, a moving and provocative presence.

No one can escape from ideology, history or the psychosexual wounds requisite to coming of age in our culture, past or present, yet some few have managed to make an intervention, no matter how slight, or with what lack of intentionality, in the seemingly monolithic structure of illusory signs and significations which construct femininity in the world of representation. Géricault, by absenting women from his representation in the way he did, and by establishing feminine presence where he did, was one of those—highly exceptional—interveners in the dominant discourse of his time.

In the middle of the nineteenth century, two major artists, Courbet and Millet, painted representations of contemporary agricultural practice. Courbet's *The Grain Sifters* was first shown in the Salon of 1855; Millet's *The Gleaners* was exhibited in the Salon of 1857.[1] The two paintings, both relatively large in scale and ambitious in their intentions and achievement, are, of course, in many ways strikingly different. Millet's is an outdoor scene, organized in terms of vast spatial extension, whereas Courbet's is an indoor one, more compactly organized on an up-tilted surface; Millet's *facture* is relatively neutral, the paint-strokes in most cases suavely blended together to create an effect of unity and continuity of form, space, light, and setting, whereas Courbet uses a dense, aggressive impasto and a discrete, more additive composition to define the picture surface. The pictorial structure of Courbet's *The Grain Sifters* is dominated by the aggressive energy of the central figure, whereas Millet's is a more relaxed, emptier structure, more lightly held together by the rhythmic repetition of similar forms. In addition, the interpretive histories of the two works are strikingly different: *The Gleaners* is so well known that it has become a kind of visual myth, a myth transparent to the multiple interpretations it has attracted over the years and inseparable from it as an experienced phenomenon; Courbet's *The Grain Sifters*, on the contrary, has been little discussed, is relatively unknown, and remains fresh and iconographically opaque. Nevertheless, both works are related in that both of these scenes of agricultural life represent the intersection of two of the most problematic issues of nineteenth-century social history: the issue of the status of the working classes and that of the position of women.

Although both works may be said to be realist, and both purport to—and in fact do—incorporate aspects of contemporary reality into their visual fabric, they are both, at the same time, historically conditioned mythic structures, replete with messages about sex, about nature, about work, about the role of women, about the nature of history. Both, in short, are documents of nineteenth-century ideology itself, mediated throughout the vision of particular artists.

What elements of ideology controlled that image of the woman-worker in the mid-nineteenth century? First of all, the notion that sheer need—the threat of poverty for herself or her children—was the only acceptable reason for a woman to work outside the domestic situation which defined her essential being.[2] Working women, like the one depicted in Daumier's famous *The Laundress* (fig. 28), who were poor, who were fated by sheer necessity to work as part of their central nurturing function, were accorded serious, sympathetic treatment. In Daumier's painting, the humble nobility of the proletarian working mother is emphasized by her pose, the self-effacing bend of the laundress toward her child; the praiseworthy altruism of this gesture is heightened further by the way it is silhouetted against the irregular urban halo behind the laundress, whose double burden of laundry and maternity is picked up by the slant rime of the composition. The middle-class woman who worked, on the contrary, was mercilessly pilloried by Daumier in his caricatures. It was an almost unquestioned assumption of nineteenth-century thought that middle-class women who worked—writers, for instance—only did so for specious and inappropriate self-fulfillment, and were therefore "unnatural" women

50 GUSTAVE COURBET The Grain Sifters, 1855

51 JEAN-FRANCOIS MILLET The Gleaners, 1857

and inadequate mothers. Daumier, for example, in a caricature like *Farewell, My Dear, I'm Going to My Publishers*[3] (1844), depicted such a woman as a frivolous, self-indulgent creature who deserts her home, leaving her child to the care of her long-suffering husband. The trope of the neglectful, middle-class mother who ignores the needs of her family for "higher things" is a commonplace in the middle of the nineteenth-century; both Daumier and De Beaumont depicted bluestockings busily writing on the joys and duties of motherhood while the baby tumbles into the bathtub (fig. 27);[4] Dickens, in the character of Mrs. Jellyby in *Bleak House*, creates the archetypal image of the reprehensible "do-gooder" whose children suffer total neglect and whose housekeeping is chaotic, as their mother works for the good of African natives oblivious to the pressing need of those who have the only rightful claim to her efforts: her long-suffering family.

Factory work for women was generally deemed a menace, not merely because the woman worker was frequently exploited, or because it might undermine her health, but, above all, because such work took her away from her role as sustainer of the family and transformed her into a social being, a human creature potentially in touch with wider issues and capable of conscious activism. Jules Simon, for example, later

52 GIOVANNI SEGANTINI The Two Mothers, 1889

to become Minister of Public Instruction and an important political figure in the Third Republic, maintains in his humanitarian tract, *L'Ouvrière*, written in 1861, that factory work for women is intrinsically bad: even if it is physically easier for them than grinding domestic labor in field or farm, it impinges on women's natural modesty and takes them away from their preordained role as guardian of the family. A woman-worker is no longer a woman, Jules Simon claims, and he repeats with emphasis Michelet's striking phrase: "The working woman, that ungodly term."[5] The woman factory worker was generally not deemed a serious subject for artists, at least not until later in the century,[6] although she was depicted as a part of the working process in articles about factory work in the popular illustrated journals of the time.

The rural woman-worker, the peasant-woman, on the contrary, insofar as she was poor, passive, natural, and understood to be content with her God-given role as mother and nurturer, served as an ideal vehicle not only for ideological definitions of femininity but for those of the good worker as well. Indeed, one might say that the female peasant, like her male counterpart, virtually embodied the positive image of the rural working class in the middle of the nineteenth century: the urban worker, male or female, was both more problematic as a moral being and ultimately far more suspect. As Robert Herbert has pointed out, in the case of the male worker, the positive image of labor was primarily a rural one in the second half of the nineteenth century.[7] In the case of the imagery of women-workers, urbanization often signified downfall: the lure of the city was visualized as a concrete moral threat to the virtuous female farmworker in a painting like Auguste-Barthélemy Glaize's *Misery the Procuress* (1860);[8] and, as Eunice Lipton has pointed out, a popular urban motif of the working-class woman, that of the laundress, was almost always viewed as an overtly erotic or, at the very least, as a sexually problematic one.[9]

The potent ideological association of the peasant-woman with a timeless, nurturing realm of Nature helped to defuse her potentiality, and, indeed, her actuality in France, where the memory of women armed with pitchforks was all too clear, as a real political threat. The assimilation of the peasant-woman to the natural order also helped to rationalize rural poverty and the necessity for grinding, continuous labor, as well as serving to justify the peasant-woman's subjugation to a tradition of male tyranny within peasant culture itself. Works like Millet's *Woman Feeding Her Child* (1861) or Giovanni Segantini's *The Two Mothers* (1889), the latter with its overt connection between the nurturing functions of cow and woman, make clear the presuppositions of a society which maintains motherhood as woman's "naturally"

53 JEAN-FRANCOIS MILLET Woman Feeding Her Child, 1861

ordained work, and demonstrates, at the same time, that the *peasant-woman*, as an elemental, untutored—hence eminently "natural"—female is the ideal signifier for the notion of beneficent maternity, replete with historical overtones of the Christian Madonna and Child. The Italian artist, Teofilo Patini, in *Mattock and Milk* (1883) creates a modern, naturalistic secular Madonna of Humility, who sits and gives suck on the same ungrateful soil her husband tills so arduously. In an image like this one, the spiritual and the animal polarities of the concept of motherhood are effortlessly conjoined. Fritz Mackensen, a member of the Worpswede colony in Germany toward the end of the century, depicts the peasant-woman in a similar way in *Der Säugling* (1892), in which the monumental nursing mother looms over the horizon, seated not on the ground this time, but on a wheelbarrow, a prop which effectively mediates between the reality of nature and the peasants' fate of obligatory toil.

The peasant-woman also served as the natural vehicle for uplifting notions about religious faith. In works like Alphonse LeGros's *The Ex-voto* (1860)[10] or Wilhelm Leibl's *Three Peasant-Women in a Church* (1883), piety is viewed as a natural concomitant of edifying fatalism. The peasant-woman served as the perfect visual embodiment of a conservative instinct to perpetuate age-old rituals, carrying them on by practice and precept from generation to generation.

Yet contradictorily—for ideology is, in effect, designed to absorb and rationalize self-contradiction—at the same time that the peasant-woman was viewed as naturally nurturing and pious, her very naturalness, her proximity to instinct and animality could make her serve as the epitome of untrammelled, unartificed, or "healthful" sexuality, as opposed to the more corrupt, damaged eroticism of the urban working-class girl. Sometimes this sexual force is veiled in idealization, as in the work of Jules Breton, who specialized in glamorizing the erotic charms of the peasant-girl for the annual Salons and for the delectation of American Middle-Western, *nouveau-riche* collectors. On occasion it is served up more overtly and crudely, as in works like Antoine Vollon's *Chicken Woman of Dieppe* (c. 1885) with its peasant-protagonist's revealing *décolletage.* But in either case, the peasant-woman's natural role as a signifier of earthy sexuality is as important an element in nineteenth-century visual ideology as her nurturant or religious roles.[11] Breton, who specialized in sweetly provocative field-workers, literally *saw* his subjects as naturally glamorous—as living, contemporary artworks, in fact. He felt that peasant-girls' figures were improved by their wholesome activity in the open air, and that their daily work in the fields helped to give them the well-proportioned bodies and the graceful, dignified posture of antique statues.[12] It is no wonder that rich American collectors in the nineteenth century were attracted to Breton's peasants: these charming young women were poor, they knew their place, they were not poor *American* working girls (which might have been unsettling); unlike many of Millet's peasant-women, they were physically attractive, and Breton's repertory was almost exclusively feminine. A work like *The Song of the Lark* (1884), bought by the Chicago collector Henry Field in 1885, became for a long time one of the most popular and frequently reproduced paintings in America.[13] One should not underestimate the role played by erotic attraction in the popularity of a work like *The Song of the Lark* and in general the appeal for collectors like Field of the image of the idealized peasant-girl. What could be a more beguiling combination for an American businessman than a sexy young body whose charms were justified by the virtue of labor and revealed by worn, coarse homespun or cotton? Ruddy peasant skin, when ladies where white; firm peasant muscles, when ladies were dainty; uncorseted peasant bodies

54 JULES BRETON The Song of the Lark, 1884

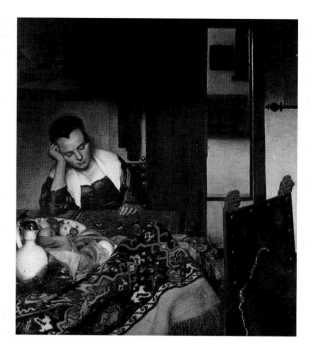

55 JAN VERMEER A Woman Asleep, c. 1657

when ladies were corseted and carapaced; bare feet and legs when women's ankles were always covered: all of these were sexually provocative in ways that are lost to us today.[14]

At times, sensual relish could be heightened by reference to the very virtue of the work contravened by the image in question, as is the case with Courbet's *Sleeping Spinner* (1853). The image of spinning is traditionally identified with female domestic virtue. Considered the most womanly of the manual arts, it was indeed so exclusively a female duty that the word "distaff" came to mean "woman." "She layeth her hands to the spindle, and her hands hold the distaff," says the Bible of the good woman.[15] A *sleeping* spinner, then, conveyed a sense of duty abandoned, womanly virtue along with it. A kind of sluttishness, or at the very least sexual availability, has been thought of as corollary to idleness in the moralizing imagery of Northern art since at least the sixteenth century. "Lady Dissolute" is the sobriquet of the neglectful spinner in a mid-sixteenth-century Flemish print *Carefree Living*, published by the Hieronymous Cock shop;[16] sleeping spinners, lacemakers and servant-girls abound in the iconography of seventeenth-century Dutch painting, all with the same implication of weakness of moral fiber, a warning to

56 GUSTAVE COURBET Sleeping Spinner, 1853

women about the dangers of sensual abandonment.[17] The theme of the neglectful spinner can be found in the repertory of popular art as well, in a print (an *image d'Epinal*) from the nineteenth century, *Good St. Lazybones, Patron of the Slothful* (fig. 57),[18] in which the moral weakness of idleness, personified by the woman who sprawls seductively daydreaming on her *chaise longue*, is heightened by her abandoned distaff and the unemptied chamber pot beneath her bed, and contrasted both with the industrious working woman outside her window and the spider who virtuously spins *her* web on the neglected window frame.

Yet it would be a mistake, and an oversimplification, to see Courbet's *Sleeping Spinner* as simply a continuation of the moralizing tradition of the past. One has only to compare Courbet's sleeping woman with a seventeenth-century "moral emblem" like Vermeer's *A Woman Asleep* to see the world of difference that separates the two. This difference is constituted not only by the plethora of meaningful symbolic allusions to the vice of sloth, personified by the sleeping girl, in the seventeenth-century painting, but to the assumptions on which such a moralizing allegory was based: the notion that, as Madlyn Kahr has put it, people have free will and must accept responsibility for their

dreams and fantasies as well as for their actions; the notion that idleness, or sloth, leads to other vices.[19] Indeed, in the most literal sense, for the traditional moral imagist, "in dreams begin responsibilities." Nothing could have been further, I believe, from Courbet's intentions in this painting than to suggest an overt moral issue, despite the fact that remnants of seventeenth-century Dutch precedents linger on in the very motif he has chosen. In addition, it is important to realize that, for the nineteenth-century admirer of Dutch art, the moral content was scarcely perceptible. Sleeping spinners or sleeping servant-girls were generally interpreted as simple realistic genre scenes, objective records of contemporary life, devoid of symbolic implications. Certainly, Vermeer's nineteenth-century discoverer, Courbet's friend, Théophile Thoré-Bürger, was far from believing that Vermeer had emblematic intentions in a painting like *A Woman Asleep*.[20] For Courbet, unlike his seventeenth-century counterparts, the sensual availability, the self-abandonment implied by the motif of work neglected in the image of a young woman who falls asleep at her spinning wheel, is a source of delight, not a cause for reproach. There is, indeed, as Werner Hofmann and Aaron Sheon have suggested,[21] something both of the fairy tale and of romantic dreaminess in the mood and attitude of Courbet's figure: overtones of the Sleeping Beauty who pricked her finger with the spindle, of the wistful songs of Schubert and Béranger on the theme of the spinner, or of Charles Nodier's dream-ridden heroine from his novel *Trilby*. And even if P.-J. Proudhon later characterized the spinner as "a real peasant-woman,"[22] contrasting her with the false and prettified versions of peasant-girls more generally shown at the Salon,[23] other observers of the work, including the critic Champfleury, have found her to be too rosy, well-fed and charming to be a truly proletarian figure.[24] Certainly, the work which is probably the immediate pictorial source of the motif, a drawing of a sleeping spinner by Vincent Vidal which had appeared in the 1850–51 Salon (the Salon in which Courbet had exhibited his *Stone-Breakers* and the *Burial at Ornans*), is decidedly Rococo and more related to the tale of the Sleeping Beauty than to the rigors of rural labor.[25] The overt setting forth of the pleasures of dreaminess and the frankly sensual, vaguely erotic aura that emanates from the richly, sensitively painted image pushed invitingly close to the spectator on the surface of the canvas are at any rate extraordinarily different from Millet's contemporary images of virtuous working women, quasi-religious icons of domesticity, depicted spinning, knitting, or sewing. Such an image is Millet's *Woman Sewing by Candlelight* (c. 1870), in

58 JEAN-FRANCOIS MILLET Woman Sewing by Candlelight, c. 1870

which the religious implications of selfless labor are made even more explicit through the juxtaposition of the sewing hands and the sleeping child in the background; it and the bent-over figure of the industrious mother are bound together by the luminous, spiritually significant vertical of the candle. The probity and self-forgetful humility suggested by Millet's depiction, as well as the alert concentration of his knitter's pose, are the very opposite of that sense of self-indulgent *disponibilité* created by Courbet in his *Sleeping Spinner.*[26]

Millet's *The Gleaners* embodies a similar notion of the near-sanctity of rural labor. The painting is, at the same time, an effective visual rationalization of the role of the peasant-woman within rural society. In *The Gleaners*, the genuinely problematic implications surrounding the issue of gleaning, though by no means completely erased, have been transformed into what might well be called a nineteenth-century realist "version of the pastoral."

Gleaning rights (the "droit de glanage") and gleaning itself, traditionally the way the poorest and weakest members of rural society were permitted to obtain their bread, had, from the Middle Ages to the nineteenth century, been fraught with controversy.[27] It was, furthermore, an area in which women had played a relatively active role, participating in the recurrent disturbances connected with the rights of gleaning: in the eighteenth century, for example, three *glaneuses* of Etampes had been condemned by the Parlement to be thrashed naked, branded with the letter "V" for *voleuse*, then forced to bear placards saying "women who stole grain at harvest-time under pretence of gleaning"[28] and finally banished. In the years closer to the time of the painting of *The Gleaners*, around the time of the 1848 Revolution specifically, the last, widespread violent resistance by the traditional peasant community to the encroachment of capitalist agriculture on their traditional rights, among them the "droit de glanage," had taken place.[29]

Yet if a few overwrought conservative critics of the time may have seen the specter of revolution hovering behind the three bent female figures in Millet's *The Gleaners*,[30] a more objective reading of the pictorial text here reveals that Millet was, on the contrary, unwilling to emphasize the expression of genuine social conflict implied by the contrast between the richness of the harvest of the wealthy landowner in the background (an absentee landowner whose presence is minutely but effectively suggested by the mounted rural guard, *garde champêtre*, in the background to the right), and the poverty of the gleaning figures bending over the rough, depleted earth in the foreground.[31] On the contrary, Millet, like most of his contemporaries it must be said, chose, by ennobling the poses and assimilating the figures to biblical and classical prototypes, to remove them from the politically charged context of contemporary history and to place them in the transhistoric context of high art. At the same time, through the strategies of his composition, Millet makes it clear that this particularly unrewarding labor must be read as ordained by nature itself rather than brought about by specific conditions of historical injustice. Indeed, the very fact that the workers in question are *glaneuses* rather than *glaneurs* makes their position more acceptable: women are more effortlessly incorporated into the natural order. Millet emphasizes this woman–nature connection in a specific aspect of his composition: as Robert Herbert has pointed out, the bodies of the bending women are quite literally encompassed and limited by the boundaries of the earth itself;[32] it is as though the earth imprisons them and condemns them to this fate, not a specific economic system such as feudalism or capitalism.

Millet's *The Gleaners*, pastoralized as they are, their work harsh and repetitive, look positively grim in contrast to the romanticized setting, rosy in the warm light of the setting sun, the poetically varied poses and the nostalgic atmosphere of Jules Breton's *The Weeders* (1860).[33] Looking at Breton's healthy, lithe young weeders (who are actually

59 JULES BRETON The Weeders, 1868 (original version painted in 1860)

gathering a food-crop rather than weeding in the usual sense of the term), it is hard to remember that the life of the female peasant in Breton's day was brutal and exhausting. Breton preferred his fieldworkers young with reason. "There is not a woman who is recognizable at the end of three years of marriage," wrote an observer of peasant life in the Hautes-Alpes in 1845. The peasant wife had to rise from childbirth almost immediately, take up demanding household tasks, do fieldwork in July and August, baby at her breast, take care of the cattle and clean the cattle barn, do the milking, and participate in the harvest in the fall. According to many witnesses, peasant-women never sat down to table with their menfolk, but stood, ready to serve those who ate at the table. Nor was classical physical beauty of the type admired by Breton considered a particularly desirable quality in a peasant-woman: it was simply not practical. Peasant proverbs of the period bear this out: "Beauty won't put food on the table" goes one; "It is better to dine with an ugly wife than to starve with a beauty" goes another.[34] Not only is there no sense of the grimness of peasant-women's lives in Breton's rosy vision of toil in the fields, there is not even a sense of the physical strain involved in bending, lifting or pulling. Breton, on the contrary, distanced his peasant-girl models from concrete effort by assimilating them to harmonious prototypes in classical antiquity, thereby reducing hard-working laborers to sentimentally sweet art-objects. Something of a poet, he articulated his aestheticized vision of one of his *glaneuses* succinctly:

> She's a child of the fields, rude, wild and proud,
> And her beautiful figure stands out clearly
> Against this simple setting.

In another poem, related to his painting *The Laundress* (1890), the sentimental classicism obfuscating his vision is made even more apparent:

> Phidias would have revealed the classical beauty
> Hidden by this boldly chiselled skirt.[35]

Neither the bent poses and pathos of Millet nor the sweetness and romanticization of Breton is evident in Courbet's *The Grain Sifters* (figs. 49, 50). It is indeed, as Courbet himself described it, a "strange picture," strange from a purely pictorial point of view that is, as well as an iconographic one. Although I do not agree with Mlle Toussaint that the oddities of the composition and color scheme are attributable to the influence of Japanese art,[36] the painting does owe much of its originality to the radical premises of this structure. Pictorial coherence is achieved here in what one might call true realist fashion by a sort of additive unity, a piecemeal but effective coherence which tends to play down what would otherwise be the total domination of the central figure. One feels an underlying relationship to Chardin in the seemingly casual placement of objects of related shape and surface texture throughout the picture. Yet Courbet's basins, bowls and containers are far more randomly distributed and more widely spread out across the surface of the canvas than the objects neatly related within a clearly receding space in Chardin's *Girl Returning from Market* (1738). As a result, in *The Grain Sifters*, the echoes are muted so that the resulting harmonies are less obvious, often verging on or actually becoming dissonance.

Perhaps, though, it is the sheer vitality of matter itself which militates most convincingly against implications of the sentimental or the grandiose in the painting and makes it unique. Despite the fact that space is implied by the corner-view, and light by the reflection on the wall above the head of the girl with the sieve, in the absence of any softening atmosphere one is far more aware of the differentiated textures of the whitewashed wall, the wooden door and moulding with a sliver of *image d'Epinal* affixed to it, the darker wood of the *tarare* (an implement into which grain is poured through a funnel at the top before falling through a series of graduated meshes which divide it from the heavier chaff) to the right, and the bulging, creamy beige sacks of grain, than of their space-creating or space-occupying functions; light itself is transformed into a tangible pattern of creamy impasto, criss-crossed by a dense granular lattice-work of shadow. In its contrast to the effect of coziness, the blurring of contour created by the atmospheric penumbra in a typical Millet interior, one can see what the critic Julius Meier-Graefe meant about *The Grain Sifters* when he referred to the "ruthless sincerity of its form."[37]

The pose of the central figure is, it is true, somewhat stylized, a little grandiose. The gesture of the sifter is assertive: the slightly over-contrived oval formed by her slender waist, the back of her straining neck and the sieve are balanced by the firm orangey pyramid of the outspread skirt and set off against the calculated pathos of white-stockinged feet, half emerging from their rough slippers. But grandiose or not, this energetic, dominating central figure is an extremely compelling image of the woman agricultural worker. The subject of *The Grain Sifters* as a whole, however, is an extraordinarily opaque one. What, exactly, is going on here? No one has ever even defined the precise nature of the subject, much less its broader ramifications. Yet before knowing exactly what the iconography of the picture is, we can respond on the most immediate level to the sheer physical force of the

60 JEAN-FRANCOIS MILLET The Winnower, 1847–48

central figure. Whatever Courbet meant by the picture, it would seem to have little to do with that mythology of resignation, piety or natural submission to the given order of things suggested by the paintings previously under discussion. Nor is the picture prettified, like Breton's, nor is it overtly erotic, although the voluptuous muscularity of the central figure, as well as various latent references to sexually charged motifs lying behind the manifest content, may, as we shall see, contribute mightily to the sheer vitality of the painting.

Even the exact title of the subject is ambiguous. Although consistently entitled *The Grain Sifters* (*Cribleuses de blé*) in the plural when shown in the nineteenth century, the work represents only a single grain sifter, the central figure: the two peripheral figures are engaged in quite different activities. In the letter Courbet wrote to a friend, the critic Champfleury, in 1854, explaining *The Painter's Studio,* he ended by

61 JULES BRETON Sifters of Rapeseed, 1860

saying: "I have a painting of rural customs which consists of grain sifters and formed part of the *Village Girl* series; it's a strange picture too."[38] When the work was shown in Brussels in 1857, it was entitled "the grain sifters, a scene of agricultural life in the Franche-Comté,"[39] and when it was shown in Besançon in 1860, "the grain sifters or the children of the farmers of the Doubs."[40] Two facts emerge: that Courbet in some way saw his painting as "strange" which suggests that he intended some sort of hidden meaning or implication; and that he was intent on recording the customs of his native region of the Franche-Comté, as he had already done in the *Village Girl* series and the *Burial at Ornans* and would later do in *Dressing the Dead Girl*—customs that were already beginning to disappear. Indeed, with particular reference to the activities depicted in *The Grain Sifters*, it is significant that by the second half of the nineteenth century, with the advent of increasing mechanization, women were being driven out of the major operations of harvesting and winnowing on more progressive farms, as Eugen Weber has pointed out. With the adoption of reaper-binders, the heavy, compressed bales of hay and straw became too heavy for women to handle, and the change from sickles to scythes demanded more strength than most women could muster.[41]

I suggest that in this painting Courbet is, among other things, creating an image of progress in the realm of agricultural operations: an image which is on the one hand personal—it may well be his sister Zöe with the *crible* and his sister Juliette to the left[42]—and on the other social. For by suggesting that methods of agricultural work do in fact change, Courbet is automatically taking the woman agricultural worker out of the realm of transcendent, unchanging nature and reinserting her into the realm of history, in which there can be change and progress. On the left, one may hypothesize, we have lazy, retrograde and inefficient hand separation of wheat from chaff, and in the center, the more progressive and energetic use of the *crible* or sieve. Millet's *The Winnower* (1847–48, fig. 60) represents a more primitive stage of the same sort of implement, incidentally: the shell-shaped wicker *van*. One is tempted to see Courbet's figure as a kind of response to Millet's monumental *Winnower*, a work which had been sold to Alexandre-Auguste Ledru-Rollin almost immediately after its completion.[43] To the right, in Courbet's painting, would be the final stage of sifting, or milling process—mechanization taking command, albeit on a simple level—with a device, the *tarare* or *blutoir*, so simple a child could run it.[44] If the notion that the theme of agricultural progress is embodied in the painting remains speculative, it does seem clear that Courbet intended to represent *three* different processes in this painting rather than merely the one, sifting.

The motif of the woman with the sieve, however, the dominant image of the picture, has a long tradition in art and text, and a tradition which tends to support the generally sexual interpretation of the painting advanced by Werner Hofmann and others.[45] Are there latent erotic implications in *The Grain Sifters*? Is the pose of the central figure "indecent," as one nineteenth-century observer called it?[46] What are the implications of the gesture of the little boy on the right who peers into the open door of the *tarare*? Are art historians like Hofmann simply reading twentieth-century Freudian meanings into a sexually innocent painting, or, on firmer ground, are they using modern psychoanalytic and psycho-historical techniques to reach deeper but nevertheless quite valid levels of meaning in the texts of the past when they see Courbet's grain sifters as a basically erotic subject?

In the case of the central figure with the sieve, the coincidence with a traditional sexual topos seems to make an erotic interpretation more justifiable. The sieve-bearer recalls the antique story of Tuccia, told by Pliny and Valerius Maximus, which recounts the exemplary fate of a Vestal Virgin falsely accused of losing her virginity who proves herself against her accusers when water fails to pass through her sieve.[47] The story was often represented in traditional art: in France, for example, by a School of Fontainebleau artist.[48] Whether or not Courbet was aware of such traditional precedents in high art is of course debatable. Yet to what degree had associations of sieve and the female sexual organ become a more available topic by the nineteenth century, perhaps perpetuated in popular sayings or folklore? And to what extent is one justified in suggesting certain "natural" associations between circular forms and female sexuality? Here, I think, we get lost in the mists of archetypal speculation, similar to those surrounding the issue of Georgia O'Keeffe's giant irises and peonies and the notion of "feminine imagery," speculation of dubious value today and even less justified in the pre-Freudian innocence of the nineteenth century.

If the subject of *The Grain Sifters* remains richly indeterminate, the sense of dominating energy of the central figure grasping the *crible* is unequivocal in its forcefulness. A similarly posed, back-view figure of a working woman from Velázquez's *The Weavers* (c. 1656), a figure which may in fact have inspired Courbet, looks positively lackadaisical in comparison, and the central figure of Jules Breton's near-contemporary *Sifters of Rapeseed* (1860, fig. 61) is a pretty, lifeless caryatid, merely holding the sieve as though it were a kind of attribute rather than really working with it.[49] Indeed, the only figures which suggest the kind of confident muscular expansiveness characteristic of Courbet's grain sifter are male ones, like Tintoretto's marvelously energetic ironworker shown from behind in his *Forge of Vulcan*. This is not, of course, to suggest a specific influence, but merely to point out that the kind of pose chosen by Courbet here is rare in the ranks of representations of nineteenth-century women-workers.

By the beginning of the twentieth century, the situation has changed. Even Courbet's monumental figure of the grain sifter seems frozen and self-reflexive in its energy compared with the wild vertical propulsiveness of the peasant-woman protagonist in Käthe Kollwitz's *Outbreak* (fig. 63), the central etching from her graphic cycle *The Peasants' War* (1899–1908). As a visual manifestation of woman's energy, self-assertion and power, it is to Millet's *The Gleaners* that Kollwitz's image offers the most startling contrast. One might even think

62 KATHE KOLLWITZ Revolt, from The Peasants' War series, 1899–1908

of Kollwitz's image as a kind of "anti-*glaneuses*," a counter-pastoral, with the dynamic, vertical thrust of its angular, female protagonist, who galvanizes the crowd behind her into action, serving to subvert the message of passive acquiescence to the natural order conveyed by Millet's composition. One might say that what Millet scrupulously avoided by resorting to the peasant-woman in his representation of the agricultural worker, and what Courbet kept cannily hidden, Kollwitz openly asserts: rage, energy, action. For her dominating figure of Black Anna, a leader of the sixteenth-century German peasant uprising, Kollwitz turned for historical as well as pictorial inspiration to Wilhelm Zimmermann's classical account, *Geschichte des grossen deutschen Bauernkriegs* (1891), which vividly described this powerful proletarian woman and, in addition, provided a popular woodcut illustration of her.[50] No doubt Delacroix's classic revolutionary image *Liberty Leading the People* lingered in the back of Kollwitz's mind when she created *Outbreak*: indeed, a similar allegorical figure had been represented by her as the inciter of peasants to riot in a much earlier version of a similar theme, *Revolt*. But the significant thing about Delacroix's powerful figure of Liberty, of course, is that she, like almost all such feminine embodiments of human values—Justice, Truth, Temperance—is an allegorical figure rather than a real human being, a perfect example, in fact, of what Simone de Beauvoir called "woman-as-other."[51] In Delacroix's painting, it is the men behind the female figure who are concretely described and realistically differentiated. Black Anna, on the other hand, as François Forster-Hahn has pointed out in her discussion of this series, is extremely concrete; the surging crowd of figures behind her are, on the contrary, relatively anonymous: perhaps the dynamic generalization of individual forms is meant to convey a sense of the active unity of the aroused proletariat. Significantly, as Forster-Hahn points out, Kollwitz has foreshortened historical distance into the present by introducing into the foreground of the scene the back-view figure of a powerful woman of the people, thereby, Forster-Hahn feels, persuading the viewer to identify with the event as the artist herself does.[52]

63 KATHE KOLLWITZ Outbreak, from The Peasants' War series, 1899–1908

Kollwitz, a feminist and a socialist who had been deeply influenced by August Bebel's pioneering document of feminism, *Die Frau und der Sozialismus*,[53] specifically identified herself with Black Anna, and told her biographer that "she had portrayed herself in this woman. She wanted the signal to attack to come from her..."[54] In *Outbreak*, for perhaps the first time in art history, a woman artist successfully pierced the structure of symbolic domination with conscious, politically informed awareness. Indeed, the whole seven-part cycle of etchings, *The Peasants' War*, although ostensibly and actually an account of the tragic sixteenth-century revolt of the German rural proletariat, is also a narrative of evolving feminine consciousness, perhaps, on the deepest level, an account of Kollwitz's own personal awakening to socialist feminism. The series progresses from the inert, helpless passivity of *Rape* to the ponderous thoughtfulness and incipient activism of *While Sharpening the Scythe*, to the explosive violence of catalytic feminine energy in *Outbreak*.

It is also significant that Kollwitz selected a narrative of outright social disorder for the representation of a powerful, directing, female figure. The topos of woman on top, to borrow the title of Natalie Zemon Davis's provocative study of sex-role reversal in pre-Industrial Europe,[55] has always been, and remained in the nineteenth century, a potent image of unthinkable disorder, as a popular woodcut like *Les Réformes du ménage* testifies. Generally, during our period, gestures of power and self-affirmation, especially of political activism, on the part of women

64 KATHE KOLLWITZ Rape, from The Peasants' War series, 1899–1908

65 KATHE KOLLWITZ While Sharpening the Scythe, from The Peasants' War series, 1899–1908

were treated with special visual viciousness. Daumier, in 1848, the very year of the democratic revolution fought in the name of greater equality, in his *There's a Woman Who...* from the *Divorcees* series (fig. 26), treats the two feminists to the left as denatured hags. Saggy, scrawny, uncorseted creatures, their dissatisfied gracelessness is vividly contrasted with the unselfconscious charm of the little mother to the right who continues to care for her child heedless of the tumult of history.[56] The working-class women activists of the Commune, the so-called *pétroleuses* (pyromaniacs), were mercilessly caricatured by the Government of Order, and depicted as frightening, sub-human, witchlike creatures, demons of destruction intent on wrecking the very fabric of the social order by burning down buildings.[57] In the sixteenth century, Pieter Bruegel had used the figure of a powerful, active woman, Dulle Griet or Mad Meg, to signify contemporary spiritual and political disorder.[58] Indeed, it is possible that Kollwitz herself may have turned to this, one of the most potent images of the menace of the unleashed power of women, for her conception of Black Anna in *The Peasants' War* series: Bruegel's image is more or less contemporary with Kollwitz's subject. Mad Meg, with her ferocious band of female followers, serves as the very emblem of fiery destruction, of brutal oppression and disorder; to borrow Natalie Zemon Davis's words once more, a visual summary of the reversal of the proper power relations and the natural hierarchy of a well-ordered world. Bruegel's *Dulle Griet*, unloosed from its contemporary political significance, might well serve as the perfect illustration for Yeats's "mere anarchy is loosed upon the world." For Bruegel, as for the nineteenth-century imagination, the most potent natural signifier possible for folly and chaos was woman unleashed, self-determined, definitely on top: this was the only image sufficiently contrary to "normal" power relations, rich enough in pure negative significance, to indicate the destruction of value itself.

In creating her image of the powerful proletarian woman, Black Anna, Kollwitz has transvaluated the values of Mad Meg, so to speak, and made them into positive, if frightening and ultimately tragic, visual signifiers. The dark, chthonic force of the peasant-woman, those malevolent, sometimes supernatural powers associated with the unleashing of feminine popular energies not totally foreign to witches, those most menacing of all female figures, here assume a positive social and psychological meaning. The force of darkness, in the context of history, is transformed into the harbinger of light.

Courbet's notion of the powerful female agricultural worker is of course vastly different from that of Kollwitz, yet though they may differ

66 GUSTAVE COURBET La Mère Grégoire, 1855

conceptually and pictorially, both the grain sifter and Black Anna share certain characteristics: both in some way subvert the acceptable nineteenth-century imagery of the woman-worker as conventionally come-hither, resigned, pious, or maternal; both imbue her, in vastly different ways and to different purposes to be sure, with unaccustomed energy and physical expansiveness, and both insist on a context for the working woman which is historical rather than atemporal. Courbet's figure, of course, is far from conveying the feminist and socialist implications of Kollwitz's cycle. His political engagement, his profound sense of rebellious independence, rarely ran to the overt expression of a precisely defined political position in his art. A figure such as Black Anna springs from a very different kind of socially conscious impulse running through art history, a more romantic, dynamic, expressive current, often depending heavily on allegorical representation and dramatic narrative to convey its message. Courbet's strategies as a subverter of the *status quo* are radically different from those of a Goya, a Delacroix or a Kollwitz. He never created a sequel or even an equivalent to Delacroix's *Liberty Leading the People.* Indeed, if he had been asked to create an interpretation of the ideals of 1848 like "Equality at the Barricades" in celebration of the 1848 Revolution, he might well have answered, as he did when asked why he had never painted an angel, that he could never paint a figure of Equality because he had never seen one.[59] At the same time, his notion of woman, as a motif for art-making, was vastly different from what might be thought of as either revolutionary or feminist in any sense of the word. His specific portraits of women are often sensitive, sometimes alluring, from time to time frankly coarse, like that of the so-called *Mère Grégoire,* but hardly innovative. His extensive repertory of sleeping women, clothed or dressed, such as the *Sleeping Spinner* (fig. 56), suggests an attitude quite opposed to that of feminine activism or heroism. His female nudes like *Sleep* (fig. 84), are, if sometimes anti-academic, often mannered and artificed, and almost always overtly sensual in their poses as well as in the richly seductive materiality of their paint surfaces. It is the nudes, ironically, which, in the context of feminine nakedness available to the high art of his day, constitute the subversive impulse in Courbet's imagery of women. But, it is an impulse which—in its overt sexual exhibitionism, its celebration of popular and semi-popular visual tastes in erotica, and its overt, unidealized presentation of women as objects of delectation for (presumably) male admirers—makes them difficult for many observers of today to accept at all wholeheartedly much less to accept as the daring essays into radical, sensual visualization that they were at the time of their creation.

Je fais penser les pierres.
GUSTAVE COURBET[1]

Allegories are, in the realm of thoughts, what ruins are in the realm of things.
WALTER BENJAMIN[2]

One can effectively undo authority only from the position of authority, in a way that exposes the illusions of that position *without renouncing it*, so as to permeate the position itself with the connotations of its illusoriness, so as to show that *everyone*, including the "subject presumed to know," is castrated.
JANE GALLUP[3]

Part One

Beginning from the Beginning: Wrestling with the Meaning

"It's pretty mysterious. Good luck to anyone who can make it out! (Devinera qui pourra!)" Courbet wrote to a friend about the big picture he was working on for the Paris Universal Exposition in 1855.[4] The painting in question is entitled *The Painter's Studio: A Real Allegory Summing Up Seven Years of My Artistic Life.* It represents, in a format reminiscent of the tripartite divisions of the traditional triptych, an oddly assorted group of people in an artist's studio, assembled around the central focus of the figure of Courbet, who is shown working on a landscape, in the company of a nude model, a ragged little boy, and a magnificent white cat. To the left are those whom Courbet described in a crucial letter to his friend and supporter, Champfleury, as "the world of commonplace life"; to the right is a less anonymous group, including such recognizable figures as Champfleury himself, the poet Baudelaire and the philosopher P.-J. Proudhon, a group which Courbet refers to in the letter as "his friends, fellow workers, and art lovers."[5] People have been struggling to figure out the meaning of the painting ever since Courbet issued his challenge. The title is almost as enigmatic as the painting itself, but it does provide an invaluable key to the interpretive strategy most suitable for unlocking the iconographic code of *The Painter's Studio*: it shows the painting to be an allegory.

According to Littré's *Dictionnaire*, the highest authority on French definitions, the term *allégorie* means: "A kind of continuous metaphor, a species of discourse presenting a literal sense but intended, by way of comparison, to convey another sense which is not expressed."[6] "In the simplest terms," says Angus Fletcher in the introduction to his magisterial study, *Allegory: The Theory of a Symbolic Mode*, "allegory says one thing and means another."[7] Even without the title, however, the visual evidence alone might lead us to suspect that Courbet was working in the allegorical mode in *The Painter's Studio*. The confluence of this oddly assorted group—a rabbinical-looking figure, a clown, a beggar-woman, an elegantly dressed couple, a ragged child, a famous poet, a naked model, and, in the center, the artist himself, natty in a bottle-green jacket and horizontally striped trousers—cannot be accounted for in terms of any sort of internal logic: clearly, this crew is not meant to represent a group of actual visitors to the painter's studio, as does a nearly contemporary work, no doubt known to Courbet, by the Montpellier painter, Glaize. Only allegory, it would seem, could account for the strangely muted, isolated, fragmentary and indeed, alienated, effect produced by Courbet's painting. *The Painter's Studio* seems bathed in a palpable atmosphere of melancholy, the melancholy of lost presence. Unlike the standard narrative painting of the time, and in contradistinction to the rules of academic composition generally, *The Painter's Studio* offers the viewer no meaningful interaction among the figures, no story-producing give-and-take of gesture or attention. Poses are, with rare exceptions, apparently unmotivated: each figure seems frozen in the way children "freeze" into odd or haphazard postures in the game of "Statues"; no figure is made to seem aware of or to pay attention to any other. This strange, frozen quality of the composition of *The Painter's Studio* tells us that the key to its significance lies somewhere outside the perimeter of the painting itself, that there is information controlling the system of meaning to which we, the viewers, are not immediately privy.

Courbet, the artist, plays a dual role in relation to the allegorical meaning of *The Painter's Studio*: he is both figured within it as one of its personifications—indeed, as its leading character—but has also chosen to play a role outside it in relation to its meaning. That is to say, in his

68 GUSTAVE COURBET The Painter's Studio: A Real Allegory Summing Up Seven Years of My Artistic Life, 1855

customary provoking way, he provided his friends and the present-day viewer with some confusing hints about his general intentions in *The Painter's Studio*, as well as a deceptively generous amount of data about the surface identities of the individual figures within it; equally, in the same long letter to his friend and supporter Champfleury (like Courbet himself, a character in this charade), the artist deliberately withholds information about the arcane, hidden meaning of the allegory, although he constantly drops broad hints about its existence, teasing the reader-viewer like a naughty child with a tantalizing secret. "I have explained all this very badly, the wrong way round," he concludes lamely after his unrevealing enumeration of almost every item in the picture to Champfleury, "I ought to have begun with Baudelaire, but it would take too long to start again. Make it out as best you can. People will have their work cut out to judge the picture—they must do their best."[8]

Although many of Courbet's contemporaries rejected the artist's attempt to suggest that his work hid profound meaning as characteristic pretentiousness and obscurantism,[9] more recent art historians have certainly taken Courbet at his word. Responding to his challenge, they have attempted to subdue the recalcitrant hidden meaning of *The Painter's Studio* like wrestlers—Courbet's own painting by that name provides a suitable painted equivalent of the situation—in hand-to-hand combat. Ever since the painting first came to the Louvre, in 1920, attempts have been made to decipher the meaning of Courbet's allegory, both as a general program and in terms of the individual elements within it. Such attempts have included the objective documentary approach of René Huyghe, the imaginative, wide-ranging interpretation of Werner Hofmann, the more empirical analyses of the late Benedict Nicolson, and of Alan Bowness and Pierre Georgel, my own reading of the work as a Fourierist allegory, and James Rubin's interpretation of it as a Proudhonian one.[10] All of these interpretations, however, were based on a more or less literal acceptance of the identity of the figures in the left-hand group, the "world of commonplace life," as Courbet had described them in the crucial letter to Champfleury: the Jew was a figure he had seen once in England; the curé was simply a curé; the huntsman a huntsman; the old-clothes man just that. Their allegorical function, it was believed, was simply to represent different aspects of the social order, to create an anonymous opposition to the world of "shareholders," constituted by the concrete portraits of Courbet's friends on the right.[11]

Then in 1977, on the occasion of the great Louvre exhibition celebrating the centenary of Courbet's death, Hélène Toussaint, the curator, made an interpretive breakthrough. Starting from a hint given by Courbet himself within the letter to Champfleury about the identity of the "weather-beaten old man" next to the curé,[12] she discovered that most of the figures on the left-hand side of the painting had specific if well-hidden identities. Far from constituting mere general references to the poor and downtrodden masses, each one referred to a specific, generally contemporary, public figure.[13] The adjective "real" describing the allegory in Courbet's title could now be understood not merely as a paradoxical allusion to the putative realism of the artist's style, but rather as a reference to the work's status as a commentary on real-life political events and positions. Its "real" meaning rescued from obscurity, *The Painter's Studio* could now be read once again—as it originally must have been, if only by a relatively small group of initiates—as a kind of political cartoon writ large.[14] The "weather-beaten old man" was now revealed to be a portrait of Lazare Carnot, once a member of the Convention, who had had a checkered career under subsequent governments;[15] the Jew was apparently a disguised representation of the contemporary financier and statesman, Achille Fould, a warm supporter of Emperor Napoleon III, who had been Minister of Finance from 1849 to 1852. The "curé" was actually the reactionary Catholic journalist, Louis Veuillot; the figure identified in the letter to Champfleury as an "under-taker's mute" was in fact the editor Emile de Girardin, who had initiated popular journalism in France in the 1830s.[16] The "old-clothes man" (*marchand d'habits-galons*) could be identified with Louis-Napoleon's close associate, Victor Persigny, who was nicknamed the "hawker" of the *Idées napoléoniennes*, a tract written by the Emperor; and the huntsman behind him to the left could be regarded as the representative of the Italian Risorgimento in the form of Garibaldi.[17] The man in the cap, in Toussaint's reading, would be Lajos Kossuth, representing insurgent Hungary, a figure not, in fact, mentioned by Courbet in the crucial letter to Champfleury but inserted later; the man with the scythe is now to be read as a portrait of Kosciusko, standing for the Polish freedom move-ment; and the laborer with folded arms next to him a portrait of Mikhail Bakunin, representing Russian socialism.[18]

Most startling of all, given Courbet's supposed animosity to the Second Empire and all that it stood for, as well as the fact that direct rep-resentation of the Imperial person in cartoons or caricatures was forbidden by the régime, was Toussaint's convincing identification of the booted and mustachioed figure with the hunting dogs who domi-nates the left foreground as a covert representation of Emperor Napoleon III himself.[19]

Having made these crucial discoveries about the hidden, and mani-festly contradictory, agenda of *The Painter's Studio*, Toussaint was understandably reluctant to draw any sweeping conclusions from them. Instead, she ended her decoding of Courbet's real allegory with a series of questions about the implications of the oddly assorted assemblage on the left-hand side of Courbet's painting. "Was Courbet", she asks, "being pessimistic or cynical when he assembled the 'betrayers of the Republic' on the left-hand side of his picture, as if to show that the best way of achieving dictatorial power is to use democracy as a stalking-horse? Is his work a testament of hope or disillusionment, an Inferno or a Paradiso, a farce or a tragedy? Is its message one of total forgiveness or total skepticism?"[20]

Shortly thereafter, a young German scholar, Klaus Herding, responding to the challenge of Courbet's allegorical conundrum (now rendered even more complicated by the presumed political identity of the figures on the left), wrested a complex and convincing solution to the meaning of *The Painter's Studio* from Toussaint's discoveries. In addition, Herding provided convincing answers to the more general questions of interpretation raised by *The Painter's Studio*. In an article entitled "The Studio of the Painter: Meeting Point of the World and Site of Reconciliation,"[21] Herding responded to Courbet's challenging "Devinera qui pourra!" with an interpretation of *The Painter's Studio* which was at once analytically incisive and synthetically inclusive. Basing his reading of Courbet's real allegory on the long but still viable tradition of the *adhoratio ad principem* or exhortation to the ruler, Herding interpreted the painting as a complex pictorial lesson designed for the instruction and edification of Emperor Napoleon III. Herding correctly and convincingly reads, and makes sense of, Courbet's hidden intentions in this work: to teach the Emperor, on the propitious occasion of the great Universal Exposition of 1855, a lesson in rulership. In Herding's view, in *The Painter's Studio* Courbet set out to construct a vast didactic panorama of reconciliation, of peaceful coexistence and harmony among opposing factions, classes and nations—to create an allegorical "balance of power" in short—organized around the redemptive and productive centering of the artist who is himself in harmony with the source and origin of all social and personal reconciliation: unspoiled nature, represented by a landscape of Courbet's native Franche-Comté on the easel before him.[22] Herding has accounted for every aspect of the painting's iconography and has satisfactorily contextualized it within the historical and discursive framework constituted by the Universal Exposition, with all its attendant hopes and ambitions. One might say that from the standpoint of art history, indeed from that of a social history of art, Herding, in his closely reasoned and masterfully inclusive argument, has finally solved the riddle of *The Painter's Studio*. The search for meaning is apparently exhausted: there is nothing left to discover. We have come to the end of interpretation.

From Work to Text, or The Allegorical Fumble

Having written this, I immediately feel a twinge of annoyance; indeed, a surge of rebellion. I have been put in a position of acute intellectual distress. It would seem that the more I know about *The Painter's Studio* the less able I am to collaborate in the production of its meaning. There would seem to be nothing more to say about Courbet's *The Painter's Studio*, no room for doubt: the interpretation is finished, the airtight case is closed; I, and by implication every other viewer, have been shut out of the house of meaning irrevocably. The only way I can get back in, it would seem, is by bowing down to authority, and I don't bow easily;

in fact, I don't usually bow at all. What I would like to do is to break down the doors, or, shades of Delacroix, storm the barricades! Partly, this feeling has to do with the role of authorial authority in allegory, an authority which calls forth a similar authoritativeness, not to say authoritarianism, in its interpreters. Allegory, to borrow the words of Angus Fletcher in his discussion of the literary variety, "necessarily exerts a high degree of control over the way any reader must approach any given work. The author's whole technique 'tries to indicate how a commentary on him should proceed'…Since allegorical works present an aesthetic surface which implies an authoritative, thematic, 'correct' reading, and which attempts to eliminate other possible readings, they deliberately restrict the freedom of the reader." Allegory, continues Fletcher, "does not accept doubt; its enigmas show instead an obsessive battling with doubt…[The reader] is not allowed to take up any attitude he chooses but is told by the author's devices of intentional control just how he shall interpret what is before him."[23] My distress may also be related to the way that the devices of allegory seem to accord so effort-lessly with the hermeneutic practices of art history itself, in which the production of meaning is all too often foreclosed by restricting its operations to the field of iconography, and within it, to unequivocal interpretations. Art history in this sense may be understood as an alle-gory of allegory: a rebus-like translation of elements in the pictorial "program" into verbal equivalents, with an edifying synthesis at the end. Meaning is understood to be finite, the interpretation of meaning restricted for the most part, as in allegory, to deciphering the intentions of the author. I seem to be faced with an open-and-shut case, the end of interpretation rather than the beginning, the suppression of doubt and ambiguity rather than an opening up to them; the death of meaning in the painting rather than its vivification.

This sort of interpretation, based on the assumed authority of the One Who Knows, while necessary from the vantage point of art history, tends not merely to close off the possibility of interpretation rather than opening it, but even more dubiously, militates against coming to terms with the myriad concrete meanings produced by the painting itself, independent of any intentions of the artist and at times in opposition to his intentions. Although Courbet may indeed have meant to create a grand vision of harmony, *The Painter's Studio* in its existence as a system of signs producing meanings is anything but harmonious. This is so for several reasons. Most importantly, allegory can be looked at from a very different viewpoint from that of authoritative closure and con-striction of meaning; it may rather be understood as a mode which operates in a theater of disjunction and disengagement. The presence of allegory signals to us the very opposite of that system of organic unity presupposed by the vision of harmony Herding has convincingly demonstrated to be present in *The Painter's Studio.*

Courbet as an artist came to maturity at a time when political revolution and, later, the failure of political revolution, destabilized all socially produced meanings, calling such meanings, including the meaning of art, into question. Like most of the interesting painters of the mid-nineteenth century, working in the uncertain space between the older Academy/Salon system and the still nascent one of free-enterprise production for an uncertain public and an equally uncertain private market mediated by dealers, Courbet realized that he had to choose a way of painting: he could not merely inherit one. It was unclear where painting was going; unclear what relation it had to tradition; unclear what constituted a new or modern direction for art. What indeed was "tradition" in the 1840s or 1850s? Could it be understood as anything but fragments, ruins, fleeting and partial visions?

Allegory, as Walter Benjamin suggested in his great study of German tragic drama, *Trauerspiel*,[24] bears a natural affinity to disintegrative moments of history: times which are not merely disorganized, but, so to speak, "dis-organicized"; when the ideological assumptions holding things together and the power structures engaging with such unity begin to fall apart—when the center no longer holds. "Allegory", says Frederic Jameson in his penetrating analysis of Benjamin's study, "is precisely the dominant mode of expression of a world in which things have been for whatever reason utterly sundered from meanings, from spirit, from genuine human existence."[25] Central to Benjamin's understanding of allegory, in his *Trauerspiel* study, is its wresting apart of the unity of signifier and signified, what is often, in the case of metaphor, and by extension, in the case of allegory, referred to as the "vehicle" and the "tenor" of the figure;[26] its insistence upon the material density and independence of the signifier; the dead, mutilated insubstantiality of the signified. Allegories like Courbet's, in attempting acts of visible reunification, inevitably show their hand: "The more things and meanings disengage, the more obvious become the material operations of the allegories that fumble to reunite them," declares Terry Eagleton in his discussion of Benjamin's *Trauerspiel.*[27] "Fumble" is certainly the operative word here since no allegory ever succeeds in its attempted reunification. Indeed, there is a certain dark, even tragic, pessimism implicit in the way allegory re-enacts the dilemmas of disconnectedness, dilemmas which perhaps, in the last analysis, are not

69 JEAN–AUGUSTE–DOMINIQUE INGRES The Apotheosis of Homer, 1827–33

merely moral and epistemological, but ontological. Given what Jameson, in the analysis of Benjamin's *Trauerspiel* already cited above, terms the "historical impossibility in the modern world for genuine reconciliation to endure in time," allegory becomes "the privileged mode of our own life in time, a clumsy deciphering of meaning from moment to moment, the painful attempt to restore a continuity to heterogeneous, disconnected instants."[28]

Of course, to return to the nineteenth century and to painting, there is allegory and allegory. Ingres, in his allegory of the position of art and the artist, *The Apotheosis of Homer* (1827–33), constructs a figural equivalent of the most rigid authority, firmly positioning each figure within the hierarchy of creative achievement on either side of Homer, the blind father-figure of all art, who holds sway in the exact center of the composition. The figure of the artist here rules over his belated cohorts with the hieratic authority of an archaic Zeus. In *The Apotheosis of Homer*, history is transformed by the allegorical impulse into an enabling myth of origins under the aegis of the classical, ordered by static symmetry into a permanent emblem of the pedigree and permanence of power. Aesthetic control in Ingres's work is overtly equated with a politics of domination. An almost desperate smoothness of surface, a near-compulsive perfection of finish here anxiously attempts to secure a conviction of the perfect unity between things and meanings. Yet it is interesting to see to what extent Ingres has failed to convince us of the absolute authority of his expression of artistic totalitarianism; how, exactly because Ingres works so hard at the *retour à l'ordre*, we are made more than ever aware of the arduousness of the effort at the expense of the assumed "naturalness" of the order he tries to instate. No more than in Courbet's far more destabilizing and imperfect allegorical image does the relation between form and meaning seem natural in Ingres's work, much less convincing. This of course has something to do with the history of the nineteenth century, not just the history of its art. To repeat Eagleton's phrase: "The more things and meanings disengage, the more obvious become the material operations of the allegories that fumble to reunite them." In the case of the allegorical mode operating in *The Painter's Studio*, its "material operations" are made all the more evident by Courbet's realist language, which calls our attention unrelentingly to the disjunctions between the things represented and their latent meanings, surely the very opposite of a "harmonious" relationship. But it is precisely in that "fumble"–that uncolonized territory between ball and hand, as it were–in the gaps between things and meanings, that is to say in the failure, spatially, to restore unity to fragments or temporally, to impose continuity on disconnected instants, that the really interesting meanings of Courbet's allegory are produced: what one might be justified in calling the "real allegory" of *The Painter's Studio*.

What is interesting to me, as a reader who has been shut out of the house of meaning, is the way in which Courbet's allegory fails, how it cannot create a complete and finished system of meaning; it is, after all, both figuratively and literally incomplete and unfinished–therefore, in Baudelairean terms, open to the infinite interpretive field of the imagination. This encourages me–and all those who insist on enjoying art as a text rather than merely consuming it as a work, to borrow Roland Barthes's terms–to collaborate in the production of meaning in Courbet's allegory.[29] For Courbet's real allegory is, in an important sense, also an allegory of the unfinished, of the impossibility of ever finishing, in the sense of imposing a single, coherent meaning on a work of art.

Because it is unfinished, it is more than ever possible to consider *The Painter's Studio* as a field of uncertainty, in which vague and more substantial incidents rise, assert themselves for a while, and then fade away on the vast projective screen of the canvas. Indeed, there is a neat coincidence between our word "infinite" and the French word *infini* (unfinished). The slippery flow of unfixed meaning, the interminable production of significance, has a material source in the painting's incompleteness. Undoing the phallic illusions of Courbet as well as the authority of the central image of the artist, an image which speaks to our own phallic illusions of plenitude, the unfinished condition of the painting counters the apparent closure of Courbet's *tableau vivant* by creating other meanings, totally apart from authorial intentions and often working against them.

The unfinishedness of *The Painter's Studio* is a major element enabling me to read it against the grain. In the most literal way possible, *The Painter's Studio* speaks itself as an unharmonious fumble: can one really speak of an incomplete harmony, an unfinished unity? The fact that *The Painter's Studio* is unfinished is rarely discussed in terms of the meaning of the work.[30] Generally, it is simply mentioned as a contingency with little or no effect, simply an empirical accident in the history of the painting's creation. Courbet, it seems, caught jaundice and, despite working day and night, was unable to bring it to completion in time for the deadline for the submission of works to the jury of the Universal Exposition.[31] Yet of course, even speaking on the level of biography and personal intention, Courbet could have finished it after the fact if he had wanted or been able to. For whatever reasons, it remains an unfinished painting and our reading of it must be based on that fact, or, rather, that it is partly sketchy, with elements barely adumbrated, and partly richly painted, quite highly wrought. This equivocal and disharmonious condition of the work must enter into our reading of it as much as its iconography, for it produces meanings as much as, though in a different way from, the iconography. *The Painter's Studio* would be a very different work, would mean something very different, if it had been completed, finished as highly as an allegorical painting like Ingres's *The Apotheosis of Homer*. Indeed, one might say that the air of "mystery" by which the work is so frequently characterized is produced just as much by its unfinishedness as by its "hidden" iconographical implications, and that the mystery produced by this sketchiness, or figural unclarity and openness, continues even after and in opposition to the clarification

70 JACQUES-LOUIS DAVID The Death of Marat, 1793

provided by the authoritative readings of the hidden message of the piece provided by Toussaint and Herding. As such, *The Painter's Studio* constitutes an allegory of unfinishedness.

So far, I have been using "unfinished" and "incomplete" as though they were synonymous. Indeed, they almost are in English, but not in French. Baudelaire, in fact, in his famous discussion of the subject, made a good deal of the difference between a work that is completed ("fait") and a work which is finished ("fini"). "In general," he maintains, "what is complete is not *finished*, and...a thing that is highly *finished* need not be complete at all."[32] Courbet's *The Painter's Studio*, however, is one of the few major paintings to be both incomplete, that is to say, left unfinished by the artist, and at the same time, not highly finished in many of the parts that the painter did bring to completion. Ironically, the painting is least highly finished, most overtly just unmanipulated pigment, exactly where one might say it is most "complete": in that part of the image of the artist where he may be said to demonstrate the originary roots of art—in the demonstrable lumps of highly visible paint on his palette.

Now there is a historical precedent for this contrast between the sketchy, with its overtones of evocation, of openness to imaginative possibility, and the finished, which implies perfection, closure and deliberateness; painters have long used this contrast to produce meanings.[33] There is one order of meaning in classical painting where a certain vagueness or sketchiness, an obliteration of clarity and specificity, has a primary function: that is, in producing significations of temporal distance or of universality. In David's *The Death of Marat* for instance, the vaguely adumbrated background removes the dead figure, with all its specificity of circumstance, from the immediate present and sets it in the vast, unclarified spaces of History and Universal Truth. The speckled, luminous surface of the background works on us like some angelic choir singing the hero Marat's praises in the background, moving us both backward in time to ennobling historical precedent and forward to a utopian future. Closer to Courbet's time, Thomas Couture, in his *Romans of the Decadence,* used the relative sketchiness of the depths of his painting to suggest a kind of pictorial pluperfect, the past within the past: a time, in fact, when the Romans had been upright and self-denying, the very opposite of decadent. In Courbet's *The Painter's Studio,* the contrast between the parts of the painting that are merely adumbrated, as opposed to those brought to completion, also work to create temporal

71 THOMAS COUTURE Romans of the Decadence, 1847

distance: his own past, explicitly stipulated in the title by the phrase "...seven years of my artistic life," is constituted by the paintings hanging on the back wall which are hardly more than ghostly presences, through whose transparent skeletons the texture of the canvas makes its appearance. Although in the letter to Champfleury, Courbet mentioned specific titles–*The Return from the Fair* and *The Bathers*–of works to be depicted on the back wall, they are hardly recognizable as individual works. Rather, there is a constant shifting taking place between our awareness of these "canvases" defining the back wall of the studio in the painting as painted images, and the intrusive presence of the actual canvas which serves as a support to the painting itself. This perceptual oscillation between represented and literal surfaces serves further to undermine the reading of *The Painter's Studio* as a finished product and to render it open to interpretation as process, a process of paint coming into being as form on canvas. Similarly, the contrast between the completeness and plenitude of the central section and the relative thinness and insubstantial vagueness of many portions of the lateral areas, as well as the light and dark contrast between them, tends to de-emphasize the social and political community "in the wings," as it were, in favor of the dominating group of the individual artist, his work and his model, along with his two wealthy patrons. Inconsistencies of scale add to the sense of floating vagueness which complicates the spatial relations of *The Painter's Studio*: figures in the rear of the painting, like the worker's wife, are so small in scale that they seem illogically distant; the position of the lovers on the right is undefined and indefinable; the back wall of the studio provides a spatially uncertain, as well as an almost transparent, boundary for the composition. The fact that Courbet based most of his images of his friends and associates–Champfleury, Bruyas, Buchon, Baudelaire–on pre-existing portraits he had made, rather than having them come and pose for him in the studio, adds to my sense of the painting as a collage of temporally fragmented and materially unintegrated parts, in this case, parts obtained by a re-appropriation of his own previous work.

As I look at *The Painter's Studio* with a full awareness that it is unfinished, that it is, in essence, a construction of fragments more or less successfully but by no means finally or definitively sutured together and hence eminently deconstructable and/or reconstructable, separate motifs begin to detach themselves or combine, insisting on their fragmentary presence and refusing to reintegrate themselves within the totalizing authority of the composition as a whole. One motif in particular floats up from the brownish, undersea depths of the painting, commanding my gaze. What thrusts itself most insistently on my attention is the motif on the left—which can be read as a miniature allegory in itself—constituted by the descending trio of the *croque-mort*, the skull on the newspaper, and the black-clad Irishwoman (fig. 72), a woman whom Courbet claimed he had seen "in a London street wearing nothing but a black straw hat, a torn green veil and a ragged black shawl, and carrying a naked baby under her arm."[34]

If an allegory is, as Benjamin has stated, in some sense a ruin, then the impoverished Irishwoman, emerging from the *non finito* of Courbet's composition, is the very epitome of allegory; at the same time, in the context of Courbet's iconography, she can be read as a figure more concretely signifying the unfinished. As Herding has pointed out, in his reading of *The Painter's Studio* as an *adhoratio ad principem*, this exhortation "implies mourning, warning and hope: a silent mourning is articulated with the mother dressed in rags, sitting near the feet of the Emperor; she proves drastically that his promise to eliminate poverty had by no means been fulfilled—after all Louis-Napoleon had written a book in 1844 carrying the title *L'Extinction de la pauvreté*."[35] The ruinous Irishwoman, then, stands for unfinished business, an incompleteness in the realm of the political as well as that of the pictorial, a fumble in the unifying modality of allegory itself—an aporia in the realm of utopian possibility.

Although Herding simply contrasts the beggar-woman with the figure of Emperor, as a signifier of unfinished political business, there are other important oppositions established by the figure. There are, first of all, intertextual readings within the history of art itself which endow this melancholy mourning figure, a figure of want *par excellence*, with new significances: the historically delimited meaning embodied in Louis-Napoleon's failure to "extinguish" poverty is only the tip of the iceberg. I propose to read the Irishwoman as a modern figure of Melancholy. As such, within the context of a feminist hermeneutics,[36] she points directly back to the great mother-figure of melancholy herself, Dürer's *Melencolia I* (fig. 73), which, in a sense, can also be figured as the mother of allegory as it has been interpreted for our times.

At the heart of Walter Benjamin's study of allegory in his great book on the German Tragic Drama lurks *Melencolia I*, that massive emblem of saturnine genius disenabled, unproductive, in mourning for what one might think of as both a lost transcendence and a damaged immanence: the loss of meaningfulness itself. A whole section of Benjamin's study of the *Trauerspiel* is devoted to the subject of melancholy, of which Dürer's *Melencolia I* is the founding image and a constantly invoked object of

72 GUSTAVE COURBET The Painter's Studio (detail of Irishwoman), 1855

contemplation. Benjamin associates melancholy with many other emblems; the prophetic wisdom of the melancholic is especially associated with the nether world: "For the melancholic," he says, "the inspirations of mother earth dawn from the night of contemplation."[37] "In Dürer's *Melencolia I*," declares Norman Bryson, pondering Benjamin's meditation on this figure, "the world ceases to be plenitude and becomes first allegory, existing piece by piece to transmit its emblematic meanings; but then once the allegory has been grasped and the content of signification has been released, the world is emptied, drained, sorrowful. Its signification has gone, the world persists but it has now lost something that can never be replaced or retrieved—its meaningfulness. After their excited discharge of meaning, its objects are *spent*, and the game of melancholy follows on the gaze of allegory. Dürer is clearly the classical source of statement of the connection between meaning and sadness..."[38] The "connection between meaning and sadness" is clearly at stake in any serious interpretation of Courbet's figure of the beggar-woman as she relates to the overwhelming precedent of Dürer's *Melencolia I*. If, in addition, like Dürer's *Melencolia I*, the beggar-woman is indeed an allegorical figure, which she surely is, then her meaning is subject to almost endless interpretation. In other words, she cannot be reduced to standing merely for poverty or the condition of Ireland or any other single "tenor." Both her meaning and

73 ALBRECHT DURER Melencolia I, 1514

her sadness are too large for this. If, says Benjamin, allegory "'enslaves objects in the eccentric embrace of meaning,' that meaning is irreducibly multiple."[39]

I am in this instance insisting upon still another aspect of allegory, one almost diametrically opposed to the one I posited above when I complained so bitterly about the authoritarian control the allegorist, Courbet in this case, maintained over the reader-viewer, and the authoritarian reductivism of the resulting "translation" of the painted text. But allegory offers the reader very different possibilities, as Eagleton points out, citing Walter Benjamin to make his point. The nature of these possibilities is important enough to justify reproducing the passage at length. Says Eagleton:

> The very arbitrariness of the relations between signifier and signified in allegorical thought encourages "the exploitation of ever remoter characteristics of the representative objects as symbols"...In an astounding circulation of signifiers, "any person, any object, any relationship can mean absolutely anything else." The immanent meaning that ebbs from the object under the transfixing gaze of melancholy leaves it a pure signifier, a rune or fragment retrieved from the clutches of an univocal sense and surrendered unconditionally into the allegorist's power. If it has become in one sense embalmed, it has also been liberated into polyvalence: it is in this that for Benjamin the profoundly dialectical nature of allegory lies. Allegorical discourse has the doubleness of the death's head: "total expressionlessness— the black of the eye-sockets—coupled to the most unbridled expression—the grinning rows of teeth."[40]

In my role of interpreter of *The Painter's Studio*, I also have a certain doubleness, *vis-à-vis* the meaning of the allegory. If I am its prisoner in one sense, I am also its creator in another. "All commentary is allegorical interpretation, an attaching of ideas to the structure of poetic imagery," declares Northrop Frye of the literary variety.[41] If, as I believe, all interpretation is in some sense an allegory, then in rereading Courbet's *The Painter's Studio*, I am in turn really allegorizing the "real allegory." I am not, however, free to read this figure in any way I choose. Just how I allegorize the beggar-woman depends on who I am and where and when I am doing the interpretation: interpretation occurs concretely, in specific historical circumstances, and, since the figure is a woman and I am a woman quite consciously reading *as* a woman, gender is a crucial issue here as well.

Beginning with the End: Reading as a Woman

For me, reading as a woman, but nevertheless reading from a certain position of knowledge and hence privilege, in the United States in the twentieth century, the Irish beggar-woman constitutes not just a dark note of negativity within the bright utopian promise of the allegory of *The Painter's Studio* as a whole, but rather, negates such promise as a totality. The poor woman—a dark, indrawn, passive, source of melancholy within the painting as well as a reference to it outside its boundaries—constitutes both a memorial to melancholy past and the repressed that returns, turning against both the triumphant harmony of Courbet's allegory, and the sermon of art's triumph that dominates its center. The Irish beggar-woman is thus the really realist vehicle of the allegory, interrupting the flow of its intentional meaning. In short, to me, reading as a woman, the beggar-woman sticks out like a sore thumb. In her, the would-be allegorical connection between thing and meaning is really fumbled. Because of the material specificity of Courbet's language, we are made aware, in the most substantial and moving way possible, of allegory's other potential: to emphasize the signifier at the expense of the signified. Embodying in a single figure the convergence of gender and class oppressions, the Irishwoman for me becomes the central figure, the annihilation-cancellation of Courbet's project, not merely a warning about its difficulty. Figuring all that is unassimilable and inexplicable—female, poor, mother, passive, unproductive but reproductive—she denies and negates all the male-dominated productive energy of the central portion, and thus functions as the interrupter and overturner of the whole sententious message of progress, peace and reconciliation of the allegory as a whole. In my rereading of Courbet's *The Painter's Studio*, the Irishwoman as a figure refuses to stay in her place and act as a mere vehicle of another more general meaning, be it Poor Ireland or the Problem of Pauperism, an incidental warning signal on the high road to historic reconciliation. In her dumb passivity, her stubborn immobility, she swells to the dimensions of an insurmountable, dark, stumbling block on that highway to constructive progress. Uneasily positioned within the composition, pressing up almost against, yet somewhat behind, the edge of the canvas that establishes a barrier between the defeated world of downtrodden anonymity and the triumphant world of the artist, her unstable spatial position acts to reinforce the spatial ambiguity of the composition as a whole, at the same time as it threatens the apparent stability of the central group. Visible only by the fitful glow cast by the pallid skeletons of Courbet's own past work on the wall behind her, radiating an ineluctable darkness which is also the substance of her body, the Irishwoman resists the light of productive reason and constructive representation, that luminous and seductive aura which surrounds the artist and his minions.

Take her legs, for instance: bare, flabby, pale, unhealthy, yet not without a certain unexpected, pearly sexual allure, the right one folded back in on itself, exposing its vulnerable fleshiness to the gaze of the viewer yet suggestively leading to more exciting, darker passages, passages doubly forbidden because this is the figure of a mother as well as an object of charity. This pose of exposure in a woman, this revealing of naked legs is, in the codes of nineteenth-century decorum, a signifier of degradation, an abandonment of self-respect. The implication of self-abasement is reiterated by the place where she sits: directly on the ground, so that her bare legs also figure in à secular and untranscendent updating of the Madonna of Humility topos. This topos, I might add, we have inscribed with our own uneasiness and guilt, having seen it often enough in the flesh, the flesh of those pale, varicose-veined, naked, unhealthy, sometimes filthy, often scabbed and scarred female legs on the sidewalks of our own cities, precisely as Courbet, it is said, saw them on the streets of England in his own time.

But the legs of the Irishwoman signify powerfully within the text of the painting itself as the antithesis of those of Courbet himself. For a long time, I have been if not obsessed, at least fascinated, by Courbet's legs–shapely, perky, aggressively thrust both forward toward the spectator and back into the pictorial space–but mostly by the green-striped trousers the artist has chosen to wear in the painting.[42] My fascination was intensified when I discovered, from what source I no longer remember, that Picasso too was fascinated by those green-striped legs, fascinated enough, so the story goes (although it may be apocryphal), to have trousers of his own made up just like them, at great expense, with the unusual horizontal, rather than vertical, stripes. Perhaps Picasso associated such stripes with a notion of criminality–horizontally striped clothing conventionally defines the convict in the United States and Courbet himself was not just an artistic rebel but condemned by the court as a bona fide law-breaker after the Commune–so that the stripes may have connoted that transgression so closely allied with the avant-garde project itself; in assuming the trousers (rather than donning the more conventional mantle) of Courbet, Picasso was symbolically assuming his role as the leader of artistic and social rebellion as well as literally stepping into the pants of an overtly phallic master-painter. This difference, then, between the legs of the deprived and the legs of mastery and possession, establishes the gender terms underpinning the meanings generated by the painting as a whole.

There are still other infratextual readings possible for the figure of the Irish beggar-woman in *The Painter's Studio*, other figures that construct its meaning. If, as a woman, I can read any other figure in *The Painter's Studio* in relation to the Irishwoman, it is inevitably Baudelaire to whom I must turn: Baudelaire, another dark negator of utopian promises, the Baudelaire who later sardonically dismissed Courbet with the phrase "Courbet sauvant le monde,"[43] and who, like the beggar-woman in the painting, is marked with the dark sign of melancholy. This crucial connection-opposition between Baudelaire and the poor woman is carried out on the formal level too, the woman all emergent but muffled roundness, created by an outpressing, foreshortened fullness of form; Baudelaire curiously flattened, planar, outlined, a surface phenomenon, as sunken in his reading as she is extrusive in her embodied misery: together they constitute a paired vehicle connoting privatized absorption versus public demonstration.[44]

There is a sense, too, in which the woman may be read as a Baudelairean type, one more exemplum of that engaging flotsam of the modern city which it is the project of the *flâneur* to glimpse in the course of his peregrinations. If she is not old enough to be one of the little old ladies of "Les Petites Vieilles" she is surely a prefiguration of one of those "singular, decrepit and charming beings" who take refuge in the "sinuous folds of old capital cities," and whose eyes harbor "mysterious charms/For him whom austere Misfortune nursed at her bosom."[45] Through the poet's eyes, or rather his diction, we can see/read Courbet's beggar-woman not merely as a conventional type, but as a figure as resonant with ambivalent values as Baudelaire's metaphoric nurse–"austere Misfortune"–nurturing yet denying in a single trope, she who nourished the poet at her breast. Especially potent in the light of Courbet's triumphant self-assertiveness as the painter-creator in the center of *The Painter's Studio* is Baudelaire's self-denying projection of himself as the artist in the figure "whom austere Misfortune nursed." If we think of the Irishwoman as in some sense identical to Baudelaire's Misfortune, then the artist (the one nursed at her breast) is reduced from masterful protagonist to almost nothing, a mere nursling beggar, whose frail and dependent existence is pitifully signified by the little white blob of the baby's cap. Almost invisible in the dark folds of the Irishwoman's shawl, the white blob refers not only to the fragile, moon-like tondo suspended on the wall slightly to the right above the central group, but, at the same time, to the ominous, shadowy skull on the newspaper to the left and behind the mother and child. Precarious life, inevitable death: what could constitute a more devastating response to the intended lesson of Courbet's allegory about the authoritative position of the artist than this alternative allegorization of the figure of the beggar-woman and her almost invisible child?

Part Two

Ending with the Beginning: The Centrality of Gender

Although Courbet's allegory may indeed have been designed to teach a lesson of peace, harmony and reconciliation to the Emperor, there is another lesson inscribed, doubtless unconsciously, at the very heart of Courbet's "Allégorie réelle": the all-important lesson about the gender rules governing the production of art, great art, needless to say. As such, it constitutes a lesson about the origin of art itself in male desire.[46] Although it is hidden to eyes blinded by the Oedipal construction of all meaning in patriarchy, there is nothing ambiguous about this lesson. No amount of analysis of Courbet's formal innovations[47] can obfuscate the message constituted by this central group, a group in which the major players literally replicate the Oedipal triangle. It is crystal clear in this, Courbet's construction "representing representation":[48] the artist-father, Courbet, with brush in hand, his Assyrian profile tilted at a confident angle, is unequivocally male, unambiguously active. The model-mother, to his right, and upon whom he turns his back, is equally unambiguously female, and passive. The pupil-son, representative of the next genera-tion, looks up at the artist's work presumably with awe and admiration, like his alter ego, the little boy artist sprawled out sketching on the floor to the right. The pupil-son is as unambiguously male as the artist himself, or as any of the youthful "ephebes" in Harold Bloom's study of the uninterruptedly male, if anxiety-ridden, chain of poetic creativity.[49] The implications are, reading as a woman, that if the next generation looks at Courbet's work, and is stirred with fires at once imitative and competitive, so did Courbet look at Rembrandt, Rembrandt at Raphael, Raphael at Rome, etc. That is how it is, how it has always been, how it is always going to be. If the artist leans from his space into ours, breaking down the barriers between fictive and actual presence, it is almost as though to reinforce this message: "As it is in representation, so it is in the real world." This too is part of the "real" in the real allegory. The only

74 GUSTAVE COURBET Portrait of Proudhon and His Family in 1853, 1865

touch of ambiguity comes in the multiple roles assigned to the female model, who may be read as either wife, mother,[50] mistress or inspiring muse: but this is relatively inconsequential, since the sign "woman" is infinitely malleable in the representation of representation, and can stand for any or all of these positions in its anonymous objecthood.[51]

Courbet, then, allegorized as the artist in the heart of *The Painter's Studio*, is definitively gendered, and this gendering is underlined by the position of his opposite, his would-be object included in the image: the female model. Here gender is overtly and blatantly positioned as opposition—and domination. One might say that Courbet goes so far as to cross out woman in the Lacanian sense by substituting "nature" for her as the signifier of his creation on the canvas-within-the-canvas. He resorts to this strategy of deletion, incidentally, quite literally in the later case of the *Portrait of Proudhon and His Family in 1853*, in which he "erases" the adult female member of the family, Mme Proudhon, from his composition, leaving only her workbasket behind as a synecdoche of her absence-presence. This easy replacement in *The Painter's Studio* of the woman's body by landscape–an incarnation of the nature/woman dyad *par excellence*–bears a precise relation to the almost infinite mutability of the feminine itself under patriarchy. "Femininity," says Klaus Theweleit in his provocative study of gender relations, *Male Fantasies*, "...has retained a special malleability under patriarchy, for women have never been able to be identified directly with dominant historical processes...because they have never been the direct agents of those processes; in some way or other, they have always remained objects and raw materials, *pieces of nature* awaiting socialization. This has enabled men to see and use them collectively as part of the earth's *inorganic body*–the terrain of men's own productions."[52] This seems to be exactly the point at issue in Courbet's real allegory: woman and nature are interchangeable as objects of (male) artistic desire–and manipulation. To reinforce this (totally unintentional) message, Courbet has underlined this powerful strategy of displacement by introducing a surrogate male beholder right into his picture in the figure of the little boy gazing, in the position of the spectator, at the picture.[53] Woman nevertheless has a role, a crucial if not an active one, in the image of origins Courbet has inscribed in the generative center of his real allegory: she stands as passive Other to the artist's active subjecthood, and, at the same time, forms an apex of the Oedipal triangle inscribed by painter, model and observing child. Here, at the generative center of the real allegory, Courbet functions unequivocally as father, enforcing patriarchal law, in this case the law of visual representation, depicted figuratively as separating the mother-figure from that of the child. If Courbet feels free, like many male artists, to "merge corporeally" with some of the female objects of his representation, as Michael Fried asserts in his catalogue essay,[54] he certainly does not wish to "feminize" himself when represented in the act of painting: on the level of vulgar Freudian symbolism, he depicts himself as fully and unequivocally phallic, actively giving form to inert matter with his probing, dominating brush. All the productive ambiguities proper to or characteristic of the murky wings of the altarpiece (dedicated to the dominant position of male artistic genius) are banished in the central portion, that part which Michael Fried has aptly seen as the place where Courbet is "representing representation": it is perfectly clear who is meant to be represented with the phallus here.[55] Thus, although Courbet may from time to time exercise the time-honored privilege of entering the bodies of the women in his paintings,[56] he rarely allows the opposite to happen–that is to say, allows women to enter *his* represented body, or lets himself be "feminized." Courbet may well have represented himself as the passive, wounded lover in *Portrait of the Artist (The Wounded Man)*[57] (fig. 76), positioning himself as castrated (i.e. vulnerable, womanish) in order to emphasize the extremity of the suffering caused by the female companion who nestled close to him in the original version of the painting, but whom he subsequently erased.[58] Reading as a woman, I might see the erasure of the woman as more significant than the suffering of the man, and the implication that being positioned as a woman functions as the unquestioned signifier for the one who suffers—the one who is abandoned, the helpless (wounded or castrated) victim—as more significant than either. Courbet constructs a position of femininity as a potent signifier for his defeated masculinity here—literally his "unmanning"; if this is an "openness" to the "feminine" side of his nature, it is a very negative formulation. "Womanishness" has always stood for a high degree of masculine failure, for the specific failure of masculinity; it is never a sought-after position in the representational schemata of heterosexual males.

Michael Fried makes a strong case for Courbet's openness to femininity, his ability, as it were, to enter into the bodies of his female subjects. Now to say that Courbet enters into the bodies of the women in his paintings is hardly to say anything new about the male representation of women, or of Courbet specifically. One could certainly say this of Delacroix and the murdered women his surrogate-self watches so coolly in *The Death of Sardanapalus*. "I am the wound and the knife," declared Baudelaire in "L'Héautontimorouménos": another way of saying "I am the vagina, I am the penis"; more literally, for Courbet, the visual artist, "I am the female flesh, I am the male brush or palette knife." Male artists have had that dual privilege for a long time; women's bodies have always served as allegorized objects of desire, of hatred, of elevation, of abasement—of everything, in short. That is the point: woman's body has never "counted" in itself, only with what the male artist could fill it with, and that has always, it seems, been himself and his desires. To assert that Courbet has "entered" the bodies of his women—the nude bodies, above all—is hardly the same as postulating a protofeminist Courbet. After all, entering and/or taking over women's bodies has been the time-honored privilege of the male artist, a privilege reinforced in the nineteenth century above all by the specific historical conditions associated with capitalism. It is a totally asymmetrical privilege; no such entry is provided for women artists. Courbet's apparent identification with the bodies of the women he represents would, in this reading, be simply more of the same thing, transgression as usual.

The gender rules inscribed in the center of *The Painter's Studio*—the artist is male and active, his model is female and passive—are, in my reading, manifestly in place in the construction of the erotic in Courbet's *œuvre* as a whole. If, as Fried contends, Courbet came close to "thematizing the activity of painting as simultaneously man's and woman's work" in the *Sleeping Spinner*,[59] it is hardly "the *activity* of painting" that is at stake here: the female figure, if it indeed thematizes painting, is notably asleep at her post. If painting is woman's, as well as man's, work, the female figure is overtly *not* engaged in it; painting as woman's work is characterized by disenablement, not activity, and the female figure, asleep at the job, whether spinning or, allegorically, painting, is thereby made available as the seductive object of the male gaze.

If, as Fried sees it, the powerful central figure of *The Grain Sifters* owes some of its unassimilability to current conventions for the representation of female labor to Courbet's projection of his own body image into the *cribleuse* in question,[60] doesn't its unusual, unsettlingly "masculine" configuration—embodied above all in the powerful musculature of the working arms—owe something to a more conventional source for deviant imagery of women at the time? I refer to what might be called the imagery of perverse desire—an underground source nevertheless readily available and pointing to certain kinds of aberrant erotic preferences in men of Courbet's time. The strong woman plays a discreet but omnipresent role in the nineteenth-century iconography of fetishism. Such a preference is embodied in the unusual collection of the Englishman, Arthur Munby, who had heavily muscled young working-class women, often wearing masculine clothing, photographed for his private pleasure.[61] Muscular arms were particularly admired. The muscular arms of the female figure in *The Grain Sifters* might suggest the identification of the artist with the representation; I might also, reading as a woman, suggest that the artist, like Munby, finds something vital, sexy, desirable in women's muscular arms. A body like that of Courbet's *cribleuse* offers something both resistant and yet ultimately yielding to the male gaze, and this something has to do with the fetishization of the signifiers of class in nineteenth-century representation. Upper-class women, ladies, never have such arms; working-class women frequently do. It is these vigorous, firmly grasping arms combined with the smallness of the waist, the inviting rich swelling of the skirt and the piquancy of the little feet that constitute the desirability of the whole image, as well as its ambiguity; the erotic persuasiveness of the composition as a whole is enhanced by the way the vigor of the central imagery is opposed by the more familiar languor of the female figure to the left.

75 H. HOWLE Hannah in Traditional Shropshire Peasant Dress, 1872
(from the Arthur Munby Collection)

Languor, sleep and resting are more characteristic modes of representation for female figures in the nineteenth century, for Courbet above
all, and in Courbet's case, as well as for other artists, like Emile-Auguste
Carolus-Duran (fig. 78) and the Catalan Realist, Ramón Martí y Alsina
(fig. 77), for occasional male ones as well.[62] There is a tendency to assim-
ilate all sleeping figures to a single signifying position within this
pictorial discourse. But surely here is where gender-as-difference is most
consequential: precisely where it is most unapparent, where the manifest content seems most similar, indeed, identical. Although sleep is
a topos representing both men and women, it is figured differently for
each. Of all the figures represented sleeping, only females are represented nude: males are always represented clothed. Courbet's only nude

76 GUSTAVE COURBET Portrait of the Artist (The Wounded Man), 1844–54

male figures, *Wrestlers* (1853, fig. 79), are only partly naked and vigorously active. The vulnerable flesh of the sleeping male figure in
Courbet's work, or that of his followers, is veiled flesh, protected from
the prying and possessive gaze of women as well as of other men; male
vulnerability is posited as momentary and conditional on a general state
of potency. The meanings produced by this difference—sleeping women
often nude, sometimes clothed versus sleeping men never nude, always
clothed—must therefore be different. Gender makes a potent difference
precisely within topical similarity or near identity: it is precisely within
the same topos that the gender differential reveals itself most vividly.
The sleeping male, with rare exceptions, does not suggest sexual availability to the male heterosexual gaze. Rather, it suggests a sort of poetic
or imaginative availability open to the male viewer through identification with the sleeping male figure, an embodiment of *le repos du
guerrier*, as it were. The process of identification for the female viewer of
the female sleeping figure, nude or clothed, however, is quite different:
such an identification is inevitably either masochistic or narcissistic
and connotes sexual availability, especially in the case of the nude, but
even in the case of the clothed female sleeper, like the *Sleeping Spinner.*

77 RAMON MARTI Y ALSINA
The Siesta, 1884

78 EMILE-AUGUSTE CAROLUS-DURAN
The Convalescent, c. 1860

79 GUSTAVE COURBET Wrestlers, 1853

The sleeping or dozing female nude is the topos *par excellence* open to and designed for the pleasure of the desiring male gaze. There is thus no symmetry between the sleeping male and the sleeping female. The naked woman can inscribe only passive available flesh. Muse or model, mistress or mother, asleep or awake, the nude female can inspire, perhaps reproduce, but cannot produce or create—that is the crucial distinction.

Paradoxically, however, it is in the representation of clothed female figures, in *The Young Ladies on the Banks of the Seine* (1857), that Courbet most vividly inscribes the discourse of female sexual availability. To be more precise, the foreground "demoiselle" is not, in fact fully "clothed," or certainly would not have been considered fully clothed by the nineteenth-century viewer; rather, she is what might be thought of as "half-clothed," committing the solecism of wearing her corset-cover and petticoat in public, a sure sign of impropriety. She is in an intermediary, and all the more scandalous, state, between being properly clothed and, for the purposes of painting, permissibly nude.[63]

The whiteness of lingerie, the very signifier of erotic availability in nineteenth-century sexual fantasy, could also serve in pictorial discourse, in its very purity—the material analogue it offers to the blank page—as an ideal symbolic field on which to inscribe acts of desecration. *The Young Ladies on the Banks of the Seine*, in its potent concatenation of whiteness, supineness, sleep and sexual scandal, offers a striking visual analogue to a passage describing the degradation of prostitutes from Flora Tristan's *Promenades dans Londres*, first published in France in 1840. In this passage from her heart-rending chapter on prostitution in London, Tristan describes in some detail the way English upper-class males make their prostitute-companions drunk and then, when the poor women are lying senseless on the floor, amuse themselves by pouring drinks on their unconscious bodies. "I have seen", declares Tristan, "satin dresses whose colour could no longer be ascertained; they were merely a confusion of filth. Countless fantastic shapes were traced in wine, brandy, beer, tea, coffee, cream and so forth—debauchery's mottled record. The human creature", she adds, "can sink no lower!"[64] The analogy with painting conjured up by Tristan's image of "debauchery's mottled record" is striking. But more striking still is the passage in which she describes the fall and desecration of a prostitute dressed in *white*, "an extraordinarily beautiful Irish woman...She arrived toward two in the morning, dressed with an elegant simplicity which only served to heighten her beauty. She was wearing a gown of white satin, half-length gloves revealing her pretty arms; a pair of charming little pink slippers set off her dainty feet, and a kind of diadem crowned her head. Three hours later, that same woman was lying on the floor *dead drunk*! Her gown was revolting. Everyone was tossing glasses of wine, of liqueur, etc., over her handsome shoulders and on her magnificent bosom. The waiters would trample her under foot as if she were a bundle of rubbish. Oh, if I had not witnessed such an infamous profanation of a human being, I would not have believed it possible."[65]

Courbet's representation of the white-clad fallen woman in the foreground of *The Young Ladies on the Banks of the Seine* does not go to the same lengths of moral allegorization as Tristan's, but lends itself quite nicely to a pejorative reading within the codes defining nineteenth-century female decorum. Is it a mere coincidence that the gorgeously painted cashmere shawl in the foreground re-echoes the position and function—veiling yet calling attention to the sexual part of the body—of the similar shawl draped about the hips of the heroine of Holman Hunt's *Awakening Conscience* (1853, fig. 9), a supreme example of Victorian morality painting on the theme of the fallen woman?[66]

The misogynistic and moralistic P.-J. Proudhon, who figures prominently among the group of friends and supporters in *The Painter's Studio*, author of the major anti-feminist text of the period, *Pornocracy, or Women in Modern Times*,[67] found ample material for allegorical interpretation in *The Young Ladies*. He deals with the painting at length in his study of Courbet, *On the Principle of Art and Its Social Purpose*.[68] For him, as for so many other male allegorists, ranging from Emile Zola to Otto Dix, the sexual (i.e. "fallen" or "vicious") woman functions as the prime allegorical vehicle of social corruption. Behind Proudhon's paranoid diatribe against the moral scandal represented by this painting, one must imagine another, very different, representation of the feminine: the good woman, married of course, plainly and soberly dressed, sitting with her spindle or standing, her children about her, at the stove; a woman completely controlled, mindless, sexless, privatized, powerless. It is hard to say what enrages Proudhon most: the fact that the women in Courbet's painting are represented as publicly available to the male gaze, that is to say, to the pleasure of *others*; or that they are represented as experiencing pleasure *themselves*, in some way independently, outside patriarchal control and authority, pressing their bodies lazily and voluptuously against the bosom of the earth. Proudhon immediately attempts to distance himself from the immediate sexual scandal of *The Young Ladies on the Banks of the Seine* by allegorizing it in terms of contemporary social failure: what Courbet really would have entitled the painting, if it had not seemed seditious at the time, was "Two Fashionable Young Women under the Second Empire." The implications of this title are, in Proudhon's reading, manifold, and ultimately political. They have to do with the moral corruption of Napoleon III's regime, a corruption centered in the venality of women: their unwillingness to marry and have children; their tendency, as embodied in the foreground *demoiselle*, to be at once "somewhat virile," and, at the same time, to "swim in erotic revery";[69] their unslakeable thirst for luxury at its most

80 GUSTAVE COURBET The Young Ladies on the Banks of the Seine, 1857

refined. But what Proudhon hates most of all about the female types he sees embodied in *The Young Ladies on the Banks of the Seine* is their grotesque attempt to be fully human, that is to say, their pre-emption of the male prerogatives of creativity: "They cultivate what is called the ideal; they are young, beautiful, adorable; they know how to write, to paint, to sing, to declaim; they are real artists." Obviously, for Proudhon's allegorical imagination, such presumption on the part of women can only reap punishment, and can only be, in visual terms, represented by the ugly: "But pride, adultery, divorce and suicide, replacing love affairs, hover about them and accompany them; they bear these in their dowry; it is why, in the end, they seem horrible."[70]

Although all of Courbet's paintings of eroticized women, like *The Young Ladies on the Banks of the Seine*, are open to allegorical interpretation based on gender difference, some of them would appear to be more resistant to the traditional, moralistic interpretation practiced by

81 GUSTAVE COURBET The Sleeping Blonde, c. 1868

P.-J. Proudhon. Often, Courbet, like many of his contemporaries and followers, seems to have turned to the theme of sleep or "resting"—*The Sleeping Blonde* or *Woman in Bed: Repose*—simply as a pretext for painting the nude female model. Often, and increasingly as the century progresses, even that pretext becomes unnecessary, and we are faced by what in English is designated by the *Reclining Nude* or simply *Nude* (female understood) *tout court.*

Detaching the female nude from its relatively constrained position within traditional iconography in the nineteenth century, positioning it—and significantly, not the male nude—outside narrative (or within the thinnest possible narrative pretexts such as "Sleeping Model," "Odalisque" or "Bather") as an object at once of desire and of formal innovation may be read as a courageous step in the progressive evolution—or revolutionary progress—of modernism. Women's naked bodies have played a major role in modern artists' enterprise of "making forays into and taking up positions on the frontiers of consciousness," their attempts to "advance further in the dialectic of outrage." This is Susan Sontag and she is in fact talking about pornography,[71] not about the high-art nude, but what she says has not a little resonance in the case of Courbet—and later, that of Manet, of Gauguin, of Picasso, of Matisse, and of the German Expressionists. The female nude is the contested site of vanguard versus conservative practices in the nineteenth century. The questions are: How different are these presumably adversarial practices from each other? and, if different, How significant are these differences? and even more germane to the point at issue, In whose reading are these differences between the vanguard and the conservative nude stipulated as significantly different? Reading as a woman, I might well come out with a different answer to these questions than if I were reading as a man.[72] Following Susan Suleiman's complex analysis of the centrality of the concept of transgression in the strategies of modernism,[73] I would suggest that in the case of Courbet's more excessively eroticized nudes—his *Sleep* (fig. 84), for instance, or his *The White Stockings* (fig. 85), his *The Woman in the Waves* (fig. 82), and certainly his part-image *The Origin of the World* (fig. 83)—we are invited by a certain modernist discourse, or, perhaps, more accurately, a postmodern one, to read the transgressive content of the work as a metaphor for the transgressive formal practices involved. Transposing Suleiman's analysis from the realm of fiction to that of art, one might say that what we see here is the transfer or slippage of the notion of transgression from the realm of experience—whose equivalent, in painting, is representation—to the realm of figuration (or form), with a corresponding shift in the roles and importance accorded to the signifier and the signified. The signified becomes the vehicle of the metaphor, whose tenor is the signifier. The sexually scandalous iconography of Courbet's *Sleep*, two naked lesbians locked together in a sexually explicit pose, is there to signify Courbet's formally scandalous pictorial practice: his tender, miraculously modulated, sensual handling of paint, the pulsating suggestiveness of the lush curves of breasts and thighs, the daring play of pearly blond flesh-tones against deeper, rose-flushed brunette surfaces, the delicate threading of blue veins into the almost imperceptible weave of pinks and umbers

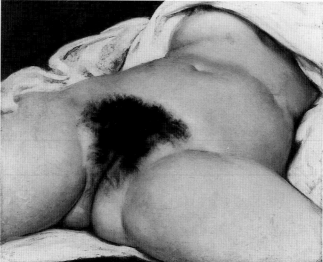

82 GUSTAVE COURBET The Woman in the Waves, 1866

83 GUSTAVE COURBET The Origin of the World, 1866

84 GUSTAVE COURBET Sleep, 1866

85 GUSTAVE COURBET The White Stockings, 1861

connoting skin, and the caress of the artist's supple brush or palette knife on the receptive surface of the canvas.[74] Yet is this an adequate analysis for a painting like Courbet's, where "effects of the real" may in fact constitute the dominant formal practice, where brushwork, intentionally, tends to vanish into palpable flesh, palette-knife work into illusory breast or thigh, and where, as much as in any *Playboy* centerfold, arousal is the issue—arousal with a certain aesthetic bonus? Reading as a woman who happens to be an art historian, I cannot entirely accept the first interpretation; reading as an art historian who happens to be a woman, I cannot wholly accept the second. Yet I must arrive at a position which maintains that simply to bracket the content and function of the work in a case like *Sleep*, or in any of Courbet's nudes, is to be blind to what they are doing, how they effect us specifically as women who view images. Surely I cannot simply take over viewing positions offered to me by men—either the creator of the picture or his spokesmen—nor can I easily identify with the women in the picture as objects of the gaze, which would necessarily involve a degree of masochism on my part;[75] nor can I easily invent some other, alternative, position. Once more, I find myself at once invited into, but shut out of, the house of meaning; uneasily hovering on the brink of, moving into, withdrawing from the potentialities of the painting: the familiar, shifty, feminine subject-position.[76] Ultimately, though, such work would seem designed to put me—the viewer who is a woman—in her place. This place, is as usual, problematic, and might best be formulated as a question: Am I going to be one of the boys (i.e. Am I going to "enjoy it" as erotic stimulation, as artistic daring, as vanguard transgression?) or one of the girls (Am I going to acquiesce to [male] authoritative interpretations? Am I going to reject it as "oppressive"? Am I going to just give up my status as viewer and lie down and identify with the bodies in the picture?)? Or to end this discussion with still another question: Why must transgression—social and artistic alike—always be enacted (by men) on the naked bodies of women?

The obvious answer to this question lies in what I have read as the Oedipal center of *The Painter's Studio*. To answer it, I have to end with a still larger question, a question posed in a different context by Susan Suleiman: "Is there a model of *textuality* possible that would not necessarily play out, in discourse, the eternal Oedipal drama of transgression and the Law—a drama which always, ultimately, ends up maintaining the latter?"[77] Reading as a woman, Courbet's vision of utopia looks less like an ideal vision of the future, or even like unfinished business, and more like business as usual; certainly, it does not seem transgressive in any deeply serious sense. Reading Courbet as a woman, it has become clear to me that it is only in gender difference that a real allegory of the transgressive can be constructed.

I can, with difficulty, imagine another scenario, a real allegory of transgression. Since it is a scenario that denies Oedipus and invokes gender reversal, it can only be read as a kind of (threatening) joke, a joke in bad taste. It will, of course, be written off as mere frivolity by serious critics and a desecration by serious art historians. I will now stop reading as a woman and write as one.

Rosa Bonheur now sits in the central position of *The Painter's Studio*. Courbet, nude, or rather partly draped, stands modestly behind her. She is wearing a striped skirt (we can leave her Courbet's jacket; with a few alterations, it will do), and vigorously painting—with her loaded brush—a bull. A ragged little girl watches her intently. Suddenly, Champfleury can't stand it any longer. He rises from his seat in the wings and approaches the center: "But she's not even a *great* artist," he protests, "Why are there no great women artists?" The little girl turns around; we see that she is, in fact, the young Mary Cassatt (or Berthe Morisot or Georgia O'Keeffe or Hannah Höch—any number of possibilities are available). Now, the anonymous women in the picture, led by the Irishwoman, begin to converge on the center of the stage; the men gradually sink into the shadows, where they take off their clothes, and, equally importantly, lose their names: no longer Champfleury or Bruyas or Max Buchon, they are just naked male bodies.[78] Little by little, they take up their positions in a series of *tableaux vivants*: one of them holds a parrot over his head, offering his substantial nudity to the audience; two others are locked in a passionate, muscular embrace on a piece of blue drapery; another displays his buttocks to us in front of a waterfall backdrop; still another displays his luminous but hairy flesh, recumbent, on white sheets before a landscape. Two of the women try to urge the naked Proudhon, misogynist author of *Pornocracy, or Women in Modern Times*,[79] to join them in a picnic on the grass, but he resists—perhaps it is still too early; they leave him alone. Now all the women are gathered together in the center of the painting; the "rich patroness" lends her shawl to the nude model. They all have names: they are Marie, Angèle, Claire. They introduce themselves to each other and engage in animated conversation; they have a lot of catching up to do. They turn to look at the naked men in their ridiculous poses and suddenly, they all burst into laughter, great gales of body-shaking, uncontrollable laughter; they laugh and they laugh and they simply cannot stop...As they laugh, as though it is a result of their laughter, the solidity of the painted matter begins to sparkle, melts, flows, diffuses "in an architecture of pure color, the sudden brightness in turn opening up color itself—a last control of vision, beyond its own density, toward dazzling light..."[80] End of scenario; but we have obviously left realism far behind for a kind of surrealism, although this is an allegory of the transgressive the Surrealists never quite got around to. This is the unreal allegory, and perhaps the never real one as well:[81] an allegory of what can never be as long as we live in the land where Oedipus rules. The absurdity of my paraphrase of Courbet's real allegory could only be paralleled by rephrasing Freud's famous question "What does a woman want?" as "What do *men* want?" It is absurd because what *men* want is what want *is*; men's want defines desire itself.

Ending with the Ending: The Politics of Place, the Place of Hope

If Courbet's *The Painter's Studio* can in no sense be read as subverting the laws of gender—the ultimate subversion—it was nevertheless successful in fulfilling its author's intention to shake up some of the social and political assumptions of its time. Such a transgressive strategy might, from a certain point of view, even appear appropriate to the occasion for which it was painted: the Universal Exposition of 1855. Courbet, following a time-honored tradition, does resort to a trope of role reversal in *The Painter's Studio*: that popular imagery of the "world upside down," the destabilizing of the accustomed social hierarchy countenanced by carnival in which all normal relations of domination and subservience are reversed. In the carnival atmosphere created by the Universal Exposition, Courbet, it would seem, felt free—indeed, called upon—to reverse the "normal" order of the world: now it is the monarch who must listen and learn, the artist who is on top, who grants the benefit of his example to the ruler. In this reversal of customary roles, his allegory and mine of gender-reversal, no matter how different in every other aspect, share a common ancestry in popular tradition, for the laws controlling gender were exactly those most outrageously violated by the carnivalesque suspension of the normal mode of life, when men could dress as women and women, as Natalie Zemon Davis has demonstrated, could, during the carnival, however briefly, find themselves "on top."[82]

There are other ways, too, in which Courbet, in *The Painter's Studio*, contravenes accepted practices: those, for example, governing the codes controlling high art. There is a sense, as I indicated at the beginning of this essay, in which *The Painter's Studio* must be read as a political cartoon writ large: an allegory of the venality, or at least the futility, of present political conduct and hope for a more positive political future.[83] In hiding politically subversive meanings under the cloak of allegory, *The Painter's Studio* looks back to a time-honored tradition connecting this rhetorical mode with political subterfuge. "Allegory", says Angus Fletcher, "presumably thrives on political censorship."[84] Certainly, Courbet's choice of an allegorical form for his painting owes a great deal to the specific political conditions, most notably, official censorship, which prevailed at the beginning of the Second Empire. But the *kind* of allegory he chose, an allegory related to the "low" form of the political cartoon rather than the "high" one of, say, classical mythology or antique epic, points to another kind of politics at work in his painting: a cultural politics involving that shifting and provocative relationship between high art and the materials of low or mass culture which has been posited as one of the defining characteristics of modernism in the recent literature.[85] In Courbet's work at the post-revolutionary Salon of 1850–51, in paintings like *Burial at Ornans*, as T. J. Clark and Thomas Crow have pointed out in different contexts, the innovations pointing ahead to fully-fledged modernism "were carried forward in the name of another public, excluded outsiders, whose own emergent or residual signifying practices these pictures managed to address."[86] By 1855, such "excluded outsiders" had to be addressed more circumspectly than they had been five years earlier, if indeed they, or they primarily, were the intended public for *The Painter's Studio.*

Indeed, the political implications of the work are impossible to grasp without a consideration of the public for which it was intended; and this notion of a public is in turn impossible to understand without a knowledge of the place and circumstances for which Courbet designed *The Painter's Studio.* It was executed for a specific historical situation: the Universal Exposition in Paris, inaugurated by Napoleon III on 1 May 1855, an exhibition to which the Emperor had devoted a great deal of detailed attention over a considerable period of time.[87]

Within the context of the Universal Exposition, a French display of technological prowess and cultural achievement to the world, in competition primarily with her arch-rival England, certain of the figures in Courbet's painting assume new importance. The "old-clothes man," for instance, positioned in the center of the left-hand group of figures, displaying his wares to exotic personifications of Turkey and China (a figure whose centrality to the allegorical message Courbet indicated in his letter to Champfleury by declaring of him: "He presides over all this...displaying his frippery to all these people, each of whom expresses great interest in his own way"[88]) can now be read as a crucial, and deflationary, figuration of that hawking of commodities which was the ultimate point of the Universal Exposition itself. If the Irish beggar-woman may be said to call into question the Emperor's economic policies on one level (see page 125 above), then the ludicrous rag-and-bone seller may be said to question it on another. This debased and parodic representative of the world of commerce—selling that which is devoid of value—provides an effective opposition to the image of the artist, who is engaged in producing that which *is* of value.

Courbet, by representing himself in his own painting surrounded by his past and present pictorial production, has created an allegory of his beneficent role as a producer of valuable cultural goods. The real allegory then, in the context of the Universal Exposition of 1855, may be read as Courbet's production of himself as a counter-commodity—a free and self-determined man producing objects of genuine value—for a new and relatively unfamiliar public. That this public might include prosperous and enlightened purchasers is indicated by the pair of wealthy patrons prominent in the right foreground of the painting as well as by the inclusion of Courbet's own patron, Alfred Bruyas, among the group of friends and supporters. *The Painter's Studio* then, in the context of the year in which it was created, 1855, and the place for which it was intended, the French section of the painting exhibition at the Universal Exposition, may be conceived of as a kind of miniature "universal exhibition" in its own right, in which the artist displays his wares to an interested public in much the same way as Napoleon III displayed his nation's commodities to would-be buyers and investors.

The public to be addressed was vast, international and socially heterogeneous and Courbet's sense of competition was keen. He intended his new painting to function as the keystone of an extended group of works, fourteen in all. But his relationship to the government-sponsored exhibition, and especially to the powerful Superintendent of the Fine Arts, Count Nieuwerkerque, was a stormy and ambivalent one,[89] which was to lead ultimately to the rejection of *The Painter's Studio* from the official exhibition and Courbet's implementation, with the financial and moral encouragement of his patron, Alfred Bruyas, of his own private exhibition. Featuring *The Painter's Studio*, this took place in the so-called Pavillon du Réalisme on the Avenue Montaigne, and competed with the official exhibition in which Courbet was also showing a group of eleven paintings. "Whether inside or outside the official exhibition," as Herding points out, "Courbet wanted to participate and to maintain at the same time his independence from the organizers."[90]

86 GUSTAVE COURBET The Pavillon du Réalisme, drawing in an autograph letter, 1854

The position of *The Painter's Studio* was thus at once marginal—Courbet's private exhibition was, so to speak "marginalized" in relation to the official one—yet central in that it dominated the space proclaiming Courbet's independence of government demands and stipulations. The real allegory then, constituted within the context of Napoleon III's Universal Exposition, declared Courbet's centrality within the terrain of the marginal, a position which vanguard artists ever since have avidly sought and established as their own. Thus, if the political allegory embodied within the painting was hidden, the allegory of cultural

politics enacted by the placing of the painting in a specific site at a concrete moment of history was far more overt. Courbet had indeed
maintained his independence, but at a price. This "price" with its
inevitable appeal to a "special" or in some sense "marginal" public—the
price of uncertainty, of non-centrality in relation to the still-powerful
government art establishment, and finally, of being in opposition to that
establishment—would eventually, transvalued, define the position of
modernist art in Paris and, indeed, the world.[91]

The cultural politics involved in the physical placement of *The
Painter's Studio* and its relation to the public—or publics—plays a major
role in the evolution of the critical discourse surrounding it. After the
exhibition in the Pavillon de Réalisme, *The Painter's Studio* languished
for more than half a century in near oblivion, until it was rescued by
public subscription for the Louvre in 1920:[92] it became, as a result of this
transaction, at once a part of the French cultural heritage, inserted into
the "great tradition" of national art production, and at the same time, as
part of the same operation, a work more or less completely divested
of political implication. As a "great work," hallowed by its position of
honor in the galleries of the Louvre, its meaning was now secured by the
elevated language of the aesthetic rather than the mundane discourse of
politics; its references to contemporary issues, though hinted at from
time to time, were, to all intents and purposes, as lost to the comprehen-
sion of a public blinded by the ideology of art-historical interpretation
as its gender lessons are today made invisible to a public blinded by the
ideology of patriarchy.[93]

If the place where a work is shown bears a crucial relationship to its
meaning, then the new location of *The Painter's Studio* in the Musée
d'Orsay rather than the Louvre would seem to demand new readings.
Whereas in the Louvre, *The Painter's Studio*—far more than the ever-
unassimilable *Burial at Ornans*—seemed to announce the end of a great
tradition, now, in the Orsay, a museum devoted to the work of the second
half of the nineteenth century, it seems to point ahead, if by no means
unequivocally, to the modernist future.[94] I say "by no means unequivocally" because there are ways in which, set against the postmodern
stoniness of Gaye Aulenti's new walls, in the company of Manet's
Olympia (if not that of Bouguereau or Bastien-Lepage) and beneath the
galleries full of Cézanne, Van Gogh, and Gauguin, *The Painter's Studio*
looks, if not precisely "traditional," at least touchingly old-fashioned in
some respects. Certainly, its iconography owes something to nostalgia
for that sweeping and totalistic, yet compulsively detailed, utopian
vision characteristic of Fourier and his disciples.[95] Yet if in the context of

its new placement in the Musée d'Orsay, Courbet's *The Painter's Studio* looks utopian, it does so not merely by preaching a pictorial lesson of reconciliation, by resorting to eccentric iconography, or even by transforming old traditions of popular resistance into new iconographic form. Rather, seen in the context of later nineteenth-century art and thus, through imaginative projection, in the context of modernism and the vanguard of the future, it is Courbet's pictorial practice in *The Painter's Studio* which seems to point ahead as a "principle of hope" (to borrow the Marxist philosopher, Ernst Bloch's, eloquent phrase). In relation to the work of the Impressionists and Cézanne, the choice of landscape, considered by progressive critics of the time as the democratic genre *par excellence*, as the motif on Courbet's easel becomes the vehicle of a progressive and liberating tenor within the allegorizing totality of the painting. The pure pigment on the palette and the insistence on the surface and substance of the painting as elements of its meaning point even further ahead to the rejection of representation itself in the modernist practices of the twentieth century. The collage-like dissonances of the composition, its fragmentation, as well as its appropriation, of ready-made imagery, and its rejection of finish and completeness all point to still other vanguard strategies of the future. *The Painter's Studio*, read in this way, is utopian in that it allegorizes the future of art and its—mostly unfulfilled—hopes of instrumentality in the production of revolutionary change. For utopia is clearly not so much a place—how could it be?—or even an ideal, but, rather, once more to borrow the words of Ernst Bloch, who spent so much of his life considering it: "the methodological organ of newness."[96]

Coda

It may be of interest to the reader to note that this two-part essay allegorizes in textual form the pictorial structure of *The Painter's Studio*. At the "heart" or "vital center" of the essay (the second half of the first part and the first of the second), I take over Courbet's role of "creator" and assume my femininity (as he has his masculinity) in the construction of a discourse of gender from the raw material offered by the visual artefact. In the "wings" (the first half of the first part and the second part of the second) I assume the "normal" voice and position of the art historian—a sort of neutro- or neutered-masculine one—and give a more empirical, and entirely ungendered, account of the painting and its context.

Chapter Five

In a brothel, both
The ladies and gentlemen
Have nicknames only.

W. H. AUDEN, "Postscript to the Cave of Meaning"

I first started thinking about Degas and the subversion of the family
when I noticed, after the removal of *The Bellelli Family* (c. 1858–60) to
the Musée d'Orsay, the existence of half a small dog scooting out of the
painting to the right. I had never noticed this detail before the painting
was moved—it is very hard to see in most reproductions—and none of the
scholars who have discussed *The Bellelli Family* have taken account of
its presence.[1] The dog must have been a last-minute addition: it does not
appear in the final Ordrupgaard sketch of about 1859. It is possible that
Degas's main reason for putting it in his painting was a formal one, to
fill up an awkward empty space in front of the figure of Gennaro Bellelli,
who might otherwise seem outbalanced by the three-figured group on
the left. Yet a formal intention does not nullify a signifying result: the
way the dog works in the construction of meaning in the painting. With
a kind of airy, heedless, cheeky *je m'en foutisme*, entirely at odds with
the almost desperate seriousness of the painting as a whole, these canine
hindquarters work to undermine the solemn balance and traditional
formality of Degas's monumental, tensely harmonized family-group
structure with a wave of a fluffy tail. The dog's vector is, in the extreme,
centrifugal; as such, it might be opposed to the reassuringly anchoring
position of Porto, the Newfoundland, wholly present—indeed, literally
part of the family—in Renoir's more cheerful and relaxed representation
of a bourgeois family group, *The Charpentier Family* (1878).

Yet it is not really the dog I wish to talk about (Degas, incidentally,
is said to have hated dogs) but rather, the relatively covert contravention
it figures in *The Bellelli Family* of what one might call conventional

bourgeois–specifically upper-bourgeois–family values such as those represented in *The Charpentier Family* and many other similar portraits of the period. Now one could point to *The Bellelli Family* as a special case: indeed it is one of course, if only in the sense that it was the representation of an unhappy family. Degas was well aware of the strains existing between husband, Gennaro Bellelli, and wife, Degas's father's sister, his aunt Laura, when he embarked on this ambitious project in the late 1850s. At the same time, he evidently wanted the portrait of the Bellellis to be a major painting with a dignified structure and a sense of traditional universality as well. The tensions proliferating among the artist's lofty intentions; his sense of the specific and the contemporary; his conscious and/or subconscious awareness of animosity between the couple; the perhaps unacknowledged strength of his feelings for his aunt and hers for her nephew; these, and the consequent insertion of the signs of dissension and instability into the superficially harmonious fabric of his representation, are what make the portrait interesting and disturbing to the modern viewer. *The Bellelli Family* (originally referred to simply as "Family Portrait" when it was first exhibited in the Salon of 1867)[2] is as much a painting about the contradictions riddling the general idea of the *haut-bourgeois* family in the middle of the nineteenth century as it is a family portrait *tout court.*

The Bellelli family portrait, then, must be read not merely as a family document but also as a representation of "The Family," its structure inscribing those tensions and oppositions, characteristic of certain familial relationships in general and the relationships existing in this family in particular, at a concrete historical moment. At the same time, the painting must be seen as inscribing those unifying codes of structural relationship–hierarchized according to age and sex, homogenized in terms of class and appearance–governing the ideal of nineteenth-century bourgeois family existence.

Within the complex web of inscriptions constituting *The Bellelli Family*, both temporal and spatial considerations play their role. For Degas has presented the family diachronically as a hierarchical continuum of generations: grandfather René, then the parents, followed by Giulia and Giovanna; and, as the presence of the recently deceased grandfather is indicated simply by an image on the wall, so the presence of the unborn next generation is merely hinted at in the costume and stance of Laura. This notion of a generational historicity is heightened by nuances of style and structure: there are references to a specifically aristocratic tradition of portraiture, that of Van Dyck and Bronzino for example, and the willed balance and geometric ordering of

88 EDGAR DEGAS The Bellelli Family, c. 1858–60

the composition suggest that it is not just to any old past that the young artist wishes to connect his family.

Yet the high tone of this reference to family continuity is interrupted or complicated by synchronic tensions. The stately procession of inheritance and succession is interrupted and called into question by contemporary and specifically psychological disharmonies characteristic of the high bourgeois family of Degas's own time and the Bellellis' particular family drama. Interestingly, these tensions are, in pictorial terms, represented not merely by the slumped figure of Gennaro and the over-erect one of Laura, but perhaps even more acutely by the figure that both separates and connects them, the awkwardly and unstably posed Giulia.

Strains there were many in the Bellelli family. The scenario of the Bellelli relationship reads like the outline of a contemporary nineteenth-century novel, one by Balzac, or later, by Zola; or perhaps it simply reveals the source of both the painting and the novels—*pace* Roland Barthes—in contemporary discourses of the family which position this institution as a problematic as well as an ideal social construction.[3]

Laura Degas had married Gennaro Bellelli as a "last resort" at the advanced age of 28, for her domineering father (standing guard in the painting on the wall behind her) had found all preceding suppliants—including one whom she truly loved and wanted to marry—insufficiently rich or distinguished to accede to the hand of this young woman who was herself both rich and beautiful. "On a particularly distressing occasion," says Roy McMullen in his biography of Degas, "an Englishman who had failed to measure up to the requirements...had lost his temper and denounced the whole proceedings as 'more like a business negotiation than an affair of the heart.'"[4]

The Bellellis' was evidently a loveless marriage, and at the time Degas was engaged in painting the portrait—first sketching in Florence, where the Bellellis lived in rented quarters, then painting the large canvas back in Paris—Laura Bellelli, whom he loved and who was startlingly open with him about her marital problems, was desperately unhappy with her husband. In 1859 and 1860, she wrote to Degas about her misery, describing her sad life with a husband whose character was "immensely disagreeable and dishonest," and declaring that "living with Gennaro, whose detestable nature you know and who has no serious occupation, shall soon lead me to the grave." In another letter, she refers to the "disagreeable countenance" of a bitter and always idle Gennaro, and declares that he has no "serious occupation to make him less boring to himself."[5]

Given the outspoken distaste of the wife for the husband, the pregnancy discreetly evoked in Degas's painting should perhaps be read not merely as the dignified suggestion of future generations carrying on the Degas–Bellelli family tradition, but as evidence of a quite different situation. From a certain vantage point, Laura Bellelli's gently expansive form may be viewed not merely as a representation of woman's predestined role as procreator, but as the subtle record of an outrage, an act committed on her body without the love or respect of the perpetrator—an act that has come to be defined as marital rape.

There is another set of facts about the family represented here that demands yet another kind of reading of the painting: a political one. Despite the surface stability of the family group, and the suggestion of elegance and settled comfort in the setting, this is a painting of a family in exile, a family which had wandered and been uprooted several times in the course of its existence. The Bellellis were living in a rented, furnished flat in Florence because Gennaro had been exiled from his native Naples and, indeed, had been condemned to death *in absentia* on account of his role in the local 1848 Revolution and his subversive political activities on behalf of Cavour, who wished to expel the Bourbons and create a greater Italy by uniting the Kingdom of the Two Sicilies with Piedmont.[6] He and his wife had fled to Marseilles, then to Paris, then to London, and in 1852 had settled with their two children in Florence. This then, is a painting not merely of a family, or of an unhappy family, but of a family torn from its native habitat. Is it merely coincidental that in his notebooks of 1858 in Florence, Degas records a plan to depict Mary Stuart's heartbroken departure from France in 1561, based on an incident in the Seigneur de Brantôme's *Vies des dames illustrés*? This was to have been a sentimental history painting which Degas described in the following terms, no doubt drawn from his source: "Without thinking of anything else, she leaned both her arms on the poop of the galley next to the tiller and began to shed huge tears while continually rolling her beautiful eyes toward the port and the land she had left, and while repeating over and over again, for nearly five hours and until night began to fall, the same doleful words: 'Adieu, France.'"[7] It is not too far-fetched to speculate that the painter conceived of his aunt as a modern Mary Stuart, melancholy in her isolation and exiled, inconsolably, from friends and family in Naples.

Yet, interesting though this painting and this family may be, it is not just *The Bellelli Family* that I will be concerned with in this text, but rather, the intersection of the particularity of the Bellelli story with the signifying structure of the painting and the relation of both to the more general and consistent practice of fragmentation and centrifugality characteristic of Degas's representations of family groups, a practice that contrasts strongly with the more unified, harmonized, and centripetally focussed representations of the subject by more conventional painters of the period. And finally, I will examine the relation of all of these issues to the problematization of the discourse of the family in the second half of the nineteenth century in France.

To begin with, *The Bellelli Family* may be contextualized as one of a number of Degas's images in which gender opposition, tension, or outright hostility is a major issue—works like the *Young Spartans* (c. 1860–62, fig. 89); the *Interior*, also called *The Rape* (c. 1868–69,

89 EDGAR DEGAS Young Spartans, c. 1860–62, reworked until 1880

fig. 90); or *Sulking* (c. 1869–71)—and in which a yawning space between the gendered opponents and/or fragmented or centrifugal composition constructs a disturbing sense of psychological distance or underlying hostility between the figures in question.

It is, oddly enough, precisely in the representation of *family* scenes—just where one would most expect a pictorial structure suggesting "togetherness"—that Degas most strongly emphasizes apartness and disjunction. In the striking portrait of his aunt Stefanina with her two daughters, for example, *The Duchessa di Montejasi with Her Daughters Elena and Camilla* (c. 1876, fig. 91), the black-clad matron stares stolidly ahead at the viewer, while the two young women, perhaps playing the piano and relegated to the bottom left margin of the painting, focus their attention away from her, out of the painting altogether.[8] In Degas's now-destroyed painting of the *Place de la Concorde* (1876, fig. 93), the Vicomte Lepic, his two daughters and their greyhound are all centrifugally deployed, and the fragmentation and disjunctiveness of the composition are made even more evident by the presence of a sliver of an onlooker in the left-hand margin and the vast empty space of the square itself in the background. This is a daringly de-centered composition, inscribing in visual terms the fragmentation and haphazardness of experience characteristic of the great modern city, but with the added poignancy that the point is made with parent and children, rather than with mere passing strangers. In the double portrait of the Bellelli sisters, *Giovanna and Giulia Bellelli* (c. 1865–66, fig. 92), the two girls turn their backs on one another, and in the portrait of Degas's close friend, Henri Rouart, with his daughter, Hélène (1871–72), the child perches uneasily on her father's knee, looking grimly out at the spectator, as he looks dully to the left. The other members of the Impressionist group, Berthe Morisot for example, or Mary Cassatt, often turned to members of their own families or those of their friends as subject matter; few of these painters indulged in sentimental family feeling. Rather, it is Degas's insistence on separation and disjunction, a formal structure of indifference as the very hallmark of the family portrait, that is so striking.[9]

90 EDGAR DEGAS Interior, c. 1868–69

91 EDGAR DEGAS The Duchessa di Montejasi with Her Daughters Elena and Camilla, c. 1876

The wistful sense of uneasiness emanating from the artist's portrait of his orphan cousin and her uncle, *Henri and Lucie Degas* (c. 1876) is a function of the same sort of psychic and compositional disjunction that marks Degas's representations of family members generally.

Even in the one work, *Carriage at the Races* (1869), in which Degas has apparently created a pastoral image of *haut-bourgeois* family felicity, a composition representing his old friend Paul Valpinçon, his wife and their infant son Henri, a group as cuddly and engaging as any sentimentalist òf the family could want, the family unit depicted, is, in a sense, a fraud. For the mother-figure at the heart of this family group, emphasized by her white dress and the solicitously adjusted white umbrella over her head, is *not*, in fact, the happy mother at all but rather, the hired help, the wet-nurse, who, like the fashionable bulldog perched on the edge of the carriage, is simply one of the necessary accouterments of the *haut-bourgeois* domestic economy. The *soi-disant* family group disguises the presence of an intruder: that of the so-called *seconde mère* who is the actual provider of nourishment to the son and heir.

It would be easy to reduce Degas's uneasy representations of the family to the projection of some sort of personal neurosis on his part,

92 EDGAR DEGAS Giovanna and
Giulia Bellelli, c. 1865–66

93 EDGAR DEGAS Place de la
Concorde, 1876

which one could attribute to the early loss of his mother, the surplus of bachelor uncles and marriages of convenience in his family or to poor communication with his father, etc., but that would be to miss the point.[10] The family was a theme considerably debated during the second half of the nineteenth century in France among men of Degas's class, and specifically within the group of sophisticated men of letters, who were his friends and associates.

After the Commune, the problematization of the family was stimulated by the nascent discipline of sociology, which took on the institution with a vengeance, claiming the Commune to be a disaster occasioned by the weakening of family authority and the resultant triumph of anarchy and greed among the lower orders. This was the interpretation not only of authorities on the right—Catholic or Royalist— but, most especially, of right-thinking Republicans of *juste-milieu* tendencies, sociologists like Henri Baudrillart, a member of the prestigious Institut and the author of the influential *La Famille et l'éducation en France dans leur rapports avec l'état de la société*, published in 1874.[11] In this important study, Baudrillart lays emphasis on the bourgeois family as the chief pillar of the state, a bulwark against the chaotic and uncontrolled energies and desires of the masses, and on the necessity for the middle-class family to instill the virtues of industry, honesty, loyalty and self-sacrifice in its members—through the instrumentality of its female members above all.

Often, in the wake of the bourgeois trauma represented by the Commune, the need for vigorous political control within the state was equated with the need for increased state intervention in the affairs of the family, that is to say, the working-class family. Such intervention became an important element of the modernization process in the nineteenth and early twentieth centuries, as Jacques Donzelot revealed in his now-classic study, *La Police des familles* of 1977.[12] This demand for the policing of the poor family was almost always accompanied by a parallel demand for self-policing, for internalized education in self-control and repression of impulse on the part of the superior levels of society.

Yet of course I am making it sound as though the family were itself a fixed, known entity, rather than a formation in the process of construction during the course of the nineteenth century. While a great deal of ink was spilled in defining family norms, which varied between the different classes to be sure, and positing family ideals, the modern family—that entity we tend to think of as relatively fixed and permanent, put in place within the individual by such structuring devices as the Oedipus complex and the superego, and socially positioned as the private sphere in opposition to the public one of politics—was still in the process of coming into being during the period when Degas was painting.

Mark Poster, in his *Critical Theory of the Family* of 1978, sets forth the most accurate, complex and nuanced model of bourgeois family structure available, making clear and raising to the level of critical consciousness just those features of family relationship and ideology that Degas and his contemporaries—and perhaps many of us as well—take as inherent to family structure, but which in fact are class- and historically specific.[13]

To summarize Poster's model of the nineteenth-century bourgeois family:

The bourgeois family by definition is located in urban areas... Family planning first began in this group. In everyday life, relations among members of the bourgeois family took on a distinct pattern of emotional intensity and privacy...Sexuality among this class, until recent changes, is one of the more astonishing features of modern history. Like no other class before, the bourgeoisie made a systematic effort to delay gratification. This led to sexual incapacities for both men and women...Among the bourgeoisie, women were viewed as asexual beings, as angelic creatures beyond animal lust. When internalized, this image of women led to profound emotional conflicts...Prostitution was required by bourgeois males... because the "double standard," which originated with this class, made sexual fulfillment impossible for both spouses.

Bourgeois marriage bound the couple forever. Social and financial interests tended to predominate in these alliances...as the soundest reason for marriage. Yet there was a contradictory drive in bourgeois youth towards romantic love. The strange thing about the sentimental pattern of the middle class is that romantic love rarely outlasted the first few years...of the union. "Happily ever after" meant living together not with intense passion but with restrained respectability.

Relations within the bourgeois family were regulated by strict sex-role divisions. The husband was the dominant authority over the family and he provided for the family by work in factory or market. The wife, considerably less rational and less capable, concerned herself exclusively with the home. The major interest of the wife for a good part of the marriage concerned the children: she was to raise them with the utmost attention, a degree of care new to family history. A new degree of intimacy and emotional depth characterized the relations between parents and children of this class. A novel form of maternal love was thought natural to women. Women were not simply to tend to the survival of their children, but to train them for a respectable place in society. More than that, they were encouraged to create a bond between themselves and the children so deep that the child's inner life could be shaped to moral perfection...As it eschewed the productive function, the bourgeois home also divorced itself from external authority. Within the family's clearly defined boundaries, authority over the relations of parents and children was now limited to the parents alone.

With new forms of love and authority, the bourgeois family generated a new emotional structure. Child-rearing methods of this family were sharply different from those of the earlier aristocracy and peasantry. During the oral stage, the mother was deeply committed to giving her infant tenderness and attention...During the anal phase, the same constant attention continued accompanied by a sharp element of denial. The child was compelled to exchange anal gratification for maternal love, denying radically the pleasure of the body in favor of sublimated forms of parental affection.

Ambivalence, according to Poster, the central emotional context of bourgeois childhood, must be seen as a direct creation of the bourgeois family structure. In fact, he maintains, "the secret of the bourgeois family structure was that, without conscious intention on the part of the parents, it played with intense feelings of love and hate which the child felt both for its body and for its parents in such a way that parental rules became internalized and cemented in the unconscious on the strength of both feelings, love and hate, each working to support and reinforce the other. Love, as ego-ideal, and hate, as superego, both worked to foster the attitudes of respectability. In this way, Poster maintains, the family generated an "autonomous" bourgeois, a modern citizen who needed no external sanctions or supports but was self-motivated to confront a competitive world, make independent decisions and battle for capital.

Poster summarizes the formative structure of the bourgeois family and the resulting sharp differentiation of gender roles as follows:

The emotional pattern of the bourgeois family is defined by authority restricted to parents, deep parental love for children and a tendency to employ threats of the withdrawal of love rather than physical punishment as a sanction. This pattern, applied to the oral, anal and genital stages, results in a systematic exchange on the child's part of bodily gratification for parental love, which in turn produces a deep internalization of the parent of the same sex. Sexual differences become sharp personality differences. Masculinity is defined as the capacity to sublimate, to be aggressive, rational and active; femininity is defined as the capacity to express emotions, to be weak, irrational and passive. Age differences become internalized patterns of submission. Childhood is a unique but inferior condition. Childhood dependency is the basis for learning to love one's superiors. Passage to adulthood requires the internalization of authority. Individuality is gained at the price of unconsciously incorporating parental norms...The bourgeois family structure is suited preeminently to generate people with ego structures that foster the illusion that they are autonomous beings. Having internalized love-authority patterns to an unprecedented degree by anchoring displaced body energy in a super-ego, the bourgeois sees himself as his own self-creation, as the captain of his soul, when in fact he is the result of complex psycho-social processes.[14]

In comparison to this psychoanalytic thematization of the formation of the family under capitalism, Jürgen Habermas's positioning of the modern nuclear family as the historically emergent institution constituting private relations within what he terms the "life world" (existing in opposition to the public, or political, sphere of this world at the same time that it is linked to and mutually dependent upon the official economic sphere of the so-called system world) emphasizes very different features of bourgeois family structure within the social, economic and political context of modernization.[15] Degas's representations of the family, it seems to me, cannot be fully understood or interpreted without taking account of this process and the ways in which the family assumes a new and important role in relation to the other institutional orders of capitalism. Nor can such representations be understood without an awareness of the important ideological role played by idealist, pictorial or literary constructions of the family in which the mutual interlinkage of the family and public life, of the family and the economy, is occluded in favor of a vision of the family which envisions it as a pure opposition to the world of getting and spending, an oasis of private feelings and authentic relationships in a desert of harsh reality. The complex construction of the bourgeois family was marked in all its phases by non-synchronous features, by failures and contradictions as well as by triumphs. For example, in Degas's time, for the upper bourgeoisie in general, the older notion of the extended family and its interests, and of marriage as a strategic cementing of economic, social and political alliances, coexisted with very different, more "progressive" notions of romantic love, freely chosen spouses, the primacy of the individual couple and their mutual interests, and so forth.[16]

I have gone into such detail in establishing an identifying model of the nineteenth-century bourgeois family because I believe it is impossible to deal with the representations and critiques problematizing this institution in the literary and artistic discourse of the time without some familiarity with various theories of the family and its historical formation under capitalism. Certainly, sharp criticism of the bourgeois family and its defining hypocrisy constituted one of the favored themes of the naturalist writers of Degas's time and circle. In these texts, it is the difference between appearance—of decorum, mutual interest, and above all, of unimpeachable respectability—and reality—sordid, exploitative, corrupt—that constitutes the favored topos, rather than what might be characterized as the Freudian figure of ambivalence. Zola's *Pot-Bouille* of 1884, for example, is just such a searching and serious critique of the corruption infecting bourgeois family relations.[17] In *Pot-Bouille*, the opposition between respectability, the appearance, and corruption, the reality, is figured in the contrast Zola establishes between the family areas and the servants' quarters of a Parisian apartment house, a setting the author characterizes as a "bourgeois chapel." But in the center of the house is the servants' staircase and inner court. Here, in this place that Zola calls "the sewer of the house," all is dank and redolent of stale odors. The servants shout malevolent gossip and vulgarities from window to window. "The façade of respectability that conceals the vulgarity of the servants' court is an analogy for the strict moral façade and inner corruption that characterize every family in the house."[18] *Pot-Bouille*, according to Demetra Palmari, constitutes a serious and devastating condemnation of bourgeois morality from the vantage point of a progressive social critique couched in the language of naturalism. From this vantage point, the failure of the family lies in the fact that although it is supposed to uphold the highest moral standards, the family does not serve this function at all. "Though the family is a central element of their lives, its members have virtually no affection for one another and are continually trying to escape its oppressive bonds, at the same time that they cling to its emotionally lifeless form, for it is the societal justification of their moral code."[19]

In those pre-Freudian days, Zola's analysis of the problems besetting the bourgeois family fastens on the contrast between appearance
and reality, between masquerade and truth, as the besetting evil; that
is to say, hypocrisy rather than internalized ambivalence is positioned
as the motor of family interaction. Love—spontaneous, natural,
unfettered—on the other hand, rather than being seen as an inherent part
of the "problem" of the bourgeois family, the most potent, internalized weapon of family control, is idealized as the (rarely available)
"solution."

This topos of appearance versus reality, of glittering performance
versus sordid *coulisse*, of masquerade as the livery of bourgeois
respectability, is one favored not merely by serious naturalists like
Zola, but by the light-hearted, cynical, worldly men of letters of Degas's
time and ambience as well. As such, it constitutes an important sub-
genre of the entire discourse of prostitution of the period, a genre
focussing on the difficulty of distinguishing between respectable women
and prostitutes.[20] Of course the Goncourts resort to the topos again
and again, both in their novels and in the pages of the *Journal*,[21] but
the apotheosis of the genre, constructing a critique of bourgeois family
values through a witty, parodic literary structure rather than a naturalistic, moralistic one, is in fact the creation of Ludovic Halévy, Degas's
close friend and fellow habitué of the *coulisses* of the Opéra: the *Famille
Cardinal* stories.

Degas created over thirty illustrations, mostly monotypes, for the
series of interrelated short stories dealing with the Cardinals: Monsieur,
Madame, and the two "petites Cardinals," Virginie and Pauline, members
of the *corps de ballet*.[22] Degas evidently admired the Cardinal stories, rel-
ishing their charm and cynicism, despite the fact that Halévy rejected his
prints as illustrations for the collected volume, *La Famille Cardinal*.
When Halévy later published the more moralizing, sentimental novel,
L'Abbé Constantin, Halévy notes Degas's negative reaction in his diary,
saying: "He is disgusted with all that virtue, all that elegance. He was
insulting to me this morning. I must always do things like Madame
Cardinal, dry little things, satirical, skeptical, ironic, without heart,
without feeling..."[23]

What Zola hypostasizes as tragedy, Halévy deconstructs as farce. It
is simply taken for granted that the "family values" represented by an
upwardly mobile lower- or lower-middle-class family with two dancing
daughters are farcical—hypocritical and corrupt—and that the desperate
need for "respectability" that apparently motivates the Cardinal parents
in their ambitions for their lovely and desirable daughters is laughable

rather than pathetic. Social critique, if it is present at all, is directed against the lower-class victims rather than the worldly men who supply these young women with material benefits in return for sexual favors: this social arrangement is simply taken as read. Its acceptability—and worldly humorousness—is underscored by the fact that the tales of the Cardinals' peccadilloes are always narrated by the author himself; Halévy figures as the observer-narrator of *La Famille Cardinal*, and Degas, rather too conspicuously for the author's taste perhaps, introduces his friend as a recognizable portrait in many of his illustrations (which were probably created during the 1870s and early 1880s). The Cardinal stories are constructed as a series of paradoxes, in which the family is figured in the form of its parodic debasement, and in which the mother enacts the role of the loving, concerned—ever-vigilant—procuress and the father that of the strict but respectable pimp, who, from time to time, because of his political ambitions, refuses to let his daughters darken his door. These paternal political ambitions serve to define the ridiculous M. Cardinal as a sort of M. Prudhomme of the left, for *La Famille Cardinal* is a parody of the radical politics of the lower orders as well as of their search for respectability. For M. Cardinal is represented as a genuine member of the Commune, a parodic Communard, and M. Prudhomme as a Communard. He is a militant atheist whose cocotte-daughters, having set him and his wife up in *confort coussu* in a suburban cottage, buy him busts of Voltaire and Rousseau as a birthday present, while their lovers provide him with fireworks and refreshments for the radical fête he has organized in the village in hopes of becoming its radical mayor. The two Cardinal daughters are hardly described at all. Their charms are a matter of suggestion, indicated by the reactions of their male admirers and the high price their sexual services fetch on the *coulisse* market. They are obviously fluff-heads, alternately dumb, tangled up in their own silly spontaneous erotic impulses, and extremely astute, making domestic arrangements that pay well and leave them free to pursue their insatiable but innocent lust for pleasure and possessions. Both Colette's *Gigi* and Anita Loos's *Gentlemen Prefer Blondes* as well as the comedy films of Marilyn Monroe are presaged in these adorably silly young creatures. In the case of these "naturally" predatory girls, Halévy implies, education—one of the cornerstones of bourgeois family aspiration—would be a drawback rather than an advantage. When Pauline Cardinal, now a *poule de luxe* ensconced in the lap of luxury, wishes to break some appointments with her wealthy lovers in order to visit her mother in the country, she has her lady's maid write to the gentlemen in question rather than doing so herself. When Mme Cardinal expresses

94 EDGAR DEGAS Ludovic Halévy Meeting Mme Cardinal Backstage, from La Famille Cardinal, c. 1880

shock over her bad manners, Pauline replies: "Hermance writes better than I do; she's been governess in a great family; she never makes a mistake in spelling. But as for me! It's a little your fault, mamma. You were much more anxious to teach me dancing than spelling." "Because I thought it was more useful and I was right," Mme Cardinal replies. "Would you be what you are if it hadn't been for the ballet? And see what spelling brings you to—to be your lady's maid."[24]

Bourgeois virtue, far from being rewarded, is in fact punished in this paradoxical mode of family satire. What you would expect the right-thinking, respectable mother to demand is never quite what Mme Cardinal, in her role of procuress-mother, is up to in her search for "respectable"—actually, high-class prostitutional—connections for her daughters.

Family feeling, that demand for harmony and mutual support usually seen as central to the respectability of the family as an institution, is wittily demeaned by such paradoxical figuration. When for

95 EDGAR DEGAS Dancers at Their Toilette, c. 1879

example, Virginie's rich and aristocratic lover, the marquis, discusses
domestic arrangements with M. and Mme Cardinal, suggesting that he
will pay the parents a little pension and set up housekeeping with
Virginie in his house on Boulevard de la Reine-Hortense, M. and Mme
Cardinal are overcome with horror. This is not because the marquis
wishes to live in sin with their daughter, as one might expect, but
because he wishes to set her up separately from them—outside the bosom
of her family—and pay them off with a measly pension. M. Cardinal

walks out in a huff, saying that nothing can induce them to part from their Virginie, leaving Madame to negotiate with her daughter's would-be keeper:

> So it was agreed, between the marquis and me, that he should hire a large apartment, large enough for the whole of us. At first the marquis proposed to take us all into his house, but I told him Monsieur Cardinal would never agree to that; and I seized the opportunity to describe M. Cardinal's character; that he was a great stickler for honor and respect and consideration before everything; that we must save appearances at any cost; that, to do that, two doors and two staircases were necessary, so that there shouldn't be any disagreeable meetings at unseasonable hours.
>
> The marquis understood it all as well as could be; the very next morning he began his search for apartments, and by noon they were found. That's where we're living now—Rue Pigalle...We are very comfortable there...Salon and dining-room in the middle; at the right, our rooms...at the left, Virginie's and the marquis's. Two doors and two staircases. The marquis did his best to induce M. Cardinal and me to take the rooms on the main staircase side; but M. Cardinal refused, with his usual tact. Tact is his strong point, you know. We took the servants' staircase.[25]

In still another incident from the same story, "Madame Cardinal," Mme Cardinal and the marquis almost come to blows about who is entitled to give the ailing Virginie her footbath.

> He seized the tub but I held on. He pulled and I pulled; half the boiling water fell on his legs and he gave a yell and dropped it. Then I ran through the door to my Virginie. "Here, my angel, here's your footbath!" And I looked the marquis straight in the eye and said: "Just try to tear a mother from her daughter's arms, will you, you grinning ape! You abandon your children, but I don't abandon mine !"[26]

This is of course cynical, *boulevardier* mockery of "family values," underscored by the shrug, wink and nudge of the worldly narrator, who shares the complicitous semiology of the *homme du monde* with his audience. This audience included Degas, who, in works like the *Dancing Lesson* (c. 1874) or *Dancers at Their Toilette* (c. 1879, also known as the *Dance Examination*) may well imply, subtly of course, that the ubiquity of the dancers' mothers behind the scenes has certain questionable over-tones and that apparent chaperonage actually disguises its opposite.

The difference between the outright procuress-mother, like Mme Cardinal, and the generic stage-mother is not a pronounced one in the eyes of the sophisticated backstage gentleman of Degas's time, and indeed, the mother represented in *Dancers at Their Toilette* bears a suspicious resemblance to Mme Cardinal in the monotype series dedicated to Halévy's stories.

Degas's climactic subversion of family values, however, occurs not in the realm of backstage shenanigans established by the *Famille Cardinal* prints, but in a setting of overt transgression: in the brothel, the family's forbidden opposite, in a pastel over monotype, *The Name Day of the Madam* (1876–77). This image, too, is related to a literary strategy of moral paradox, specifically that employed by Guy de Maupassant in his *nouvelle* of 1881, *La Maison Tellier*, in which prostitutes play the role of *grandes dames* at the first communion of the madam's niece, and where the comic tears of sentimental whores create a moment of genuine emotion in the little church in Normandy where they have gathered for the celebration. "The convention," writes Edward D. Sullivan in his analysis of this work, "to be sure, is the convention of farce and develops the conceivable consequences of the singular proposition of a bawdy house closed because of a first communion."[27] Right from the beginning, however, Maupassant emphasizes the "family atmosphere" of the brothel in question: the Maison Tellier is constructed as a site of warmth, good fellowship and even of respectability. "There were always about six or eight people there, always the same, not cut-ups, but honorable men...and they took their chartreuse teasing the girls a little or else they talked seriously with *Madame*, whom everyone respected...The house was familial, very small, painted yellow...*Madame*, born into a good peasant family...had accepted that profession absolutely as she would have become a milliner or a seamstress..."[28]

Degas, although he too relies on the figure of reversal in *The Name Day of the Madam*, pushes things a bit further. It is not the image of respectability that he wishes to construct, but its opposite. In one reading, this might be construed as a grotesque reversal of the notion of family piety, the madam, the "mother figure" of the piece, inscribing a notion of maternal abjection, to borrow Kristeva's locution. The whole brothel setting, with the naked girls pressed together, proffering both their sexual charms and their congratulatory bouquet, creates a sense of family values displaced: the house is certainly a home in terms of warmth, of the pressing together of bodies in a fleshly intimacy impossible to the chilly decorum governing the behavior of a "real" bourgeois family like the Bellellis, but it is nevertheless a house of scandal, of

96 EDGAR DEGAS The Name Day of the Madam, 1876–77

debasement. Perhaps it is irony which is the figure at issue here, as Victor Koshkin-Youritzin suggests in his extremely suggestive article entitled "The Irony of Degas." Characterizing this, among all the bordello monotypes created by Degas, as a "serious and poignant aspect of irony," he points out that this seriousness can only be appreciated to the full if "one recalls the entire body of Degas's work, especially the many family scenes (*Bellelli*, *Mante*, *Lepic*, etc.) with their piercing sense of isolation. Very simply," Koshkin-Youritzin concludes, "is there not a rather exquisite irony to the fact that here—not in a private home or polite social gathering, but a mere bordello—one finds probably the

97 EDGAR DEGAS In the Salon, c. 1876–85

fullest expression of human warmth, inter-relationship, and general happiness to be found anywhere in Degas's work—and moreover, perhaps the only specific example of human *giving*?"[29]

It is unexpectedly enlightening to examine Degas's whole series of brothel monotypes (c. 1876–85)—for example, *In the Salon* (J 82)—from the unexpected vantage point of the problem of "family values" as it was constituted in the later nineteenth century.[30] It seems to me that Degas's strategies *vis-à-vis* the representation of the family are best read against the foil of their apparent opposite, the brothel, the one functioning as the parodic supplement of the other. The family as the site of alienation and disconnection; the brothel as the last refuge of living warmth and human contact; or the family as the place where women are sold for money as in the brothel, but with greater hypocrisy, under a veneer of social virtue, and above all, bourgeois respectability: these are the topics suggested by Degas's representations.

The brothel monotypes are too often considered as a unified group of works, inscribing a single discourse of prostitution and transgression, yet as a group, they are far from unified. They range from alienating, caricatural coarseness and animalism—see, for example, *Two Girls in a Brothel* (J 81, fig. 100); *In the Salon* (J 82); or *Waiting I* (J 64, first

98 EDGAR DEGAS Two
Women, c. 1876–85

99 EDGAR DEGAS Waiting I,
c. 1876–85

100 EDGAR DEGAS Two Girls in a Brothel, c. 1876–85   101 EDGAR DEGAS Relaxation, c. 1876–85

version)—to representations of relaxed conviviality among women on their own, or women with a male client, or women enjoying each other's bodies—*Siesta in the Salon* (J 18); *Naked Women* (J 118); *Two Women* (J 117, fig. 98); *Conversation* (J 106)—to a kind of melting bodily unification, a dark, dreamy, fingerprinted figuration of flesh finding satisfaction in flesh, inscribed in compositions in which centripetality—in one case, around a hearth in *The Fireside* (J 159)—is often the controlling compositional feature, and formal blending, dissolution of borders, and material unity are the strategic constructive principles—for example *Relaxation* (J 73) or *Brothel Scene, In the Salon* (J 71, fig. 104). Boundaries and oppositions are obfuscated in these amazing prints, suggesting an almost palpable yearning for that ultimate, even pre-Oedipal, unification with the object of desire—a total and fantasmic satisfaction of the flesh—utterly forbidden by bourgeois family codes, and any others that we know of for that matter.[31]

In Degas's most typical works, for example *The Dancer with a Bouquet*, also known as *Ballerina and Lady with a Fan* (1878, fig. 105), the figure of relationship—of "togetherness"—is always stipulated as a

102 EDGAR DEGAS Siesta in the Salon, c. 1876–85

103 EDGAR DEGAS The Fireside, c. 1876–77

104 EDGAR DEGAS Brothel Scene, In the Salon, c. 1876–85

purely formal one, constituted here by the way tutu and fan echo and
re-echo each other as formal entities, not as signs of human connection.
The "closeness" is specified as that of shapes on paper or canvas,
certainly not that of individual psychology or communitarian solidarity:
on the contrary, it is precisely the social and psychological *distance*
between the dancer on the stage and the elegant spectator in the box
that is at once elided, and at the same time, evoked, by the formal
echoing, even overlapping, of the semicircular shapes that bind them
in a completely fortuitous rapport. This rejection of conventional psychological connection, of traditional narrative, constitutes for us an
essential part of Degas's modernity: his making strange of human relat-
edness; his insistence on isolation, disjunction and unexpected
"meaningless" conjunction as the norms for the pictorial construction of
contemporary social existence. His rejection of the clichés—and the presumed hypocrisy—of the discourse of the family and of women in
general seems like one aspect of this modernity. It is only in this sense,

I believe, that one can speak of some of Degas's representations of women as "positive," in that they call into question, by means of unconventional structures of composition and expression, the notion that the family is the natural site of feminine existence, rejecting the standard codes and pictorial conventions of the time, even those informing many of the engaging family representations of his Impressionist colleagues.

Pursuing the implications of this negative dialectic even further, Degas went so far as to locate the purported virtues of the bourgeois "home" in the "house," so to speak, on the very site—both seductive and repellently grotesque—of the family's transgressive Other. In so doing, he undermined the oppositional authority of both as imaginary spaces of moral distinctiveness.

105 EDGAR DEGAS The Dancer with a Bouquet, 1878

Mary Cassatt's *Lady at a Tea Table* (1883–85, fig. 107) is one of the most remarkable American portraits of the nineteenth century. A subtle combination of strength and fragility, the painting represents Mrs. Mary Dickinson Riddle, Cassatt's first cousin once removed. The sitter, who had a reputation as a great beauty, in fact rejected the work, apparently because she and her daughters felt it was not flattering enough. And indeed, it is not a flattering portrait, in the sense that John Singer Sargent's almost contemporary portrait of *Lady Agnew* (1892–93, fig. 109) is. The pose is far more rigid, the costume and decor more severe; the tell-tale signs of age, especially about the mouth and chin, are observed, if not exaggerated; the wonderfully quirky nose's sharp tip is enhanced by a dab of white highlight; the horizontal flare of the nostril is anything but classic in its idiosyncratic structure. What Mrs. Riddle has is *character*, something as different from the slightly vapid elegance of Sargent's sitter as it is from the explosive primitivism of an almost contemporary portrait like Vincent van Gogh's *La Mère Roulin* (1889).

Cassatt has been criticized for paying attention to the lives of only a very restricted circle of women: a privileged circle, like that represented by Mrs. Mary Dickinson Riddle, women who could afford to spend their days enjoying genteel accomplishments, mutual entertainment, and mild, leisure activities; women who did not have to work, and who, on the whole, did not engage in the arts on a *professional* rather than an amateur level. Cassatt herself was divided about this: she aspired unswervingly toward professionalism and the serious work it entailed but nevertheless honored the feminine sphere of activity, those "spaces of femininity"[1] so aptly named by Griselda Pollock, that private sphere of family, friends and decorous sociability which engaged most women of Cassatt's time and class.

The taking of tea with elegant accouterments seems to have attracted her more than once, as the painting *The Cup of Tea* (1880, fig. 108) demonstrates. Perhaps it seemed paradigmatic to her of that other kind of "work" or more accurately, art, that leisure-class women engaged in, in addition to running fairly complicated, large-scale

107 MARY CASSATT Lady at a Tea Table, 1883–85

households: the art of organizing domestic ceremonies. Tea is here represented as a sort of ritual occasion in the feminine, what Yeats has referred to as a "ceremony of innocence." As such, presiding over the tea table may be seen as a major instance of what the great modern novelist, Dorothy Richardson, in her *roman-fleuve, Pilgrimage* (the first volume of which was published in 1915), has called women's crowning achievement—"the creation of atmospheres."[2] Like Cassatt, Richardson both yearned for women's emancipation, and, at the same time, honored and cherished her domestic role as creative director and maintainer of the "spaces of femininity." Miriam, the heroine of *Pilgrimage*, in conversation with an enlightened male advocate of women's emancipation, states: "There's no emancipation to be done. Women are emancipated." "Prove it, Miriam," her male suffragist friend challenges. "I can," Miriam replies,

> Through their pre-eminence in art. The art of making atmospheres. It's as big an art as any other. Most women can exercise it, for reasons, by fits and starts. The best women work at it the whole of the time. Not one man in a million is aware of it. It's like air within the air. It may be deadly...So is the bad art of men. At its best it is absolutely life-giving. And not soft. Very hard and stern and austere in its beauty...Just as with "Art"...It's one of the answers to the question about women and art. It's all there. It doesn't show, like men's art. There's no drama or publicity...It's hard and exacting; needing "the maximum of detachment and control." And people have to learn, or be taught, to see it...[3]

108 MARY CASSATT The Cup of Tea, 1880

109 JOHN SINGER SARGENT Lady Agnew, 1892–93   110 NICOLAS POUSSIN Self-Portrait, 1650

Yet Miriam (who is really the authorial voice in the novel), like Cassatt, somehow reveals the paradoxical nature of her defense of women as atmosphere-makers versus art-makers by admitting at the end of this passage: "Lots of women hold back. Just as men do—from exacting careers. I do. I don't want to exercise the feminine art."[4] And later, in an article, Richardson articulates that divided position *vis-à-vis* women's domestic role which so unites her with Cassatt, by pointing out that the demands of atmosphere-making offer precisely the greatest obstacles to women's creative achievement:

Art demands what, to women, current civilization won't give. There is for a Dostoyevsky writing against time on the corner of a crowded kitchen table a greater possibility of detachment than for a woman artist no matter how placed. Neither motherhood nor the more continuously exacting and indefinitely expansive responsibilities of even the simplest housekeeping can so effectively hamper her as the human demands, besieging her wherever she is, for an inclusive awareness, from which men, for good or ill, are exempt.[5]

The article, published under the rubric "Women in the Arts," is entitled, significantly: "Some Notes on the Eternally Conflicting Demands of Humanity (*Not* 'Femininity'!) and Art."

In a sense, one might speculate that Cassatt, in the painting *Lady at a Tea Table*, sees her sitter's vocation–manipulating the tea things, pouring, arranging her clothing and decor, running her household with a sure grasp, a keen aesthetic sense, and long years of experience, of building a seemly and even exquisite atmosphere–as an analogue to her own task of painting a portrait: constructive, subtle, full of choices and decisions, a formal work as well as a social occasion.

And indeed, it is through the knowing manipulation of the formal means of *her* art, the art of painting, that Cassatt has made this portrait into a masterpiece, not merely a likeness. Like Poussin's great self-portrait in the Louvre (1650), it is also a painting about art and the making of art. Like Poussin, Cassatt sets off her sitter's head in a series of enframements which both rivets it in place and calls attention to the relation between the rectangles within the painting (one of which is, indeed, a framed picture itself) and the rectangular shape of the canvas support.

A similar use of the frame to provide compositional stability and self-reference exists in Degas's *The Bellelli Family* (figs. 87–88), a family portrait of the late 1850s and early 1860s, where Laura Bellelli offers a striking analogue to the figure of Mrs. Riddle in both her dignified pose and her dark pyramidal shape; Degas, a friend of Cassatt's, used the painting-within-a-painting motif again, with quite different implications, in his 1868 portrait of another friend, the artist James Tissot.

Yet oddly enough, it is a painter whom Cassatt seems not to have admired strongly whose work offers the best analogy for her sense of the frame-within-a-frame in her work. Cézanne, in his seated portrait of Choquet (1877), locks the figure in place with exactly the same tightly-knit planar grid that Cassatt constructs for her portrait, although he emphasizes it more through constant reiteration. Cassatt, on the contrary, softens any impression of pictorial geometry through strategies of texture and color, playing the blue-and-white drip patterns of the Chinese Export tea set, so strikingly deployed in the foreground, against the differentiated swirls and textures–also blue and white–of the delicate, transparent lace *coiffe* of the sitter. The glitter of the porcelain is picked up, in a different modality, by the subdued glow and coloristic striation of light playing on the sitter's face. Indeed, the painting could, with perfect justice, in a Whistlerian vein, be thought of as a "Symphony in Blue and White." Cassatt also avoids any sense of over-rigidity by

111 BERTHE MORISOT Mme Pontillon, 1871

playing the asymmetry of pose and carefully deployed china against the slightly off-center position of the figure as a whole, loosening the bonds of would-be symmetry into an interesting off-centeredness.

This sense of a firm skeletal structure controlling the portrait composition is quite different from the looser one used by Berthe Morisot in her portrait of her sister, Mme Pontillon (1871). This firmness of structure is characteristic of all of Cassatt's most distinguished portraits of women, like that of Miss Mary Ellison (1879), where the gilt-edged mirror plays the same enframing role as the picture in *Lady at a Tea Table* and the semicircle of the fan is echoed in the answering curve of the sofa back, or the *Young Lady in Black* (1883), where the striking female figure is doubly enframed by elements of the background.

But although Cassatt can certainly demonstrate her brilliance and formal inventiveness as a portrait-painter of women, it must neverthe-

112 MARY CASSATT Miss Mary Ellison, 1879

less be admitted that it is upon her images of mothers and children that
her reputation seems to rest today.

My graduate student who sent an image of the painting *Emmie and
Her Child* (1889, fig. 113) as a Mother's Day card to his mom is certainly
typical, even if his appreciation is on a higher level, of the perception
of Cassatt's work today. For many people, Cassatt is representing the
"natural mother" in *Emmie and Her Child*, a maternal image cast in the
timeless one of the Madonna and Child of Italian Renaissance painting–
say, for example, Raphael's *Madonna del Granduca* (1500)–but made
contemporary, secular and intimate.

Yet of course, there is no "natural" way of representing motherhood,
any more than motherhood itself can be thought of outside the specificity of a particular historical, social, and imagistic context.

Within Cassatt's own time, representations of the mother and child
theme could range from the iconic ferocity of Van Gogh's *Mme Roulin*

113 MARY CASSATT Emmie and Her Child, 1889

114 MARY CASSATT After the Bath, 1901

115 VINCENT VAN GOGH Mme Roulin and Her Baby, 1888

116 MAX ERNST Virgin Spanking Infant Jesus, 1926

117 PAULA MODERSOHN-BECKER Mother and Child, 1907

and Her Baby (1888, fig. 115) to the saccharine traditionalism of William Bouguereau. Other epochs have envisioned motherhood, under duress, as either fierce or alienating, as is exemplified by Goya's *They Are Like Wild Beasts* (c. 1810, fig. 24) or Dorothea Tanning's *Self-Portrait (Maternity)* (1946, fig. 6). And of course not all mothers are "good," nor have they been represented as such—for example, Delacroix's *Medea* (1838) or Max Ernst's *Virgin Spanking Infant Jesus* (1926, fig. 116)— although their transgressive power arises precisely from the memory of the "good mother" images they violate, in the case of the Delacroix, Andrea del Sarto's *Charity* in the Louvre, in the case of the Ernst, some- thing like the Raphael *Madonna* mentioned above.

And if Cassatt's mother and child images speak openly of the sensual fleshly delights of maternity as is the case with *After the Bath* (1901, fig. 114)—far more, for instance, than Morisot's more distanced, delicate image, *The Cradle* (1872, fig. 4)—they seem repressed or at least sublimated in relation to Paula Modersohn-Becker's animalistic, earthy carnality in the painting *Mother and Child* (1907), where the naked maternal body, itself curled into an almost fetal position, seems almost to merge with the naked form of her young.

And certainly, Cassatt never deals with misery, poverty and anguish as conditions of the maternal relationship. She does not represent the tragedy of the proletarian mother who cannot care for or succor her young as does Kollwitz with characteristic expressive power in such images as her etching of *Dead Child and Mother* (1903) or the *Portraits of Misery IV* (c. 1903). Cassatt's is the mother of the cozy, well-provided upper-middle-class bedroom or parlor, in which her curving body can provide shelter and sustenance, not the mother of the back alley or the urban slum.

But there is another kind of mother that Cassatt's art engages with, a very different mother—her own mother, but, perhaps equally importantly, a mother *without* a child. Despite the fact that Cassatt's painting of her mother, *Reading "Le Figaro"* (1877–78, fig. 120), shares certain formal characteristics with Whistler's (fig. 119), and despite the fact that,

118 KATHE KOLLWITZ Portraits of Misery IV, c. 1903

119 JAMES MCNEILL WHISTLER Arrangement in Gray and Black: The Artist's Mother, 1871

from a coloristic point of view, Cassatt's painting, playing on a subtle scale of whites tinged with gray, could, like another famous painting by Whistler, also be called "A Symphony in White," her mother is represented not staring blankly into space, in disembodied profile, an object within a world of objects, but rather in solid three-quarter view. She is represented reading with great concentration, not some fluffy novel, but the rather serious and politically and literarily oriented *Le Figaro*, its title prominent if upside down in the foreground.

In her classic text, "Motherhood According to Bellini,"[6] the French theorist Julia Kristeva meditates on the Virgin's body, its ineffability and the way it ultimately dissolves into pure radiance. In other writings, she and other French, psychoanalytically oriented "feminists" stress the maternal body as the site of the pre-rational, the incoherent and the inchoate. Cassatt's portrait inscribes a very different position *vis-à-vis* the maternal figure; for this is a portrait-homage not to the maternal body, but to the maternal *mind*. Put another way, one might say that finally, we have a loving but dispassionate representation of the mother not as nurturer but rather, the mother as logos. It doesn't really matter whether the real Mrs. Cassatt was an intellectual or not—for all we know, she may have been absorbed in the racing news—it is the power of the representation that counts. Instead of the dazzling, disintegrative,

120 MARY CASSATT Reading "Le Figaro," 1877–78

ineffable colorism with which Kristeva inscribes the maternal body according to Bellini, Cassatt reduces the palette of the maternal image to sober black and white—or its intermediate, gray—the colors of the printed word itself. Sight, of course, is the sense most closely allied with mental activity, associated with (usually, but not always) masculine power in the nineteenth century; and the black-framed pince-nez—the instrument of visual power—is prominent, reiterating the black of the printed page below and the hair above.

121 MARY CASSATT Portrait of Katherine Kelso Cassatt, 1889

122 MARY CASSATT Woman in Black at the Opera, 1877–78

Shortly before, in *Woman in Black at the Opera* (1877–78), Cassatt had associated femininity and the active gaze. Her young woman in black, armed with opera glasses, is all active and aggressive-looking. She holds the opera glasses, those prototypical instruments of masculine specular power, firmly to her eyes, and her tense silhouette suggests the concentrated energy of her assertive visual thrust into space. Even in a portrait painted when her mother was sick and visibly older, *Portrait of Katherine Kelso Cassatt* (1889), Cassatt creates an image of power, framing and setting off the head and giving her mother's body a certain amplitude, placing her in the traditional "thinker" pose.

What I am trying to suggest is that, while they might often, in the nineteenth century, be the antithesis of the spaces of thought and action in the public (and predominantly masculine) sphere, the spaces of femininity might also, for some women, actually serve as sites of intellectual and creative production, and eventually, even of political militancy. Or to put it another way, these spaces can suggest the psychoanalytic maternal position, inscribed in the presymbolic, symbiotic relation of mother–child in a world of their own, apart from a public, patriarchal sphere of reason and power—the symbolic order, to which the (male) child gradually accedes with the acquisition of language, a process brilliantly recorded in Mary Kelly's *Post Partum Document* (1978-79). This psychoanalytic construction of the maternal position is radically different from the multiple positions historically assumed by actual mothers in the historical world, including such women as Mary Cassatt's close friend, Louisine Havemeyer, a mother who collected the most advanced art of her time and went to jail for the cause of women's suffrage, or Mrs. Potter Palmer, also an active feminist and suffragist and an organizer of the Womens' Building at the Chicago World's Fair of 1892-93. Not that Mary Cassatt's mother was a political activist, far from it; I am merely saying that for her daughter, she could serve as a powerful if understated metonym of thought, directed attention and intelligence and at the same time inscribe the position of motherhood. This duality might not be without its contradictions—they stay with us today, as any professional or politically active woman who is also a mother knows—but it was a position within the privileged world in which the Cassatts lived, and even within less privileged ones. It is not without significance that Gertrude Stein chose to call her remarkable play based on the life and

123 MARY KELLY Post Partum Document,
Documentation VI, 1978–79

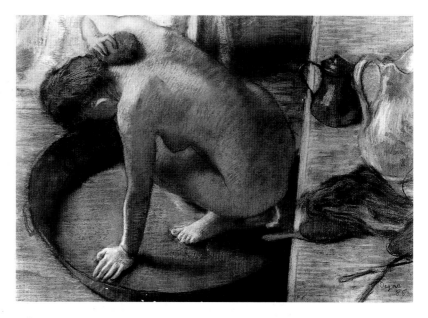

124 EDGAR DEGAS The Tub, c. 1886

achievements of Susan B. Anthony, later an opera with music by Virgil Thomson, "The Mother of Us All." And as far as the psychoanalytic take on the maternal position is concerned, even that has been recently challenged by Marie Christine Hamon in her book provocatively entitled *Pourquoi les femmes aiment-elles les hommes? et non pas plutôt leur mère?*[7]

Yet even when Cassatt confronts the more conventional aspects of motherhood—the mother caring for her child, bathing it, as in the painting *The Bath* (1891–92) or the drypoint *The Bath* (1890–91, fig. 127)—at her best she avoids the sentimentality, the roly-poly clichés of form and conception, including the animalistic "earth-mother" physiognomy, of Renoir's *Motherhood* of the same period.

Indeed, it is to another contemporary, Degas, and his adult women "Bathers," specifically *The Tub* (c. 1886), that one must turn for an equivalent to Cassatt's formal boldness in her 1891–92 painting *The Bath*, which shares with Degas the high horizon, the view from above and the psychological restraint, as well as that sense of the formal demands of the surface, which move our eye up and across the canvas rather than into it. The bold yet controlled use of multiple patterns and sophisticated color relationships in the formal construction of the image, however, is Cassatt's own: the pattern of the wallpaper in relation

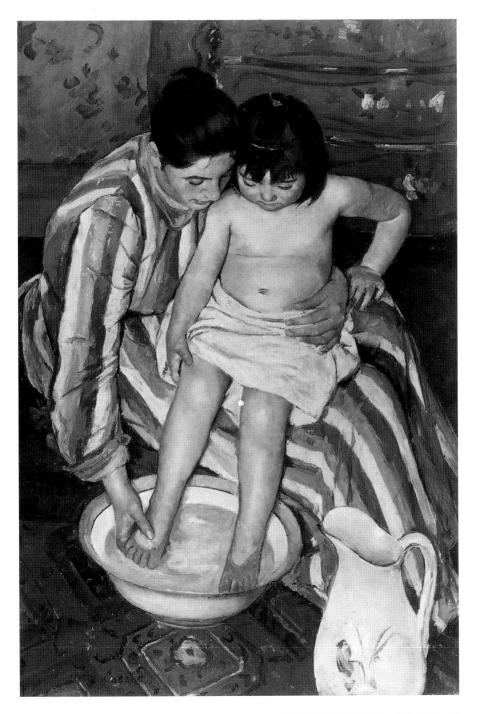

125 MARY CASSATT The Bath, 1891–92

**126 KITAGAWA UTAMARO Young Mother Bathing Her Baby,
from Customs of Women in the Twelve Hours series, c. 1795**

to that of the bureau in the background; the two different rugs, one at the front and one at the back; the recherché harmony of the dress striped in mauve, olive and white, the stripes picked up differentially by the pattern of the fingers of mother and of child, the folds of the towel and, now circular, in the mauve border of the footbath; all this set into play by the exaggerated scale of the pitcher in the foreground leading the eye up and onto the pictorial surface.

One must not, of course, underestimate the role of the Japanese print, like the eighteenth-century example by Kitagawa Utamaro, *Young Mother Bathing Her Baby*, in mediating and transforming scenes of intimate life, which in the Western art of the nineteenth century were susceptible to sentimental convention, into works of formal rigor and emotional distance. This relationship is particularly noticeable in the

127 MARY CASSATT The Bath, 1890–91

print version of the image, and is another predilection that Cassatt shared with Degas, as well as with her friend Louisine Havemeyer from whose collection this print (fig. 127, a trial proof from between the 9th and 10th states) comes.

Yet neither should one underestimate the rich current of sensuality marking Cassatt's treatment of the infant body, her delight in the luscious tactility of baby flesh. I asked a student at a recent doctoral examination which was a more sensual treatment of the naked body, the Cassatt or Degas's pastel, *Woman Bathing in a Shallow Tub* (1886). She was stumped. The two other women professors on the committee agreed that it was a hard decision, but interestingly enough, the solitary male member of the committee confessed that as a man and a father he had been so indoctrinated into the taboo nature of the girl-child's body that he could hardly even look at the image, much less consider it a sensual one! Cassatt transcribes her own impatience with convention in one of her early representations of the child alone, *Little Girl in a Blue Armchair* (1878). How well she has captured the irritation of the nicely dressed child, that particularly annoying quality of wiggliness that afflicts the young when, nearly going mad with boredom, they are forced to sit still for a long time against their will. Against the angular movement of the child, Cassatt has contrasted the immobile form of the sleeping puppy to the left; one can imagine the desperate parent saying to the little prisoner: "See how nicely Fido sits for Miss Cassatt." The young girl's restless pose is in marked contrast to the conventional, dull and angelic manner in which Rudyard Kipling's little daughter sits for Cassatt's contemporary and academic rival, Elizabeth Gardner Bouguereau. This same kind of sentimentalized innocence marks Angèle Dubos's child-portrait, *Happy Age* (1877). Rather than being an individual feature, it is a convention of the representation of childhood for the academic art of the period.

In a certain sense, Cassatt's *Little Girl in a Blue Armchair* might be said to contain an autobiographical reference as much as the *Woman in Black at the Opera* with her avid glance: a portrait of the artist as an impatient semi-rejector of traditional feminine roles and decorum as well as the conventional representation of female subjects, young or mature; although the real, grown Mary couldn't wiggle like that, a certain amount of spiritual wiggling, and verbal tartness, was permissible—and useful.

Berthe Morisot, a friend of Cassatt's, also takes steps to deconventionalize the child-portrait in her image of her daughter, *Julie and Doll* (1884), both in terms of style and in choice of pose and dress—sagging stockings and rucked up skirt—though the brushwork is far looser and more expressive and the image more benign than Cassatt's. It is, of course, possible for the modern viewer to read a certain undertow of prepubescent sexuality in the sprawling, straddle-legged pose. Again, one might point to precedents in the history of French art. In Théodore Géricault's *Portrait of Louise Vernet as a Child* (c. 1818, fig. 38) for instance, also known as *L'Enfant au chat*, the child is shown with seductively revealed shoulder and knee, gripping a very knowing—or even human-looking—cat with her arm. Courbet's *Portrait of Béatrice Bouvet* (1864, fig. 39), is marked by a perverse, doll-like stiffness, a perversity which surfaces violently in the representations of young girls by Balthus (fig. 40), though his sitters are a little older to be sure; note the presence of the cat and the echo of the seductive pose in the raised arms.

128 MARY CASSATT Little Girl in a Blue Armchair, 1878

It has rarely been noticed how many of Cassatt's children—babies mostly, but some more than that—are stark naked and sexually identifiable, or if it has been noticed, it has not been commented on as anything out of the ordinary. Nor has it been pointed out how frankly provocative the glances and gestures of mother and infant son are in the aptly named *Baby's First Caress* (1891, fig. 129). This is partly because of the justifying precedent provided by the naked or semi-naked Christ child in the Virgin and Child imagery of the Renaissance; but of course, the myth of the asexuality of these figures was exploded once and for all by Leo Steinberg in his brilliant study of the sexuality of Christ.[8] But we also avoid the issue of the child-nude in Cassatt's paintings because, in the light of psychoanalytic theory, the subject has too many disturbing undertones and overtones. The sexuality of Mary Cassatt is not something we want to think about, just as we prefer to think of the childish body as innocent, prelapsarian in fact, despite evidence to the contrary. The nineteenth century, like our own, was a time of deep ambiguity about the naked body of the child although the inscriptions of repression are far from identical.

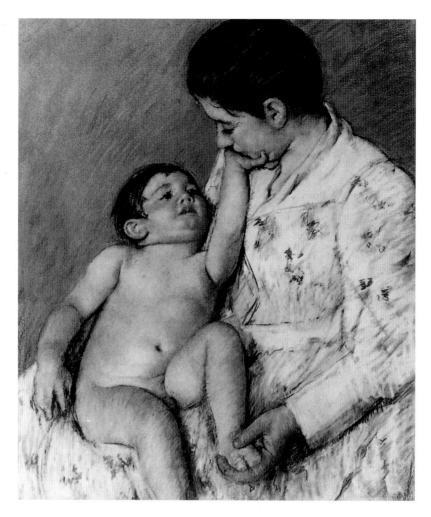

129 MARY CASSATT Baby's First Caress, 1891

In Cassatt's passionate devotion to the nude child's body, as in the painting *Mother and Child (Mother Wearing a Sunflower on Her Dress)* (1905), one cannot rule out the presence of desire. One might almost speak of Cassatt's lust for baby flesh, for the touch, smell and feel—intimate touching plays an important role here—of plump, naked, smooth-skinned bodies, a desire kept carefully in control by formal strategies and a certain emotional diffidence; in some cases, the less successful ones, displaced and oversweetened as sentimentality.

130 MARY CASSATT Mother and Child (The Oval Mirror), c. 1899

131 MARY CASSATT Mother and Child (Mother Wearing a Sunflower on Her Dress), 1905

The psychoanalytic terms "displacement," "repression" and "sublimation" inevitably creep into the discourse when the subject of sexuality is broached in relation to the works of Cassatt. Yet we must be wary of anachronistic readings of the mobility of desire and its objects. For the nineteenth century, the naked bodies of children were often envisioned as simultaneously pure *and* desirable, as is exemplified by the seductively nude or nearly nude photographs of little girls by the Reverend Dodgson, otherwise known as Lewis Carroll, such as his *Portrait of Evelyn Maud Hatch* (1879, fig. 132).

Though it is tempting to see Cassatt's lusciously nude babies, such as the *Mother and Child (The Oval Mirror)*, as examples of Freudian "displacement"—to assert that in the absence, in the representational codes of the time, of socially acceptable *mature* objects of female desire, she simply displaced that desire onto immature ones—this may not be the case at all. Desire takes many different forms at different historical moments and in different situations and we decide what is "normal," what "displaced" or "repressed" at our peril. Although the Reverend Dodgson might shy away from the adult female nude, he, his youthful

132 LEWIS CARROLL Portrait of Evelyn Maud Hatch, 1879

sitters, and their cooperative mothers seem to have felt quite at ease with the child-nude, reserving the sexual fantasies we deem appropriate only to *adult* objects for the realm of childhood.[9]

Why should a nude photograph by Robert Mapplethorpe of the young Jessie McBride of 1976 be considered obscene, or even placed in the category of "child pornography" by some extremists? Why are such images as these, or ones like them, considered—by our postal authority even, officially—dirty pictures? And why are Sally Mann's photographs of her own children considered more than equivocal—offensive, even, by some people (and I'm not saying, in an absolute sense that they don't hover on the dark border of the forbidden)—and Cassatt's not? Is the issue at stake the indexicality of photography? Clearly, Cassatt's youthful sitters sat naked as much as Sally Mann's daughter posed likewise.

Or maybe we should think more about the equivocal sexuality present in both and realize that we are living through an age of almost unparalleled repressiveness and prudery where the child's body and its visual representation is concerned; our much vaunted sense of sexual liberation has gone at least ten steps backward in that area since the time of the Reverend Dodgson and Mary Cassatt.

In the years between 1890 and 1893, Cassatt created two of her major works: one of them, small-scale and private, in the form of a series of prints, was unparalleled for its subtlety, inventiveness and technical

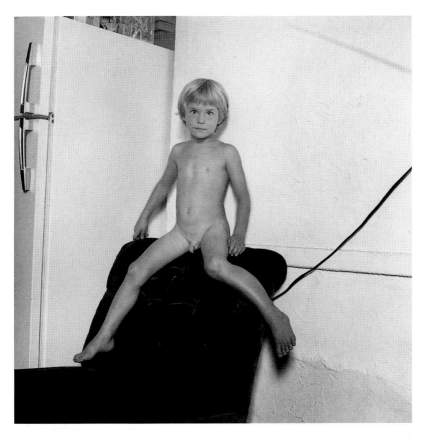

133 ROBERT MAPPLETHORPE Jessie McBride, 1976

daring; the other, a large-scale, public and allegorical mural, alas lost, is
known to us only through inadequate black-and-white photos.

Indeed, one might say that Cassatt's masterpiece was the series of
color prints she executed in etching, drypoint and aquatint at the beginning of the 1890s, at the height of her career. Prints such as *Mother's
Kiss* (1890–91, fig. 134) or *Maternal Caress* (1890–91) encapsulate the
undramatic events constituting the daily life of the upper-class woman,
the woman of refinement and leisure. These include playing with the
baby, the private preparations of the body or clothing, letter-writing,
visiting, and riding on the omnibus. Despite the fact that the last two
demand venturing into the outside world of a great city, the female
subject is always represented existing within a protected and enclosed—
even encapsulated—world.

134 MARY CASSATT Mother's Kiss, 1890–91

In such prints as *The Coiffure* (1890–91) and *The Fitting* (1890–91)
the closed, protected world of genteel womanhood is daringly filtered
through the stylized and elliptical rendering of reality characteristic of
the Japanese print, whose lessons her friends and fellow Impressionists
Degas and Pissarro were also taking seriously at this time; the three
artists often shared ideas, technical data and criticism. Cassatt trans-
poses the *yukio-e* idiom into her own modern and Western terms, terms
in which feminine experience functions as a complete language system,
with its own tropes and inventions. Here Cassatt completely erases the
meaningful narrative implications of temporality (traditionally produced by shadow, modeling or deep space, signifiers of the unfolding of
time in painting), in favor of surface, presentness and anti-narrative
surface in a series of subjects, which, because of their very unimpor-
tance, their anti-heroic qualities, lend themselves perfectly to the idiom
of modernism. The transformation of intimate spaces into formal elegance by means of bold reduction and sophisticated patterning is one
of Cassatt's many achievements in these works, as both *The Letter*
(1890–91) and *The Lamp* (1890–91) indicate.

135 MARY CASSATT The Fitting, 1890–91

136 MARY CASSATT The Coiffure, 1890–91

137 MARY CASSATT The Letter, 1890–91

138 MARY CASSATT The Lamp, 1890–91

139 MARY CASSATT The Omnibus, 1890–91   140 MARY CASSATT Afternoon Tea Party, 1890–91

Worldly sociability, the tête-à-tête of two fashionably dressed ladies—that "creation of atmospheres" that Dorothy Richardson, and Cassatt herself at times, saw as woman's highest artistic achievement—could serve as the basis of *Afternoon Tea Party* (1890–91), a print of great coloristic and compositional subtlety which plays the black of the visitor's jacket against the white of the hostess's gown, a white of course identical to the white of the paper itself. In *The Omnibus* (1890–91), a trip into the outside world is represented as so protected that the public vehicle, whose open windows provide an admirable formal scaffolding for the composition, is figured like a traveling parlor for elegant mother, baby and nursemaid, and the city of Paris itself, locus of so much Impressionist attention, functions as a mere backdrop for the domesticated interior.

Cassatt's other major project in the early 1890s was the vast allegorical mural she created for the Woman's Building at the Chicago World's Columbian Exposition (1893). Cassatt's mural, dedicated to the subject of *Modern Woman* (fig. 141), was set across from its pendant, *Primitive Woman* (fig. 142), by Mary Fairchild MacMonnies, another American artist living in Paris. Both of these monumental works seem to have survived into the twentieth century, but the last traces of them disappeared shortly after the First World War according to recent archival detective work by Carolyn Kinder Carr and Sally Webster.[10] The murals, set in the tympana of the Hall of Honor of the Woman's Building, were grand in scale—about sixty feet long and twelve to fourteen feet high at the highest point—and tripartite in conception.

Cassatt's mural in the south tympanum was divided into three parts by a prominent decorative border: the central panel represented a scene of young women picking fruit in a blooming garden, allegorizing the notion of "Young Women Plucking the Fruits of Knowledge and Science"; to the left, in "Young Women Pursuing Fame," young women were again represented allegorically—and rather humorously—running after what looks like a kite but is actually a little winged figure, with geese nipping at their heels. To the right, "Arts, Music, Dancing" are represented by young women engaged in these activities. "Nothing of St. Cecilia," she specified wryly of the "music" figure.[11]

Despite the loss of the original, a near-contemporary oil sketch related to the theme of the central panel, *Young Woman Picking Fruit* (1892, fig. 143), provides some notion of the brilliance of the color, a brilliance unexpected in the more conventional mural projects of the period, and associated at the time by conservative critics with an assertive modernist stridency of form.

In a recent article in the *Art Bulletin*,[12] Judy Sund critiques Cassatt's mural, *Modern Woman*, on a variety of grounds, both formal and iconographic, summing up her criticism by asserting that "Cassatt, by depicting modern woman in symbolic terms, neglected real women and their actual achievements. Rather than singling out notable individuals", Sund continues, "or even distinctive types—for instance, the sorts of scientists, educators, homemakers and suffragists who attended the Women's Congress—in representative domains, Cassatt presented the viewer with clusters of young, resemblant women, homogeneous in class and race..."[13]

While it is certainly true that Cassatt resorts to the types and the class of women with which she is familiar, and while she is far from being "politically correct" in terms of present-day conceptions (a rather anachronistic demand!), Sund's alternative program, though worthy, sounds depressingly familiar: a sort of conventionalized "upward-and-onward" iconography, iterated in various forms, on the walls of public buildings and high-school assembly rooms in particular.

Cassatt, on the contrary, was attempting, if not entirely successfully, to create a really modern allegory, to take up Courbet's "Allégorie

141 MARY CASSATT Modern Woman mural for the south tympanum of the Hall of Honor, Woman's Building, World's Columbian Exposition, Chicago, 1893

réelle"—an allegory in terms of reality—in her own terms, a cultivated, cosmopolitan, *fin-de-siècle* woman's terms. Her work bears the signs of modernity in its very ambiguousness. Like Courbet in his "Allégorie réelle" of 1855—also created for a World's Fair—she may have thought it prudent to conceal her own strongly felt political views, feminist in her case, her high aspirations for women, in the public space of a major monument. *Modern Woman* was light, humorous and up-to-date in its modern if not modish dress.

If Cassatt, in her own words, "tried to express the modern woman in the fashion of our day and…to represent those fashions as accurately and as much in detail as possible,"[14] she did not by any means resort to the frivolities of Parisian Haute Couture as did Tissot in his allegorical series *The Woman of Fashion* of ten years earlier, which was also devoted, from a very different point of view, to Modern Woman. Cassatt had the dresses made by Doucet and Worth according to her own instructions, and they are neither constrictive or sexy but rather, modern without being precisely fashionable.[15] In short, Cassatt's is one of the few ambitious monumental allegorical paintings of its time I know that, although serious in its total intent, is not weighed down with deadening solemnity and moralism.

About the central portion of her mural (fig. 144), Cassatt wrote that she intended to demonstrate that in *her* garden the picking of the fruit of knowledge by women was *not* a condemned activity: on the contrary, it was strongly to be encouraged. The promoters of the Woman's Building had stated their purpose as follows: "We [women] have eaten of the Tree of Knowledge and the Eden of Idleness is hateful to us. We claim our inheritance, and are become workers not cumberers of the earth."[16] And, if the theme of fruit picking depicted in the central panel of Cassatt's mural allied her figures more closely to the realm of nature than the

142 MARY FAIRCHILD MACMONNIES Primitive Woman mural for the north tympanum of the Hall of Honor, Woman's Building, World's Columbian Exposition, Chicago, 1893

realm of culture, as Sund asserts, it is nevertheless true that it was a theme to which many of the most advanced artists of her day turned in the later part of the nineteenth century, and not necessarily just those who believed in some old-fashioned notion of pastoral beatitude as an alternative to modern reality.

Degas, for instance, turned to the theme of apple-pickers for an unusual bronze funerary monument, while Morisot saw it as a theme of contemporary summer activity in the country for well-brought-up

143 MARY CASSATT Young Woman Picking Fruit, 1892

144 MARY CASSATT Central panel of Modern Woman, 1893

145 CAMILLE PISSARRO Apple Picking at Eragny-sur-Epte, 1888

young girls, as devoid of allegorical implications as possible; and, it must be admitted, Morisot's young women are picking cherries, not apples. Pissarro, at the height of his pointillist period, gives the theme certain specifically moral overtones in *Apple Picking at Eragny-sur-Epte* by centralizing the tree and emphasizing the contemplative gesture of the woman at the right—and these are peasants, not middle-class girls.

Like Cassatt, Gauguin, in his monumental mural-scale painting *Where Do We Come From? Who Are We? Where Are We Going?* (1897), constructs the motif in modernist, in his case primitivist, language, making it the center of a frankly allegorical, and frankly ambiguous, iconographic scheme—either fruit picking unconnected with sin in an island paradise, or the opposite, that even an island paradise may be infected with sin through the plucking of the fruit of the tree of the knowledge of good and evil.

Apple picking offers a theme that is at once decorative and primitivizing in Paul Sérusier's vaguely medievalizing triptych, *Gathering of Apples* (1891), with its Breton and female cast of characters. But here, the conjunction of women and apple picking signifies in exactly the opposite way from Cassatt's modern allegory: in a medievalizing context, it is hard to escape notions of Eve and the Fall.

Cassatt's interpretation of the apple picking theme comes closest in its positive allegorization and the modernity of decor and formal language to Paul Signac's utopian scheme for a mural for the Town Hall at Montreuil (1895), *Au Temps d'Harmonie*. In this anarchist hymn to working-class family values, however, it is of course a man, in the left foreground, who is privileged to pick the transvaluated fruit of the tree of knowledge, not a mere woman.

In refusing to make her allegory grim or moralistic, in rejecting old-fashioned notions of allegory, in her fidelity, above all, to the formal inventiveness of the vanguard of her day, Mary Cassatt was taking big risks in Chicago. In concerning herself with the effects of a large-scale, decorative ensemble, she was participating in one of the major vanguard enterprises of her time. To borrow the words of Carol Zemel: "From mural painting to industrial design, art as '*décoration*' had enormous

146 PAUL SIGNAC Au Temps d'Harmonie, 1895

currency...in the final decades of the century."[17] By 1891 when "Albert Aurier's essay on Gauguin made *décoration* a major plank of the Symbolist platform, the emphasis was on decoration's ideational force: the unity of surface that guaranteed a picture's immediate...impact and effect. With this embrace of the decorative within the avant-garde, an important shift had taken place. Decorative painting now...had become an important and specifically modern domain."[18]

Cassatt was certainly aware of the various debates about the decorative that engaged so many of the advanced painters and critics of her time. Her correspondence contemporary with the painting of *Modern Woman* makes this evident, be it a rather technical exchange about the role of the decorative border with Mary MacMonnies or a more general discussion with Mrs. Potter Palmer about aspects of form, scale and color in the Woman's Building. Most interestingly, perhaps, in a letter to Mrs. Palmer of 11 October 1892, Cassatt makes clear her commitment to a specifically *gendered* aspect of the discourse on decoration and the decorative when she states, about the color: "My idea would have been one of those admirable old tapestries—brilliant yet soft."[19] Now in the decorative parlance of the time, especially among the Nabis, tapestry (and stitched work in general) were associated exclusively with the feminine realm. As Laura Morwitz has pointed out, "The tapestry...became a paradigmatic art form during the *fin de siècle*, connoting the feminine, private spaces of bourgeois life and was associated with female production."[20]

In the same letter, the artist justifies her omission of men from her mural with some crispness: "An American friend asked me in a rather huffy tone the other day, 'Then this is woman apart from her relations to man?' I told him it was. Men I have no doubt are painted in all their vigor on the walls of the other buildings; to us the sweetness of childhood, the charm of womanhood, if I have not conveyed some sense of that charm, in one word if I have not been absolutely feminine, then I have failed."[21] A modernism which is a specifically *feminine* modernism: that is Cassatt's ambitious goal in her Chicago project. If the contradictions seem apparent to us—an experimental public art extolling private joys and virtues, the equation, perhaps, of feminist with feminine, not by any means the same thing in today's parlance—we must remember that these associations were made by many advanced women of Cassatt's time, and many feminists as well.

For it seems to me that Cassatt was undeniably a feminist. Writing to Sara Hallowell, she declared, "After all give me France. Women do not have to fight for recognition here if they do serious work"; she refers positively to women's determination to "be *someone* rather than *some-thing*."[22] Cassatt was a woman who became increasingly radical in her politics with the passage of time. She was a supporter of Dreyfus at the time of the Affair, and more and more felt herself allied with the cause of feminism.

Indeed, it was Cassatt, according to Frances Weitzenhoffer, who had initially encouraged her friend Louisine Havemeyer to "go in for the Suffrage."[23] In 1914, she wrote from war-torn France to Mrs. Havemeyer, by now a prominent member of the Women's Political Union and more than ever a suffrage activist:

> Of course, every question is subordinated to the war, but never more than now was suffrage for women the question of the day—the hope of the future. Surely, surely, now women will wake to a sense of their duty and insist upon passing upon such subjects as war, and insist upon a voice in the world's government![24]

Cassatt helped Mrs. Havemeyer to organize the important loan exhibition "Masterpieces by Old and Modern Painters" at Knoedler's Gallery, New York, in 1915, and showed eighteen of her own works along with a large selection of Degas's paintings and some Old Masters for the benefit of women's suffrage.

Yet in the last analysis, it is for her art that Mary Cassatt will be remembered, her production, to borrow the words of Griselda Pollock, of a "body of works about women, an *œuvre* which was both feminine in its fidelity to the social realities of the life of a middle-class woman and thoroughly feminist in the way it questioned, transformed and subverted the traditional images of Women..."[25] And this transformation was wrought through the language of the most advanced painting movements of her time. It is in this sense that, looking back from the vantage point of a century, we, women art historians, critics, and yes, women artists, can say of Cassatt as Gertrude Stein did of Susan B. Anthony (another unmarried, childless woman, incidentally): she was "The Mother of Us All."

In his two versions of the *Poseuses*, the larger in the Barnes Collection (figs. 147, 149), the smaller in the Berggruen Collection (fig. 148), Seurat problematizes one of the central themes of later nineteenth-century painting, the female nude.[1] Although at first glance, the paintings appear to be fairly conventional, deploying as they do the traditional topos of the model in the studio, visual analysis and historical contextualization reveal that these are slyly subversive works, calling into question both the epistemological and the social status of the subject. One might say that Seurat's *Poseuses* constitute a critical politics of the representation of the female body in the later nineteenth century.

What do I mean by "body politics" in the title of this essay? I will offer some examples. In *La Belle Noiseuse* (1991), a highly praised film by the French director Jacques Rivette, the audience was regaled for four hours with the spectacle of an ageing painter attempting to reignite his flickering genius by working on an ultimate masterpiece under the inspiration of a beautiful model-muse. Although based specifically on Balzac's early nineteenth-century novel, *Le Chef d'œuvre inconnu*, the motif of the artist who must prove himself through the masterful representation of the naked body of a woman—or women—is understood to be a timeless and universal topos for signifying the highest challenge of genius. That the female nude is the major subject for artistic creation is taken for granted—by the director, his cast, and presumably his audience—as being as valid today as in Balzac's time. The artist, the naked model, and the audience sweat it out to the sound of Michel Piccoli's scratching pen and scraping brush, until the masterpiece is achieved. That the artist must be male and of a certain age and the model in question must be a beautiful young woman is of course integral to the accepted myth of creativity in the visual arts. It is the cornerstone of a conventional body politics.

Yet if we examine the history of the nude in art, we find that the *female* variety did not always occupy such a central position in artistic creation. From the time of Michelangelo's *David* in the Renaissance, down to the early nineteenth century, in the work of David and his

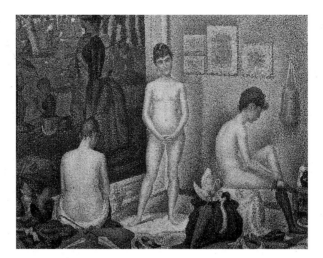

148 GEORGES SEURAT Poseuses, 1888

school, it was mastery of the *male* nude, not the female, that constituted the most serious challenge to the aspiring artist.[2] Indeed, the subjects for the crucial Prix de Rome invariably involved the representation of the heroic male nude; and the single-figure composition contest—that of the so-called "Académie"—was invariably based on the male and not the female model. Heroism, sublimation, knowledge of anatomy and antique exemplars were the issues at stake rather than overt sensuality and the embodiment of desire.[3] It was not until later in the century, with the rise of the art market and the dealer system and the fall in importance of history painting itself that the female nude came to take the dominating position which it has occupied ever since, to the extent that today when someone says "this is a show of nudes," the show is invariably understood to feature naked *women*, unless otherwise specified. Body politics then, can be understood on one level as being a politics of gender, specific to a certain period and certain practices in the history of art, rather than being a universal given of the creative act. As such, Seurat's choice to create a major painting featuring the female nude, and, above all, his decisions about how to represent this subject inscribe a politics of the body rather than a purely aesthetic position.[4]

First of all, Seurat has positioned the naked models in his painting in such a way that they bear a problematic, even parodic, relation to the elevated nudes of tradition or of the recent past: that vast array of naked *Susannahs*, *Dianas*, or *Three Graces* or *Bathers* that had seemed to constitute a self-justifying category of elevated physical and spiritual

149 GEORGES SEURAT Poseuses, 1886–88

beauty. While it is certainly true that Manet's *Déjeuner sur l'herbe* and the *Olympia* gave a salutary jolt to the notion of the nude as timeless and elevated, even these revolutionary works did so in terms of a justifying subject matter: the nude in nature in the former case, the naked prostitute in the latter. Seurat's models, despite their overt reference to traditional prototypes, are represented as nothing but models posing as off-duty models. These are, in Seurat's terms, simply contemporary and rather unidealized bodies for whom the state of nature is anything but natural, as is revealed by their abandoned chemises, hats and umbrellas which form an important part of the composition.

How, specifically, in the *Poseuses*, does Seurat problematize the female nude? First of all, he refuses to represent the subject as a natural and timeless one, a position which secures the traditional politics of the

150 PIERRE-AUGUSTE RENOIR The Large Bathers, 1887

body and is the unspoken assumption behind a project like Renoir's *The Large Bathers* (1887), an equally ambitious and large-scale composition of exactly the same date as the *Poseuses*, and like it featuring three female nudes. Here the connection between woman and nature, particularly the naked female and the unhistoric, bucolic setting, is foregrounded by composition and setting: the female nude, conceived of as part of nature, is at the same time a natural topic for the artist. Nor, like more overtly academic painters, does Seurat attempt to tie his nudes to nature by means of classical reference, as does Bouguereau, for example, in *The Nymphaeum* (1878), or to allegorize them as embodiments of the "natural" cycle of the seasons, as Puvis de Chavannes did in his *Autumn* (1865). Seurat means his nudes to be seen as contemporary urban working women and thereby shakes up the topic in a variety of ways: not merely does he insist that a naked woman is not a natural phenomenon but he also asserts that these naked women are workers who are paid for posing, a fact which renders their social as well as their aesthetic position equivocal. In their literal and not very glamorous status as models working standing around and waiting to pose within the self-referential world of the artist's studio, they serve to body forth, literally

151 PIERRE PUVIS DE CHAVANNES Autumn, 1865

152 WILLIAM BOUGUEREAU The Nymphaeum, 1878

153 J. E. DANTAN The Model's Lunch, 1881

to embody, *the* central issue of art and art-making itself at the end of the nineteenth century: the relation between the artist and his subject and, ultimately, between the artist and his public.[5]

In rethematizing the topic of the artist's studio in a large-scale, ambitious composition, we may say that Seurat takes over where Courbet left off in his provocative *The Painter's Studio* (1855, figs. 67–68), a similarly confrontational statement of the major issues confronting the artist couched in contemporary terms. In Courbet's painting, however, the focus is the working artist; the model merely looks on. Courbet, unlike Seurat, is hesitant to break the connection between naked woman and nature; indeed, despite the studio setting, the model is still materially connected to nature by means of the landscape on Courbet's easel, which serves as a partial background for her body. And if the model is represented as contemporary and unclothed, rather than idealized and classically nude, she nevertheless functions as a kind of updated inspiring muse, playing a subordinate role in Courbet's fiction of creation, rather than being its whole subject, like the models in the *Poseuses.*

Now Seurat was not alone in attempting to modernize the theme of the model in the studio in the later nineteenth century. Many of his academic contemporaries tried to update the topic by means of naturalistic

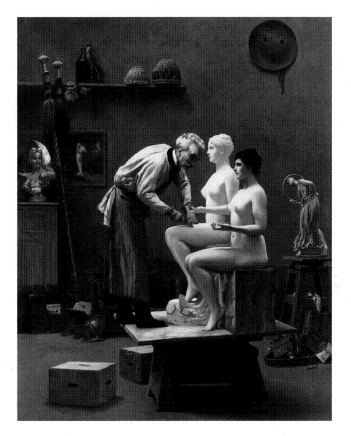

154 JEAN-LEON GEROME The Artist and His Model, c. 1890–93

detail or by emphasizing juicy, sexually charged anecdotes relating to the theme in a desperate attempt to assert their originality; a good example of this is *The Model's Lunch* (Salon of 1881) by the prolific J. E. Dantan. Their paintings are unvaryingly vulgar, banal and anecdotal, and, unlike Seurat's, in these Salon works the artist himself is usually present, playing a provocative if not a dominating role. Sometimes, as in Jean-Léon Gérôme's *The Artist and His Model* (c. 1890–93), the artist represents himself as actually at work with the nude model. In Gérôme's painting, the question of touch is a primary factor in the body politics controlling the scenario. If the artist is represented as only touching the work, not the model herself, the gesture presumably provides the observer with an enjoyable little *frisson* over this close call, and a sense of power, however fleeting, through identification with the all-powerful artist in the painting who at once exercises such complete control and

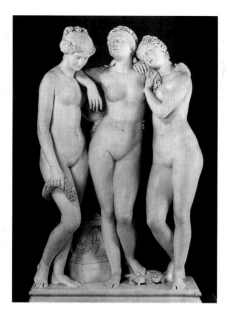

155 JEAN–JACQUES PRADIER The Three Graces, 1831

yet such admirable restraint in his dealings with an unclothed woman. In other versions of the theme, it may be the innocence and potential sexual initiation of the model, the violation of her natural modesty, which lies at the crux of the scene, as it does in Maurice Bompard's *A Début in the Studio* (1881) or Rémy Cogghe's *Anxiety* (c. 1887).

In Seurat's *Poseuses,* on the contrary, there is no titillating incident, no prurience, no hint of delicious victimization. These women are represented as professional, even blasé posers, not terrified novices, their thin, unseductive bodies matter-of-factly stripped for work. Within this context of ordinariness, there may be a hint of a certain specificity of class and ethnic type. We know something of the institution of modeling during this period: who did it, where the models were available. There seems to have been a whole industry of Italian models during Seurat's time, for example, and different ethnic types were often remarked upon.[6] Indeed, the naturalism with which the central model is represented in the large version of the *Poseuses* made at least one contemporary spectator, Gustave Kahn, himself a Jew and later the owner of the painting, refer to her "tête juive"—Jewish head—"beneath a flat coiffure of black hair," when he wrote about the work on its first appearance.[7]

Yet what constitutes the politics of the painting, and its confrontational novelty as well, is not mere naturalism, by a long shot, but

156 J. MOULINS The Three Graces, c. 1855

something far more interesting and provocative. What Seurat achieves in the *Poseuses* is a feat of visual demystification. He does this, first of all, by playing tradition and its weight of authority against the challenge of modernity and contemporaneity. If the poses of the *Poseuses* recall the art of the past—the Three Graces, most notably, with their front, side and back view or some such variation of the theme, updated in the nineteenth century, like the sculptor Pradier's—that past is appropriated and transformed by Seurat in a gigantic, joky meiosis: he makes sure we know it is the banal *act* of posing itself, not the traditional elevated mythological topic, that is at issue.[8]

Primary, it seems to me, in the construction of the *Poseuses*, especially the large version in the Barnes Collection, is the representational modernity offered by the relatively new medium of photography. Seurat, absorbed as he was in the perceptual discoveries of modern science, must surely have been interested in photography as a medium, as a new way to conceive of the perceptual field.

While photography quickly took over the representation of the nude female figure and disseminated it to a greatly extended market of eager *amateurs*—including *amateurs* of overt pornography—this branch of photographic representation also made its appeal to professionals. Artists made use of this cheap and convenient source of ready-made, two-dimensional models, models available in a wide variety of poses, often aping the themes of traditional art itself. There were, for example, many photographs (fig. 156), based on the classical threesome by mid-century. Stereoscopic photography in particular, with its emphatic, indeed illusionistic, three-dimensionality, underscored the notion of possession of the image through the gaze of the individual beholder.[9] Hand-tinting of the nude figures added to the immediacy of the illusion.

It seems to me that Seurat is attempting to some degree to duplicate this visual effect of illusionistic space through optical means in the large version of the *Poseuses*, by all accounts his most naturalistic painting and the one in which the effects of divisionism and the *pointillé* are least in evidence.[10]

Other aspects of photography are also suggested by specific features of the painting: for example, the pose of the profile-view model to the right duplicates a specific artist's photograph of the time, J. E. Lecadre's *Profile Model Kneeling in the Clouds* (c. 1890). The deliberate variety of poses offered by Seurat's painting recalls the photographed artist's "sheets" of the period, such as A. Cabaras's *Sheet of Nude Studies* (c. 1895), with their convenient multiple views of the nude body; and, if we think of Seurat's *Poseuses* as a single woman in three different poses, as several authorities have suggested,[11] the relation to Eadweard Muybridge's or Etienne-Jules Marey's near-contemporary photographic experiments with the human body in motion might seem apposite.

Yet despite its unusual degree of visual naturalism, art and artifice lie at the heart of Seurat's ambitious project in the *Poseuses*. Indeed, as Françoise Cachin has suggested in her excellent catalogue essay on the painting, Seurat's very choice of the title *Poseuses* for his painting creates, in the French viewer at least, certain expectations of deliberation or artifice. "Poseuse" is not the term normally used in French to indicate the studio-model—that term is "modèle"—but signifies rather "one who...seeks to attract notice by an artificial or affected manner."[12]

Throughout the composition, Seurat establishes an ambiguous interplay between art and reality, asserted first of all by the overwhelming presence of his own major masterpiece of contemporary life, *A Sunday Afternoon on the Island of La Grande Jatte* (1884–86, fig. 159), on the wall to the left. There is constant visual badinage deployed between elements of the real and those of the artificial: "real" in this case referring to the world of the studio and "artificial" to that of the painting-within-the-painting. On the most obvious level, it is implied that the naked models in the *Poseuses* are the same women who posed, in contemporary dress, for the *Grande Jatte*; these women are now stripped for

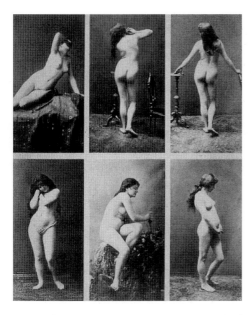

157 A. CABARAS Sheet of Nude Studies, c. 1895

158 J. E. LECADRE Profile Model Kneeling in the Clouds, c. 1890

action as "nudes," thereby reminding the viewer that there is nothing particularly natural about being naked. Even in small details, Seurat reinforces the interplay between the two paintings. For example, although it is extremely difficult to see when the *Poseuses* is *in situ* at the Barnes Collection, the "painted" dog from the *Grande Jatte* jumps up at the ribbon bow on the handle of the "real" parasol in the studio in which the models are posing. In addition, recognizable items of clothing—hats, dresses, parasols and gloves—from the *Grande Jatte* are strewn around the foreground of the *Poseuses*. Seurat plays with the polka-dot skirt in the foreground, punning on the relationship between the dotted technique of the *pointillé* and the "real" polka dots—red/orange on blue—of the printed fabric.

He also plays with other color relationships existing between the *Poseuses* and the *Grande Jatte*. The predominant green of the grass and trees of the latter is picked up by the unexpected and deliberate notes of green in the stockings and bag hanging on the wall which unite the left of the painting with the right, and which, at the same time, imply that the single color green—associated with grass, trees and the natural order in the earlier painting—now refers to the far from natural world of man-made artefacts in the later one.[13]

159 GEORGES SEURAT A Sunday Afternoon on the Island of La Grande Jatte, 1884–86

Seurat emphasizes the perceptual basis of his artistry, and his controlling role in the construction of the perceivable in the work, by playing with visibility and invisibility or ambiguous visibility. Although it is easy to make out that there are at least four small pictures hanging on the studio wall opposite the *Grande Jatte*, the spectator is not allowed to make out the precise identity of these images. Peer as I might—and I had binoculars with me at the Barnes Collection—these images defied identification with maddening obstinacy. I could only speculate what they might be until I found external assistance in the form of a description of Seurat's studio on the Boulevard de Clichy written by his admirer Gustave Kahn, the first owner of the picture. Kahn's description of the studio represented in the *Poseuses* is amazingly accurate and tells us what the works on the wall might be: "There was scarcely anything in it except a little iron bed, the red divan, the angle of which appears to the left of the great canvas, the tiny cast-iron stove which is visible to the right, and everywhere, drawings and canvases: hung on the white wall, there were his own drawings which Seurat had made at the Ecole des

Beaux-Arts, works by Guys, by Guillaumin, several Forains, and even a poster by Chéret, so different from our painter and yet so admired by him. There was finally, covering a whole side of the studio, the *Grande-Jatte...*"[14] Obviously, Seurat wished to record the appearance of his studio without making explicit the works of art it contained, aside from the dominating *Grande Jatte.* And of course the group of pictures hanging on the wall provides a reiterated abstract compositional balance of varied square and rectangular shapes for the larger geometric form of the painting dominating the left-hand side of the work. In denying us access to the specificity of the little pictures, the artist asserts his control over every conceivable aspect of picture-making.

Space and the manipulation of spatial illusion play an important role in that foregrounding of artifice and system so central to Seurat's project in the *Poseuses*; contradictory clues to space and flatness are carefully juxtaposed. This is more visible in the less three-dimensional, more abstract small version, where the vertical, shaded line on the wall to the right at first seems to indicate the corner of the room, contradicting the perspectival clues presented by the floor and the frame of the *Grande Jatte*, which indicate that the two walls meet behind the standing model. Then you realize that you can—indeed you *must*—read this superfluous "corner" as an enframement of the seated profile figure (presumably created by the removal of a large painting from the wall behind

160 GEORGES SEURAT Bathers at Asnières, 1883–84

her), as part of the two-dimensional structure of the room. But despite what we know, or rationalize, about this element, a strange sense of contradiction and doubleness nevertheless lingers, forcing us into active perception rather than passive reception of the visual evidence.

The artifices of femininity are everywhere in the *Poseuses*, establishing at once the picture's location in the contemporary world of commodities and Seurat's familiarity with the niceties of fashion. Modernity in this sense may be said to be figured as up-to-dateness, an allusion to the newly available world of mass-produced women's accessories offered by Parisian department stores. Seurat sometimes seems to be obsessed by clothes. He often gives abandoned garments a surprising, even disturbing vitality. All the *poseuses*, it should be noted, pose in or on their own undergarments, defined by pink ribbons on the chemise that serves as a base for the central figure and blue ribbon on that beneath the right-hand figure.

Clothing figures in and in connection with Seurat's earliest works, from the time of the *Bathers at Asnières* (1883–84, fig. 160), the *Grande Jatte* (fig. 162), and in works (such as the drawing *Still Life with Hat, Umbrella and Clothes on a Chair* [c. 1887]) from during the period when he was working on the *Poseuses* itself. An exaggerated emphasis on

161 GEORGES SEURAT Still Life with Hat, Umbrella and Clothes on a Chair, study for Poseuses, c. 1887

162 GEORGES SEURAT Drawing of a Bustle, study for A Sunday Afternoon on the Island of La Grande Jatte, 1885

163 GEORGES SEURAT Young Woman
Powdering Herself, 1890

164 GEORGES SEURAT Le Chahut, 1889

elements of costume continues in the two major paintings of modern life that follow: the *Young Woman Powdering Herself* (1890) and *Le Chahut* (1889). The *Young Woman Powdering Herself*, with her ruffles, bracelet, earrings, and emphatically constrictive corset, thematizes the act of feminine self-decoration, and, more slyly perhaps, the transformative craft of the artist himself, within a setting of supreme and spindly artificiality. In *Le Chahut*, especially the finished version in the Kröller-Müller Museum, Otterlo, the insistent and repetitive contours of bows on shoes, tails on coats and ribbons at shoulders in their flying, frozen upward movement, make strange these familiar elements of sartorial decoration and impart a freakish, almost hysterical vitality to the nightclub scene.[15]

In the *Poseuses*, it is almost as though the vivid dynamism of the shapes and forms of inanimate clothing—deployed in lightning flashes, exaggerated curves and sharp diagonals—is far more alive than the static contours of the living models themselves. This strategy, a pathetic fallacy of sorts, anticipates that of the Surrealists, inscribing the return of the repressed, making strange the familiar appurtenances of daily life and fetishizing objects associated with women's bodies like gloves, hats

and stockings. Here, two hats seem to "put their heads together" in sur-
reptitious gossip on the left; a pair of abandoned shoes seems to await its
occupant disconsolately in the center foreground, and a dropped glove
makes an arch contortion to the right.

Individual figures also instate ambiguity by occupying an equivocal
position between the elevation of the traditional icons of high art and
the banality of everyday contemporary existence. It seems clear, for
example, that Seurat meant the left-hand model as a homage—or a
parodic reference—to Ingres's famous, mysterious, back-view nude, the
Valpinçon Bather (1808). Ingres's Orientalist sphinx, however, is clearly
understood to be doing nothing at all but creating a sense of erotic mystification within her harem setting; in the case of Seurat's model, one
may well ask: "Just what is this *poseuse* doing to while away the time?"
She is, after all, figured as an ordinary modern woman, sitting with her
chemise draped about her haunches, waiting to pose. It would be easy to
imagine that she is knitting or sewing, like the figures in Seurat's earlier
drawings, the Conté crayon portrait of his mother of 1882–83, or the
study for the Knitting Woman from the *Grande Jatte*, and that the bag
hanging on the wall is her work-bag.

In the preliminary painted sketch for Seurat's figure (fig. 167), now
in the Musée d'Orsay, the image is far more abstract; in this respect, it is

165 JEAN–AUGUSTE-DOMINIQUE INGRES
Valpinçon Bather, 1808

166 GEORGES SEURAT Knitting Woman, study for A
Sunday Afternoon on the Island of La Grande Jatte, 1885

167 GEORGES SEURAT Back View of a Poseuse,
study for Poseuses, 1886

more like the *Valpinçon Bather*. But in all other respects, the painted
sketch for the left-hand *poseuse* is very distant from Ingres's painting
and from the high-art tradition generally. The little sketch ($9^5/_8 \times 6^1/_8$ in.)
is a miracle of diaphanous impalpability, of floating atomic particles of
color, perceptual atoms that at once deconstruct the solid mass of the
body yet merge to suggest form and volume, veiling and constructing
the body at the same time. The painted sketch embodies a totally modern
conception of form, not in the sense that it naturalistically represents
contemporary life, but in that it inscribes new scientific ideas about the
nature of color, of perception and the signs of visibility itself.[16] As
Robert Herbert has astutely observed, color, previously relegated—in
theory at least—to the trivial, secondary or even "feminine" side of art-
making, now becomes primary, amenable to the systematic rigor
associated with the most advanced optical discoveries of the scientists of
the time.[17] In addition, Seurat's deployment of color demands a new
activism on the part of the spectator. To put it another way: Seurat looks

168 GEORGES SEURAT Poseuse de face, study for Poseuses, 1886

to modern science to justify a new inscription of the role of color in the creative process, an inscription demanding a new kind of response. Here, it is color, or rather its particles, which is active, calling forth a corresponding activism on the part of the perceiving subject. While the pose of this *poseuse* may be static, the perceptual field is extraordinarily activated and depends on an equally active subject for its organization, for making sense of the discrete, dazzling data offered by the painting. Nothing could be more different from Ingres's traditional notion of form as closed, fixed, and held in place by continuous and perfected contour.

The central figure of the frontal, standing model may be based on the classical *Venus Pudica* (*Venus of Modesty*) in its general posture, with the hands shielding the pubic region. But there is little that is either classical or overtly modest about the deportment or proportions of the figure. In fact, in the preliminary Conté crayon drawing for the work (fig. 168), a *poseuse de face*, both the defiantly symmetrical, anti-classical pose and the adolescent immaturity of the body bring to mind the general conformation of Degas's recent—and shocking—*Little Dancer*

Aged Fourteen (1880). If the central figure in the final version is more mature, and the pose more reminiscent of classical *contrapposto*, nevertheless the unidealized naturalism of the figure and the self-conscious awareness it conveys of posing *as* a model, or even, in a bored way, collaborating in the creative process, removes the figure from the realm of tradition to that of modern consciousness.[18]

The right-hand, profile figure, the most abstract and most androgynous of the three models, may indeed refer back in a general way to the classical precedent of the *Spinario* or thorn-picker in its pose, as Robert Herbert has suggested,[19] but she is clearly figured as a contemporary woman with an 1880s coiffure and a skinny body, pulling on a strikingly green stocking. Notably androgynous, in pose and figure type the profile *poseuse* most pointedly refers back to an adolescent *male* represented in profile, the boy seated on the river bank from Seurat's own earlier work, the *Bathers at Asnières* (fig. 160). This is an interesting choice of pose and type, in that the topos of the pulling on (or off) of

169 EDGAR DEGAS Little Dancer Aged Fourteen, 1880

stockings is usually firmly located within the genre of female erotica. The stocking-puller is usually unequivocally feminine, as exemplified in a work which, like the *Poseuses*, is in the Barnes Collection: Courbet's *The White Stockings* (1861, fig. 85). Here the activity of removing the stocking provides the artist, and the viewer—male understood—with the opportunity of glimpsing forbidden bodily territory. Seurat, on the contrary, constructs this as a figure of the most unassailable modesty, locating it at the opposite pole of visual representation from the deliberate prurience often associated with the theme, and in addition, he plays down the femininity of the figure by referring it to a masculine, rather than a feminine prototype. Little satisfaction for the desiring male gaze is offered by this *poseuse de profil*, which Seurat plays so skillfully against the erotic grain of thematic expectations.

As one of the major pictorial monuments of its time, Seurat's *Poseuses* is clearly related to the future of the modernist enterprise. It takes up where Manet left off in problematizing the nude in the 1860s with the *Déjeuner sur l'herbe* and *Olympia*. By the *fin de siècle*, it was clear that the female nude was the proving ground for artistic ambition: it had become the topos that stood for art itself. Seurat certainly rose to the challenge in the *Poseuses*. Yet in its politics of the body, frustrating male desire, blocking erotic fantasy, or displacing it onto items of dress, and its rejection of figures of either debasement or transcendence, the *Poseuses* swims against the tide of the avant-garde creation of its painter's time.

Offering an escape neither into nature, the past, nor an erotics of exoticism, like Gauguin's *Fatata te Miti* (1892), the *Poseuses* sticks with the urban workaday world, with science and the culture of commodity, in which both artist and model—and the work of art itself—participate: our own inheritance. There is nothing easy or harmonious about Seurat's view of modernity and the position of women's bodies within it—on the contrary, through the formal complexity of his work, he constructs the female nude in the artist's studio as a socially and psychologically charged, disturbingly contradictory theme.

This is quite different from the sense of cool mastery projected by Matisse in his version of the theme, *Carmelina* (1903–04). Here, the voluptuous model is positioned directly before the spectator, pressed close to the picture plane, and, as in Rivette's film *La Belle Noiseuse*, the watchful gaze of the male artist is asserted by Matisse's reflected presence in the mirror in the background. In a pioneering article, published in 1973, Carol Duncan revealed the extent to which the assertion of virility and the will to dominate were controlling assumptions behind the art production of the early twentieth-century avant-garde, using this painting among others to demonstrate her point. Says Duncan: "From his corner of the mirror he (Matisse) blazes forth in brilliant red—the only red in this somber composition—fully alert and at the controls. The artist, if not the man, masters the situation—and also Carmelina, whose dominant role as a *femme fatale* is reversed by the mirror image."[20]

Seurat's intentions, and his achievement in the *Poseuses*—although far from being consciously feminist in any conceivable sense of that term—lie at the opposite pole of the aesthetico-political spectrum of their time. Both veiled and yet revealed by the tropes of work and artifice (there is evidence that Seurat, while he was painting the work, wished to think of himself, like his models, as a wage laborer, working for a daily fee[21]), the bodies of Seurat's *Poseuses*, although they can never entirely escape the objectifying regime of the male gaze, may nevertheless intervene in this regime by calling both its naturalness and its unhistoric approach into question. This seems to me to be an accomplishment indeed within the politics of representation, today as much as it was in Seurat's day.

170 HENRI MATISSE Carmelina, 1903–04

Notes and Sources

Chapter One
Notes to pages 34–57

1. For the Freud-fetishism interpretation, see Kaja Silverman, *The Acoustic Mirror: The Female Voice in Psychoanalysis and Cinema* (Bloomington: Indiana University Press, 1988), pp. 18–19.
2. For more information about this painting, see the detailed catalogue entry for the small version, now on loan from the reserves of the Musée Carnavalet in Paris, in the Musée des Beaux-Arts, Place Stanislas, Nancy in *Cahier*, no. 4 (1988), cat. no. 3, pp. 14–15.
3. For the Diderot reference to Le Barbier's painting, see Diderot, *Salons*, ed. Jean Seznec (Oxford: The Clarendon Press, 1967), IV, no. 201, p. 336. The painting was very well received on the whole, one critic proclaiming it "one of the most beautiful paintings in the Salon," although Seznec (p. 337) cites some adverse opinions as well.
4. For reproductions of the sketch, the destroyed painting itself, and the lithograph after it, see the brief article by Jean Vergnet-Ruiz, "Une Inspiration de Delacroix? La Jeanne Hachette de Le Barbier," *La Revue du Louvre et des Musées de France*, 21: 2 (1971), pp. 81–85.
5. See Barthélemy Jobert, "The 'Travaux d'encouragement': An Aspect of Official Arts Policy in France under Louis XVI," *Oxford Art Journal*, 10: 1 (1987), pp. 3–14.
6. Despite the fairly large number of subjects dealing with the heroism of women of antiquity commissioned under Louis XVI, including at least one painting by Le Barbier, *Aristomenes and the Spartan Women* (1787), only one other modern French subject featuring a heroine was chosen, *Blanche de Castille Delivers the Inhabitants of Chatenay*, by Le Monnier in 1787. And certainly none of the paintings dealt with the heroic deeds of modern, French middle- or lower-class women as did Le Barbier's painting. See *ibid.*, p. 8.

7. For a lengthy discussion of negative and positive opinions about the historical existence of Jeanne Hachette, and a great deal of information about this heroine and her putative role in the Siege of Beauvais see M. Renet, "Siège de Beauvais: Jeanne Hachette," in *Beauvais et Les Beauvaisis dans les temps modernes: Epoque de Louis XI et de Charles de Téméraire (1461–1483)* (Beauvais: Imprimerie Professionnelle, 1898), pp. 136–195 and 550–628.
8. "Les femmes et filles...portoient ausdits gens de guerre, sur la muraille, grande habondance de grosses pierres de faix, pots de terre pleins de chaux vives, cercles de queues et gros muids et autres tonneaux, croisez l'un parmi l'autre, avec chausse-trappes, cendres, huilles et graisses toutes chaudes, pour jetter sur lesdits Bourgugnons, afin qui'ils ne pussent monter sur la muraille." Cited in *ibid.*, p. 191.
9. See M. [Jean-Antoine] Roucher, *Les Mois, poème en douze chants* (Paris: Imprimerie de Qe Quillan, 1779, 2 vols.). For more information about Roucher, see Antoine Guillois, *Pendant la Terreur: Le Poète Roucher (1745–1794)* (Paris: Calmann Lévy, 1890).
10. "Quoi! Vous pouvez combattre, et vous versez des larmes!/Laissez à vos maris la peur et les allarmes./Marchons; et les forçant à rougir devant nous,/Soyez Hommes pour eux, s'ils sont Femmes pour vous." Roucher, *Les Mois*, I, p. 266. My translation.
11. Letter from Le Barbier to d'Angiviller, 14 March 1782, Archives Nationales O1 1916 (1782/80).
12. See note 3 above for references to critical opinion, including that of Diderot.
13. For example, women's nascent feminist activity, their attempt to create all-female political organizations to fight for their rights, was suppressed by the laws of 1793. For further discussion of the anti-feminist tenor of the French Revolution, see Lynn Hunt, *Politics, Culture and Class in the French Revolution*

(Berkeley and Los Angeles: University of California Press, 1984) and Joan B. Landes, *Women and the Public Sphere in the Age of the French Revolution* (Ithaca and London: Cornell University Press, 1988).

14. Lynn Hunt has pointed out the gradual substitution of the figure of Hercules for that of an allegorical Republic in the official representations of the Revolutionary period and has related this to a cooling of enthusiasm on the part of the Convention for any expression of feminine, much less feminist, solidarity in terms of women's clubs or groups seeking to certify the social and political rights of women as well as those of men. Women were increasingly deprived of access to public space, both literally and figuratively, as the Revolution progressed. See Hunt, *Politics, Culture and Class*, pp. 93–119.

15. For the "great masculine renunciation," see John Carl Flugel, *The Psychology of Clothes* (London: L. and V. Woolf at The Hogarth Press, and the Institute of Pscyhoanalysis, 1930). For a discussion of this topic, see Silverman, *The Acoustic Mirror*, pp. 24–25.

16. Zoffany's painting has been variously identified as *The Women of Paris Dancing on the Bodies of the Swiss Guards After the Assault on the Tuileries, 10 August 1792* by David Bindman in *The Shadow of the Guillotine: Britain and the French Revolution* (London: British Museum Publications, 1989), p. 60; as *The Massacre of the Champ-de-Mars of July 1791* by Marrin Angerer in *La Révolution Française et L'Europe, 1789–1799* (Paris: Grand Palais, 1989), cat. no. 607, p. 45; and by Philippe Bordes, as the *Parisians at Versailles on Oct. 5, 1789.*

17. Erving Goffman, *Gender Advertisements* (New York: Harper and Row, 1976).

18. For an interesting and detailed reading of the *Horatii* in terms of gender difference and historical specificity, see Landes, *Women and the Public Sphere*, pp. 152–158.

19. For the actual influence of Le Barbier's painting on Delacroix's *Liberty Leading the People*, see Vergnet-Ruiz, "Une Inspiration de Delacroix?"

20. See Natalie Zemon Davis, "Woman on Top," in *Society and Culture in Early Modern France* (Stanford, California: Stanford University Press, 1975).

21. Champfleury, *Histoire de la caricature moderne*, Paris, n.d., pp. 168–169, and

"Concours des Républiques: Daumier et Préault" in *Œuvres posthumes*, Paris, 1894, pp. 97–100. For more recent and complete information, see Bernard Lehmann, "Daumier and the Republic," *Gazette des Beaux-Arts*, 27 (February 1945), pp. 105–120 and Albert Boime, "The Second Republic's Contest for the Figure of the Republic," *Art Bulletin*, 53 (March 1971), pp. 68–83.

22. Boime, "The Second Republic's Contest," p. 76.

23. P.-J. Proudhon, "Notes," in *Œuvres complètes de Proudhon*, eds. C. Bougle and H. Moysset (Paris: M. Rivière, 1939), p. 421, for the remarks on the 1848 Revolution and women.

24. The celebrated formula, "menagère ou courtisane" may be found in more than one place in Proudhon's writing, most notably in *La Pornocratie, ou Les Femmes dans les temps modernes* in *Œuvres complètes de Proudhon*, p. 306.

25. Freud, in his *Jokes and Their Relation to the Unconscious*, first published in 1905, lays great stress on the unconscious sexual hostility and aggression embodied in jokes and certain forms of humor. It would be interesting to analyze Daumier's caricatures of women's aspirations in the light of Freud's essay.

Chapter Two
Notes to pages 58–79

1. "La figure de la jeune fille est ravissante, et elle est presque une exception dans l'œuvre du grand maître." Charles Clément, *Géricault: Etude biographique et critique*, intro. Lorenz Eitner (Paris: Laget, 1973; reprint of definitive edition of 1879), pp. 217–218.

2. The latest candidate for the (much-contested) representation of Géricault's lover, his aunt Alexandrine Modeste Caruel, may provide an addition to the rare corpus of female portraits by the master. The work, *Portrait of a Young Woman* (c. 1816), which was published in a Sotheby's New York catalogue of 17 October 1991, has been partially attributed to Géricault by Lorenz Eitner.

3. The *Scene of Mutiny* is now in the Historisch Museum, Amsterdam. It is reproduced in *Géricault* (Paris: Grand Palais, 1991)—hereafter *Géricault*, 1991—no. 191, ill. 231, p. 145.

4. Both of these drawings are entitled *Study for the Group of a Father Holding His Wife and Child*. One is in the Marillier Collection, Paris,

and the other, the most finished, is in the Fogg Museum, Cambridge, Massachusetts. Both are reproduced in Lorenz Eitner, *Géricault's Raft of the Medusa* (London: Phaidon, 1972), nos. 34 and 35, ills. 26 and 28.

5. The *Scene of Cannibalism* is reproduced in *Géricault*, 1991, no. 189, ill. 234, p. 147.

6. J. B. Henri Savigny and Alexandre Corréard, *Narrative of a Voyage to Senegal in 1816...Comprising an Account of the Shipwreck of the Medusa* (London: Henry Coburn, 1818, 2nd edition). This English translation of the *Naufrage de la frégate la Méduse faisant partie de l'expedition du Sénégal en 1816...* (Paris: Hocquet, 1817) is extremely accurate.

7. See, for example, the account of Géricault's quest for accuracy in Eitner, *Géricault's Raft*, pp. 18–20; 22–24; 36–37.

8. Both women and a family were present on the frigate *Medusa* and escaped to the African shore in boats. These included the heartless and snobbish daughters of the captain and the "famille nombreuse" of one M. Picard, the *greffier* (clerk of court) of Senegal. All in all there were 18 women and 8 children on the frigate. The raft itself, after the shipwreck, set out originally with about 150 aboard: 120 soldiers, including officers; 29 men, sailors and passengers; and one woman.

9. Savigny and Corréard, *Narrative of a Voyage*, p. 90.

10. *Ibid.*, p. 93.

11. *Ibid.*, p. 119. There is a great deal more in this vein.

12. One "Jean Charles, black soldier" is noted in the list of fifteen who were "alive when we were saved." He is listed as "dead" under the heading of "Notice of their subsequent fate." *Ibid.*, p. 145.

13. See an unpublished manuscript by Norman Bryson, "Géricault and Masculinity." "...However much the markers of the masculine proliferate, what subtends that proliferation is lack within the position of the masculine and lack at its very centre," (p. 18). I am grateful to Professor Bryson for making his important insights available to me.

14. See *Géricault*, 1991, cat. no. 280, ill. 291.

15. See, for example, his *Execution in Italy*, in *Géricault*, 1991, cat. no. 106, ill. 156 and *Gibbet*, in *ibid.*, cat. no. 226, ill. 325.

16. Tania Modleski's book is entitled *Feminism Without Women: Culture and Criticism in a "Postfeminist" Age* (New York and London: Routledge, 1991).

17. *Horses' Rumps and One Head*, private collection. See *Géricault*, 1991, cat. no. 27, ill. 65.

18. *Ibid.*, cat. no. 246, ill. 349.

19. *Ibid.*, cat. no. 127, ill. 178.

20. *Ibid.*, *hors* cat., ill. 188. The work is in a private collection.

21. See *Monomania of Envy*, in *ibid.*, cat. no 308, ill. 380; *Monomania of Gambling*, *ibid.*, cat. no. 306, ill. 379.

22. For a different and far more critical interpretation of Géricault's portraits of the insane, see Albert Boime, "Portraying Monomaniacs to Service the Alienist's Monomania: Géricault and Georget," *Oxford Art Journal*, 14: 1 (1991), pp. 79–91.

23. See Jane Kromm, "Marianne and the Madwomen," *Art Journal*, 46: 4 (Winter 1987), pp. 299–304.

24. See *Géricault*, 1991, cat. no. 296, ill. 369.

25. Yale graduate student Beth Handler has, however, a very different and more critical reading of Géricault's representation of blacks in her unpublished seminar report, "Blacks and *The Raft of the Medusa*," in a seminar on "The Body in the Nineteenth Century," Fall 1991.

26. Clément, *Géricault*, p. 218.

27. It seems to me that this print, like others of this series, owes a good deal to popular prints of the period, and specifically to English ones. See *Géricault*, 1991, cat. no. 222, ill. 327.

28. Clément, *Géricault*, pp. 217–218.

29. Michael Fried has suggested that the missing words on the poster are "evil eye," making the complete message "For all sickness and the evil eye." I would agree with this part of his interpretation, but not with the broader continuation of it, in which he suggests that this is in fact a representation focussed on seeing and looking. Michael Fried, "Géricault's Romanticism," *Colloque Géricault*, Paris, Louvre, November 1991. Proceedings published in *Géricault* (Paris: Louvre/La Documentation française, 1996), pp. 641–659. See p. 649 for his "evil eye" suggestion.

30. See William Hogarth, *The Harlot's Progress*, plate V, "Harlot Expires with Doctors Disputing" for the print in question.

31. William Blake, *Poetry and Prose*, ed. Geoffrey Keynes (London: Nonesuch Press, 1927), p. 76.

32. "Il ne semble pas que le peintre audacieux et savant ait compris la beauté féminine dans ce

qu'elle a de délicat et de distingué," and "Il a dit lui-même: 'Je commence une femme, et ça devient un lion." And even more revealingly: "et aussi, très-familièrement, en frappant sur l'épaule d'un de ses amis: 'Nous deux X..., nous aimons les grosses f...s'" Clément, *Géricault*, p. 218.

33. See, for example, *The Embrace*, in *Géricault*, 1991, cat. no. 90, ill. 134.

34. "Il lui fallait des formes amples et robustes, des mouvements accusés et violents, des expressions énergiques: toujours le drame et la passion avec une nuance d'ardeur, de sensualité, de brutalité même, que l'on trouve dans ses *Femmes enlevées par des centaures*, dans les bacchantes du *Silène*..." Clément, *Géricault*, p. 218. For the materialization of these qualities in Géricault's erotic art, see especially the recently published *Scène d'intérieur: Couple enlacé auprès d'une femme étendue*, a small painting formerly in the collection of Dantan Jeune. Ader Tajan, Sale Catalogue, Paris, Hôtel Drouot, 26 June 1992, no. 48, with a notice by Philippe Grunchec. I am grateful to Robert Simon for having brought this work to my attention.

35. "...par cent preuves l'élévation de son caractère, la sensibilité, l'excellence, la tendressse de son cœur." Clément, *Géricault*, p. 219.

36. Peter Brooks, "The Revolutionary Body," in *Fictions of the French Revolution*, ed. B. Fort (Evanston: Northwestern University Press, 1991), p. 39. For specific examples and documentation, see Lynn Hunt, *Politics, Culture, and Class in the French Revolution* (Berkeley and Los Angeles: University of California Press, 1984), *passim.*, and Joan B. Landes, *Women and the Public Sphere in the Age of the French Revolution* (Ithaca and London: Cornell University Press, 1988), *passim*.

37. Dorinda Outram, *The Body and the French Revolution: Sex, Class, and Political Culture* (New Haven and London: Yale University Press, 1989), p. 127.

38. For a quite different, but not necessarily contradictory, Freudian interpretation of these drawings as implicated in Géricault's experience of the primal scene, see Stefan Germer, "'Je commence une femme et ça devient un lion.' Fantasmes érotiques dans l'œuvre de Géricault," *Colloque Géricault*, Paris, Louvre, November 1991. Published in *Géricault*, 1996, pp. 423–447.

39. See, for example, Thomas Crow's exploration of new constructions of the male body during and after the French Revolution in "Revolutionary Activism and the Cult of Male Beauty in the Studio of David," in *Fictions of the French Revolution*, pp. 55–83.

Chapter Three
Notes to pages 80–105

1. For the most recent and complete discussion of and references to the literature on Courbet's *The Grain Sifters*, see *Gustave Courbet, 1819–1877* (Paris: Grand Palais, 1977); hereafter *Courbet*, 1977. Also see Werner Hofmann's briefer discussion of the work in "Courbet's Wirklichkeiten" in *Courbet und Deutschland* (Hamburger: Kunsthalle, 1978), pp. 600–601. For Millet's *The Gleaners*, see *Jean-François Millet (1814–1875)* (Paris: Grand Palais, 1975)–hereafter *Millet*, 1975– no. 65, and "Le dossier des 'Glaneuses'," pp. 143–149. See also *Jean-François Millet* (London: Hayward Gallery, 1976), pp. 84–116. Both of these catalogues owe much of their information to Robert Herbert, who also was a major contributor to the smaller catalogue, *Millet's "Gleaners"* (Minneapolis: Minneapolis Art Institute, 1978). For a more sociological examination of Millet and his work, see Jean-Claude Chamboredon, "Peintures des rapports sociaux et invention de l'eternel paysan: les deux manières de Jean-François Millet," *Actes de la recherche et sciences sociales*, nos. 17–18 (November 1977), pp. 6–28.

2. For a discussion of the complex issue of women's work in the context of the early period of industrialization, see Louise A. Tilly and Joan W. Scott, *Women, Work and Family* (New York: Holt, Rinehart and Winston, 1978).

3. "Adieu, mon cher, je vais chez mes éditeurs."

4. For an excellent study of Daumier's anti-feminist caricatures, see Caecilia Rentmeister, "Daumier und das hässliche Geschlecht" in the catalogue *Honoré Daumier und die ungelösten Probleme der burgerlichen Gesellschaft* (Berlin, Schloss Charlottenburg, 1974), pp. 57–79. Also see Françoise Parturier's unfortunately titled *Lib Women* (Paris: Leon Amiel, 1974). Rentmeister discusses the topos of the baby who falls into the bathtub on p. 6 and illustrates the works in question. Daumier was, of course, perfectly capable of producing

a monumental, allegorical representation of a woman nurturing her young to stand for the Republic in 1848 (see note 56 below). It was real women as activists or as independent forces apart from their maternal function that were anathema to him, and to most "right-thinking" men of his time.

5. "L'ouvrière, mot impie." Jules Simon, *L'Ouvrière* (Paris: Hachette et cie., 1861). Not all authorities agreed with Simon, however. For other opinions, see Tilly and Scott, *Women, Work and Family*, pp. 1–2.

6. See such paintings as Max Liebermann's *Women Working in a Canned Food Factory* (1879); A. Zorn's *The Large Brewery* (1890); or Edouard Rosset-Granger, *The Sugar-Crushing Machine* (1891). These are reproduced in Edward Lucie-Smith and Celestine Dars, *Work and Struggle: The Painter as Witness, 1870–1914* (New York and London: Paddington Press, 1977), figs. 27, 29 and 30.

7. Robert L. Herbert, "City vs. Country: The Rural Image in French Painting from Millet to Gauguin," *Artforum*, 8 (February 1970), pp. 44–55.

8. See nos. VI–61 in the catalogue *The Second Empire 1852–1870: Art in France Under Napoleon III* (Philadephia: Philadelphia Museum of Art, 1978) for a discussion of Glaize's painting and contemporary reactions to it.

9. Eunice Lipton, "The Violence of Ideological Distortion: The Imagery of Laundress in Nineteenth-Century French Culture," *Heresies: On Women and Violence*, no. 6 (Summer 1978), pp. 77–81, 85.

10. Alphonse LeGros's *The Ex-voto* was originally intended as a representation of a funeral and then repainted. See Monique Geiger, "Alphonse Legros, *L'ex-voto*. Etude radiographique," *Bulletin du Laboratoire du Musée du Louvre* (1971), pp. 18–23. See also *Alphonse Legros: Peintre et fraveur, 1837–1911* (Dijon: Musée des Beaux-Arts, 1957), no. 2.

11. Perhaps nowhere is the connection between raw sexuality and the daily life of the *paysanne* more forcefully asserted than at the beginning of Zola's novel *La Terre* (1887), in which the adolescent farm-girl, Françoise, nonchalantly inserts a bull's penis into the waiting cow with her hand. See Emile Zola, *La Terre* in *Les Rougon-Macquart*, IV (Paris: Bibliothèque de la Pléiade, 1966), pp. 374–375.

12. See Marius Vachon, *Jules Breton* (Paris: A. Lehure, 1899), p. 100, 115, 127–128.

13. I am grateful for this information to Madelaine Fidell Beaufort who permitted me to see her unpublished article "Jules Breton: Some American Appreciations."

14. The most extensive and provocative study of the erotic allure of this working-class woman, in England, rather than France, is found in Derek Hudson's *Munby: Man of Two Worlds* (Boston: Gambit, 1972). The subject of the book, Arthur J. Munby, gentleman, civil servant and minor literary figure, was obsessed with the muscular charms of the working women whom he interviewed and photographed in male attire. Eventually, he married, secretly, his servant Hannah. His biographer characterized his attitude as "benign perversity" (p. 77), but, in exaggerated form, it epitomizes the erotic stimulus provided for middle- and upper-class men by lower-class characteristics. Christopher Isherwood makes the same point, from a homosexual viewpoint, about the allure of working-class boys to upper-class Englishmen in *Christopher and His Kind, 1929–1939* (New York: Farrar, Straus, Giroux, 1976).

15. Marilyn Kluger, *The Joy of Spinning* (New York: Simon and Schuster, 1971), p. 107.

16. For a reproduction, see Walter S. Gibson, "Some Flemish Popular Prints from Hieronymus Cock and his contemporaries," *Art Bulletin*, 60 (December 1978), fig. 1, p. 673.

17. See, for example, Steven van Duyven's *Eingeschlafene Spitzen-Klöpplerin*, 1677, in W. Bernt, *Die Niederländischen Maler des 17. Jahrhunderts* (Munich: F. Bruckmann, 1962), vol. IV, no. 77. The theme continued in eighteenth-century France. See, for example, the photograph of a sleeping spinner, not unlike Courbet's in its pose, attributed to Françoise Duparc in the files of the Witt Photographic Survey, London. (See Anne Sutherland Harris and Linda Nochlin, *Women Artists: 1550–1950* [Los Angeles: Los Angeles County Museum, 1976], p. 172. I am grateful to Professor Harris for calling this work to my attention.) In addition, Michael Fried has reproduced a related but not exactly similar figure, after Greuze, *La Tricoteuse endormie* from the Salon of 1759, engraved by Jardinier, in *Eighteenth-Century Studies*, 9 (1975/6), pp. 139–177. For studies of the moral implications of the sleeping servant-girl, particularly Jan

Vermeer's *A Woman Asleep*, see Seymour Slive, "'en Dronke Slapende Meyd aen een Tafel' by Jan Vermeer," *Festschrift Ulrich Middeldorf* (Berlin: W. de Gruyter, 1968), pp. 52–459, and Madlyn M. Kahr, "Vermeer's Girl Asleep: A Moral Emblem," *Metropolitan Museum Journal*, 6 (1972), pp. 115–132. For an analysis of the theme of the spinner in Dutch seventeenth-century art, see *Tot Lering en Vermaak* (Amsterdam: Rijksmuseum, 1976), pp. 40–43 and 48–49.

18. "Bonne Ste. Fainéante, Protectrice des paresseuses."

19. Kahr, "Vermeer's Girl Asleep," pp. 126–127.

20. Slive, "'en Dronke Slapende Meyd aen een Tafel' by Jan Vermeer," p. 454 and Kahr, "Vermeer's Girl Asleep," pp. 115–116.

21. Werner Hofmann, "Über die 'Schlafende Spinnerin'," in *Realismus als Widerspruch: Die Wirklichkeit in Courbets Malerie*, ed. Klaus Herding (Frankfurt am Main: Suhrkamp Verlag, 1978), pp. 212–222 and "Courbets Wirklichkeiten" in *Courbet und Deutschland*, pp. 605–608. Aaron Sheon, "Courbet, French Realism and the Discovery of the Unconscious," *Arts*, 55 (February 1981), pp. 114–128. Sheon also discusses a related drawing, Millet's *Sleeping Girl* (c. 1846), very similar to Courbet's *Sleeping Spinner* in pose and composition, a work that has now disappeared, to which Robert L. Herbert had called his attention.

22. "Une franche paysanne."

23. P.-J. Proudhon, *Du Principe de l'art et de sa destination sociale*, in *Œuvres complètes de Proudhon*, eds. C. Bougle and H. Moysset (Paris: M. Rivière, 1939), p. 173.

24. Champfleury, *Le Réalisme*, eds. Geneviève and Jean Lacambre (Paris: Hermann, 1973), p. 190.

25. Vidal's work had appeared as no. 5046 in the Paris Salon catalogue of 1850, under the title *Le Fil rompu*. I am grateful to Professor Beatrice Farwell for calling the work to my attention. Other representations of spinners, knitters, and related fiber-workers had appeared in the Salons immediately preceding that of 1853, in which Courbet's *Sleeping Spinner* figured as no. 301. These included, in the Salon of 1850, François Bonvin's *La Tricoteuse* (no. 295); Mlle Marie-Laure Forestier's *La Tricoteuse* (no. 1089); François Montfallet's *Une Fileuse* (no. 2239) as well as his *Le Sommeil* (no. 2238), a suggestive combination; and in the Salon of 1852,

Léon-Joseph Billotte's *Une Brodeuse* (no. 116) and Louis-Alexandre Marolle's *Fileuse du Béarn* (no. 877).

26. A most interesting (possible) offshoot of Courbet's *Sleeping Spinner*, although in some ways more relatable to Millet in mood and style, is the even more overtly eroticized and far sweeter *The Spinning Wheel*, signed and dated 1859 by the English painter John Philipp, now in the Burrell Collection in Glasgow Art Gallery. Philipp's sleeping spinner has a frankly open, light-revealed *décolletage* and "fortuitously" clutches her heart with her right hand, as she smiles in dreaming.

27. The most complete historical examination of the issue of gleaning is Paul de Grully's monumental doctoral dissertation, "Le Droit de glanage, grappillage, ratelage, chaumage et sarclage," written for the Law Faculty of the University of Montpellier, 1912. The dissertation is subtitled "Patrimonie des pauvres."

28. "Voleuses de grains pendant la moisson sous prétexte de glaner," *ibid.*, p. 66.

29. See Albert Soboul, "La Question paysanne en 1848," *La Pensée*, 1948, and Roger Price, *The French Second Republic: A Social History* (Ithaca: Cornell University Press, 1972), pp. 117–118.

30. Jean Rousseau in *Le Figaro* of 1857 wrote: "Derrière ces trois glaneuses se silhouettent... les piques des émentes populaires et les échafauds de '93." Robert Herbert points out that this painting also offended the middle class, for whom Paul de Saint-Victor spoke in *La Presse*, accusing the gleaners of having "des prétentions gigantesques" and denominating them "les trois Parques du paupérisme" (*Millet*, 1975, p. 101). Ironically, left-wing critics who admired the painting like Castagnary, defended it by saying that it was not "une harangue politique ou une thèse sociale, mais un œuvre d'art, très belle et très simple, franche de toute déclamation." Castagnary further removed the painting from the context of contemporary conflict by declaring that the motif "...s'élève au-dessus des passions de parti et reproduit...une de ces pages de la nature vraies, et grandes, comme en trouvaient Homère et Virgile" (*Millet*, 1975, p. 102).

31. For Millet's refusal to accept political interpretations of his work, in contradiction to Courbet, as well as the question of a socially

provocative contrast between foreground and background in *The Gleaners*, see Chamboredon, "Peintures des rapports sociaux et invention de l'eternel paysan," pp. 15–16, and note 19, p. 16.

32. This is especially true of the woman to the right: "enplaçant la ligne d'horizon au ras de cette tête, Millet, du même coup, exclu la femme du ciel et l'intègre à la grande horizontale de la moisson..." *Millet*, 1975, p. 102.

33. The location of the original version of *The Weeders* of 1860, exhibited in the 1861 Salon is unknown. A reduced version of the work, of 1868, is in the Metropolitan Museum in New York. See Charles Sterling and M. M. Salinger, *French Paintings: A Catalogue of the Collection of the Metropolitan Museum of Art* (New York: Metropolitan Museum, 1966), vol. II, pp. 179–181. Breton himself wrote about the event that inspired the painting in the most high-flown terms, referring to "a group of weeders...crouched on their knees...their faces haloed by the pink transparency of the violet hands, as if to venerate the fecundating star." He notes the "svelte body," "long and supple," of the girl to the left. Later, he talks of the "religious tremor" the scene aroused in him: "Not one detail was bothersome, not one tone disrupted the harmony. It was", he declared, "like a natural transfiguration of the most humble of labors." Jules Breton, *Un Peintre paysan: Souvenirs et impressions* (Paris: A. Lemerre, 1896), pp. 110–111. Cited in *Millet's "Gleaners,"* p. 46.

34. For contemporary nineteenth-century reports on the realities of life of women peasants, see E. Shorter, "Différences de classe et sentiment depuis 1750: L'Exemple de la France," *Annales*, 29 (July/August 1974). The observer of 1845 was one Barthélemy Chaix of Grenoble. Reports about peasant-wives serving the men at table are by Jean Baptiste Déribier-du-Châtelet, *Dictionnaire statistique...ou histoire du département de Cantal* (Aurillac: Imp. de Picut. 1853), vol. II, p. 133, and Carlo Bossi, *Statistique générale de la France, département de l'Ain* (Paris: 1808), p. 311. See Shorter, "Différences de classe et sentiment depuis 1750," p. 1048. There are other examples. The peasant proverbs ("La beauté ne se mange pas à la cuillère" and "Il vaut mieux dire: Laide, allons souper que lui demander: Belle, qu'avons nous à souper?") are taken

from Dr. Charles Perron, *Les Francs-Comtois: Leur Caractère national, leurs mœurs, leurs usages*, Besançon, 1892, p. 85. Yann Brekilien, in *La Vie quotidienne des paysans Bretagne au XIXᵉ siècle*, Paris, 1966, remarks that the farmer's wife "n'asséyait même pas à table, restant debout pendant tout le repas à servir les hommes. Usée par les travaux et les maternités, ignorant le repos, elle ne recevait même pas l'encouragement d'une parole affectueuse. Elle semblait réduite du rang d'esclave" (p. 69). The situation of oppression seems widespread and fairly universal. Recently, Eugen Weber has summarized the low status and hard lot of the nineteenth-century peasant-woman in his *Peasants into Frenchmen: The Modernization of Rural France, 1870–1914* (Stanford, California: Stanford University Press, 1976), pp. 171–174. Weber maintains that an opportunity for relative independence only arose when women could earn independent wages.

35. "C'est une enfant des champs, âpre, sauvage et fière/Et son galbe fait bien sur ce simple décor..." "Phidias eut révélé le chef d'œuvre que voile/Cette jupe taillée à grands coups d'ébauchoir." Vachon dates to 1877 both the poem from which the first lines are taken, and the painting, a *Gleaner*, which it accompanied. The next lines of verse are from a poem of 1890. See Vachon, *Jules Breton*, p. 85. Vachon, echoing Breton, declares: "Les femmes de l'Artois sont grandes, vigoreuses et imposantes dans l'ampleur des formes auxquelles le développement par le travail des champs donne une grace fière et robuste" (p. 100).

36. *Courbet*, 1977, p. 134. Among other "oriental" elements Toussaint finds present in the work are the high viewpoint, the monochromatic gray-and-blond color scheme, and the poses of the figures. Aside from the fact that, as she admits, 1854 is rather early for the presence of such elements in Courbet's art, I find no visual affirmation of such influence in the painting itself: the colors are not really *that* monochromatic, but markedly warm and bright in certain areas, like the skirt and bodice of the protagonist, or her yellow neckscarf; nor is there any sense in *The Grain Sifters* of that decorative flattening or suave linear emphasis characteristic of the Japanese print.

37. Julius Meier-Graefe, *Modern Art*, trans. Florence Simmonds and George W. Chrystal (New York: G. P. Putnam's Sons, 1908), vol. I, p. 233.

38. "J'ai un tableau de mœurs de campagne qui est fait de cribleuses de blé qui entra dans la série des *Demoiselles de village*, tableau étrange aussi." Cited in *Courbet*, 1977, p. 134. He also described it as a "tableau de mœurs de paysan" when writing to Alfred Bruyas in an undated letter, probably from early 1855. See Pierre Borel, *Le Roman de Gustave Courbet, d'après une correspondance originale du grand peintre* (Paris: E. Sansot, 1922, 2nd edition), p. 61.

39. "Les Cribleuses de blé, scène de mœurs agricoles, Franche-Comté."

40. "Les Cribleuses ou les enfants des cultivateurs du Doubs," Borel, *Le Roman de Gustave Courbet*. It was also shown in Nantes in 1861. What was perhaps a sketch for the work was evidently shown in Le Havre in 1858 and perhaps in London in 1859: Francis Haskell found a reference to what may have been the latter work in a London catalogue of 1859. See *Courbet*, 1977, pp. 134–135. Professor William Gerdts has informed me in personal conversation that *The Grain Sifters* was exhibited in New York in 1859.

41. Weber, *Peasants into Frenchmen*, p. 125.

42. These are traditional identifications, reiterated by Hélène Toussaint in *Courbet*, 1977, p. 13. Toussaint also hypothesizes that the boy to the right is Courbet's illegitimate son, Désiré Binet, born in 1847, hence 6 years old when the painting was begun. She finds the figure comparable to that of "l'enfant qui dessine dans *L'Atelier*...dont nous disons qu'il est très vraisemblablement le petit Désiré que Courbet a toutes sortes de raisons d'introduire dans l'œuvre qui est l'histoire de sept ans de sa vie."

43. For a detailed examination of the function, structure and history of both the *van* and the *crible*, see *Cours complet d'agriculture théorique et pratique...*, eds. Francois Rozier and M. le Baron de Morogues et al. (Paris: Marchant, Drevet, Crapart, Caille and Ravier, 1785–1805). For the *crible*, see vol. 7, pp. 371–372 and pl. cxxcii; for the *van*, vol. 17, pp. 265–269 and pl. cccxxvii. Millet's original *Winnower* (not illustrated) was sold out of Ledru-Rollin's collection to an American in 1854. See Kenneth Lindsay, "Millet's Lost Winnower Rediscovered," *Burlington Magazine*, 116 (May 1974), pp. 239–245. In later versions, Millet toned down the subversive implication of the *bonnet rouge* and the *tricolor* color scheme of the original. See T. J. Clark, *The Absolute Bourgeois: Artists and Politics in France 1848–1851* (Greenwich, Conn.: New York Graphic Society, 1973), p. 64 and Lindsay, "Millet's Lost Winnower Rediscovered," pp. 240–241 and note 12, p. 240.

44. The instrument has been denominated a *blutoir*, a closely related implement, by Suzanne Tardieu, in her important article "Un Blutoir du Berri," *Bulletin des Musées de France*, XII, no. 2 (February 1947), pp. 10–13, in which she illustrates the *blutoir* in question and points out a similar implement in Courbet's *The Grain Sifters*. The *blutoir*, however, is generally meant for the refining of flour. See Paul Dubreuil, *Dictionnaire populaire d'agriculture pratique* (Paris: Jouvet et Cie., 1895), p. 220, whereas the *tarare*, like the *van* and the *crible*, was intended more exclusively for the cleaning of grain. It was an extremely popular device during the nineteenth century, effecting, according to the authors of the *Cours complet d'agriculture* (vol. 17, p. 265), "une immense économie dans le travail de main d'œuvre nécessaire pour nettoyer des rains [et] aussi la moyen d'opérer ce nettoiement avec une bien plus grande perfection qu'il n'est possible de la faire par les procédés employés précédemment."

45. See especially Hofmann, "Courbets Wirklichkeiten," pp. 600–603.

46. The critic Edmond About evidently found the pose of the grain sifter not only indecent but trivial as well, *ibid.*, p. 600. Hofmann, for example, sees *The Grain Sifters* as multidimensional in its metaphoric implications, *ibid.*, p. 600 and note 36, p. 613. For example, he compares the kneeling figure of the grain sifter with her outstretched implement to that of Danaë awaiting the shower of gold and connects the figure to a universal mythology of fertility embodied in the female's symbolic embrace with the male principle, a theory articulated by J. J. Bachofen in *Mutterrecht und Urreligion*, ed. V. Rudolf Marx (Leipzig: A. Kroner, 1926).

47. According to Andreas Pigler, *Barockthemen: Eine Auswahl von Verzeichnissen zur Ikonographie des 17. und 18. Jahrhunderts* (Budapest: Verlag der Ungarischen Akademie der Wissenschaften, 1956), vol. II, p. 346,

Tuccia was a vestal who carried water in her sieve to demonstrate her purity. Her story is recounted in Valerius Maximus, VII, 1, 5 and Pliny, *Natural History*, XXVII, 12. She evidently served as an emblem of chastity for Ripa and appeared as a personification of virginity in works by Rubens, Coypel and Suvée as well as in images by Mantegna, Beccafumi, Parmigianino and Tintoretto.

48. The work, an engraving, has been attributed to François Gentil and many others. The composition has been connected to Ruggiero da Ruggieri, a mysterious artist of the School of Fontainebleau, although John Schloder has told me in correspondence that Giovanni Francesco Penni is a possible author. The engraving may be found at the Metropolitan Museum in the Maniette Scrapbook of Parmigianino and is mentioned in Félix Herber, *Les Graveurs de l'Ecole de Fontainebleau* (1896–1900), viii, p. 33, no. 10. Republished by B. M. Israel, 1969 (Amsterdam). I am grateful to Sylvie Béguin and John Schloder for this interesting information.

49. Breton's *Sifters of Rapeseed* was originally shown in the 1861 Salon. A version of 1866 is now in the Corcoran Gallery, Washington, D.C.

50. This illustration has been reproduced in *Käthe Kollwitz*, 2nd edition (Frankfurt: Frankfurter Kunstverein, 1973), fig. 17.

51. De Beauvoir discusses the notion of "woman-as-other" in great detail in the section dedicated to myths in *Le Deuxième Sexe* (Paris: Gallimard, 1949), pp. 185–278, pointing out that female mythic or allegorical figures can "stand for almost any quality, good or bad, as long as it, and they, are defined exclusively in relation to men" (p. 192).

52. Françoise Forster-Hahn, *Käthe Kollwitz, 1867–1945: Prints, Drawings, Sculpture* (Riverside, California: University Art Galleries, 1978), p. 6. Forster-Hahn discusses the whole *Peasants' War* series with great penetration, pp. 15–19.

53. Bebel's *Die Frau und der Sozialismus* was a most successful popularization of the essentials of social democracy as well as those of women's liberation. First published in 1883, it had reached over fifty editions in the original German by the time its author died in 1913. Bebel argued that women's emancipation could only take place in a socialist society. August Bebel, *Woman under Socialism*, 33rd edition, trans. D. de Leon, introd. L. Coser (New York: Schocken Books, 1971), p. vii and Forster-Hahn, *Käthe Kollwitz*, p. 4.

54. Otto Nagel, *Käthe Kollwitz* (Greenwich, Conn., New York Graphic Society, 1971), p. 35.

55. Natalie Zemon Davis, "Woman on Top," in her *Society and Culture in Early Modern France* (Stanford, California: Stanford University Press, 1975), pp. 124–151, esp. p. 129.

56. The two figures may be caricatural references to two of the most prominent feminists of the day, Jeanne Déroin and Eugénie Niboyet. Rentmeister feels that in the entire *Divorcees* series Daumier simply bodies forth the attitude of *Charivari* and its middle-class readers. See her "Daumier und das hässliche Geschlecht," pp. 69–71, as in note 4 above.

57. For a discussion of caricatures of women of the Commune, see James A. Leith, "The War of Images surrounding the Commune" in *Images of the Commune*, ed. James A. Leith (Montreal and London: McGill/Queen's University Press, 1978), pp. 135–138. For the role of women in the Commune, see Edith Thomas, *Les Pétroleuses* (Paris: Gallimard, 1963).

58. For a complete analysis of the complex contemporary political and religious references contained in or implied by Bruegel's *Dulle Griet*, see Margret A. Sullivan, "Madness and Folly: Pieter Bruegel the Elder's *Dulle Griet*," *Art Bulletin*, 59 (March 1977), pp. 55–66.

59. It is significant that his own little image of the barricades of 1848, a frontispiece for *Le Salut public*, no. 2, shows a perfectly ordinary man in ragged contemporary dress leading the charge up the barricades. Daumier, however, contributed an allegorical half-nude figure of the Republic to a government-sponsored contest at the time. See Bernard Lehmann, "Daumier and the Republic," *Gazette des Beaux-Arts*, 27 (February 1945), pp. 105–120, and Albert Boime, "The Second Republic's Contest for the Figure of the Republic," *Art Bulletin*, 53 (March 1971), pp. 68–83.

Chapter Four
Notes to pages 106–151

1. Cited in Champfleury, "Lettre confidentielle à mon ami Courbet," 30 July 1870, in *Le Réalisme*, eds. Geneviève and Jean Lacambre (Paris: Hermann, 1973), p. 190.

2. Walter Benjamin, *The Origin of German Tragic Drama*, trans. J. Osborne (London: NLB, 1977), p. 178.

3. Jane Gallup, *Reading Lacan* (Ithaca: Cornell University Press, 1985), p. 21.

4. The letter, cited by Hélène Toussaint in *Gustave Courbet (1819–1877)* (Paris: Grand Palais, 1977), pp. 246–247—hereafter *Courbet, 1977*—was written to his friend Français to ask the latter to persuade the Universal Exposition jury to extend the time limit for the submission of his pictures.

5. For more specific information about the cast of characters see the complete text of the letter, available in English translation in Hélène Toussaint et al., *Gustave Courbet, 1819–1877* (London: Royal Academy of Arts, 1978), pp. 254–255. All of the English translations of material from *Courbet*, 1977 are taken from this source.

6. Emile Littré, *Dictionnaire de la langue française*, ed. J. Pauvert (Paris: Hachette, 1936), 2: 317. ("Sorte de métaphore continuée, espèce de discours qui est d'abord présenté sous un sense propre et qui ne sert que de comparison pour donner l'intelligence d'un autre sense qu'on n'exprime point.")

7. Angus Fletcher, *Allegory: The Theory of a Symbolic Mode* (Ithaca: Cornell University Press, 1964), p. 2. He continues: "It [allegory] destroys the normal expectation we have about language, that our words 'mean what they say'. When we predicate quality X of a person Y, Y really is what our predication says he is (or we assume so); but allegory would turn Y into something other (*allos*) than what the open and direct statement tells the reader."

8. *Courbet*, 1977, pp. 246–247.

9. See, for example, the opinions of critics and men of letters from 1855 and after—A.-H. du Pays, Champfleury, Charles Perier, Paul Mantz, Jules Buisson and many others—gathered together as "Appréciations" in René Huyghe, Germain Bazain et al., *Courbet: L'Atelier du peintre, allégorie réelle, 1855*, Monographies des peintures du Musée du Louvre, III (Paris: Editions des Musées Nationaux, 1944), pp. 24–28. Delacroix, who greatly admired *The Painter's Studio* when he saw it in Courbet's exhibition in 1855, referring to it as "one of the most singular works of our time," simply refused to deal with its meaning at all. *Journal*, 3 August 1855, cited in Huyghe, Bazain et al., *Courbet*, pp. 24–25.

10. For interpretations of *The Painter's Studio* see Werner Hofmann, *The Earthly Paradise* (New York, George Braziller, 1961), pp. 11–49; Benedict Nicolson, *Courbet: The Studio of the Painter* (New York: The Viking Press, 1973); Alan Bowness, *Courbet's "Atelier du peintre"* (University of Newcastle-upon-Tyne, 1972); Linda Nochlin, "The Invention of the Avant-Garde: France, 1830–80," *Art News Annual*, 34 (1968), pp. 13–16; Pierre Georgel, "Les Transformations de la peinture vers 1848, 1855, 1863," *Revue de l'art*, 27 (1975), pp. 69–72; James Henry Rubin, *Realism and Social Vision in Courbet and Proudhon* (Princeton, N.J.: Princeton University Press, 1980), especially pp. 38–63. This list is by no means exhaustive. See *Courbet*, 1977, p. 243 for further references.

11. This opposition between the side of the shareholders and friends on the right and the masses, "wretchedness, poverty, wealth, the exploited and the exploiters, people who live on death" (*Courbet*, 1977, p. 246), to the left, perhaps—not merely coincidentally—repeats the opposition between the blessed to the right of the Judging Christ and the damned to his left in the Christian iconography of the Last Judgment.

12. Courbet's description of this character in the letter is as follows: "...A weather-beaten old man, a diehard republican (that Minister of the Interior, for instance, who was in the Assembly when Louis XVI was condemned to death, the one who was still following courses at the Sorbonne last year) a man 90 years old with a begging-bag in his hand, dressed in old patched white linen and wearing a broad-brimmed hat" (*Courbet*, 1977, p. 246).

13. Toussaint supported each of her specific identifications with a contemporary photograph or print of the public figure in question (*Courbet*, 1977, pp. 252–258).

14. Toussaint maintains, in considerable detail, that the crucial letter to Champfleury actually contains many hints about these hidden identities, hints available only to those who have a really idiomatic knowledge of the meaning of certain French turns-of-phrase of the period. For example, she explains, in support of her contention that the scythe-man is a portrait of Kosciusko, representing insurgent Poland, that in 1855 the French term "faucheur" signified "above all, a Polish

patriot." She convincingly explains the double meanings of many other phrases used by Courbet in his letter of explanation. These hints were, she feels, certainly understood by Courbet's friend and champion Castagnary, when he declared in 1881 that *The Painter's Studio* "contains a whole side of topical reference which is escaping from us through the death of almost all its audience." See Hélène Toussaint, "A propos d'une Critique," Les Amis de Gustave Courbet, *Bulletin*, 61 (1979), pp. 10–13.

15. See *Courbet*, 1977, p. 253.

16. *Ibid.*, pp. 252–254.

17. *Ibid.*, pp. 254–255.

18. *Ibid.*, pp. 256–257. Toussaint originally identified the laborer representing Russian socialism as Alexander Herzen, who had worked with Proudhon in Paris until 1851. She later admitted to me, in conversation, that this figure was more likely to be based on a portrait of the anarchist Bakunin.

19. *Ibid.*, pp. 257–258. Toussaint's identification of this *braconnier* or poacher-figure with Napoleon III, based on similarity of appearance and meaningful hints in accouterments—the seated figure is wearing the jack-boots which often "stood for" the forbidden image of the Emperor in cartoons—is extremely convincing.

20. *Ibid.*, p. 264.

21. Klaus Herding, "Das *Atelier des Malers*: Treffpunkt der Welt und Ort der Versöhnung," in *Realismus als Widerspruch: Die Wirklichket in Courbets Malerei*, ed. Klaus Herding (Frankfurt am Main: Suhrkamp Verlag, 1978), pp. 223–247.

22. It is of course impossible to summarize Herding's whole article in a few sentences. I have, however, attempted to draw out the main points of his piece. I am grateful to Benjamin Buchloh for his translation of Herding's article.

23. Fletcher, *Allegory*, pp. 304–305 and 322–323. The author cites Northrop Frye, *The Anatomy of Criticism: Four Essays* (Princeton: Princeton University Press, 1957), p. 90, to prove his case.

24. See note 2 above.

25. Frederic Jameson, *Marxism and Form* (Princeton, New Jersey: Princeton University Press, 1971), p. 71.

26. Angus Fletcher refers to I. A. Richards's introduction of these terms in the latter's lectures, "The Philosophy of Rhetoric," in 1936. See Fletcher, *Allegory*, p. 11 and note 19.

27. Terry Eagleton, *Walter Benjamin or Towards a Revolutionary Criticism* (London: Verso Editions, 1981), p. 19.

28. Jameson, *Marxism and Form*, p. 72.

29. For the distinction between the work and the text, see Roland Barthes, *Le Plaisir du texte* (Paris: Editions du Seuil, 1973) and "De l'œuvre au texte," *Revue de l'esthétique*, 24: 3 (1971), esp. pp. 230–231: "L'œuvre est ordinairement l'objet d'une consommation... le texte demande qu'on essaye d'abolir...la distance entre l'écriture et la lecture...Le lecteur joue, lui, deux fois: il *joue au Texte* (sense ludique), il *joue le Texte*...Le Texte est à peu près une partition...il sollicite au lecteur une collaboration pratique. Ceci amène à poser...une dernière approche du Texte: celle du plaisir."

30. Hofmann, in *The Earthly Paradise*, pp. 11–49, is a rare exception. Hofmann does not, however, discuss the sketchy quality of the work in relation to allegory. For a passing reference to the fact that the painting is incomplete, see Nicolson, *Courbet: The Studio of the Painter*, pp. 18–20. For a first-rate analysis of the role of sketchiness, color and brushwork in Courbet's *œuvre* as a whole, see Klaus Herding, "Farbe und Weltbild: Thesen zu Courbets Malerei" in *Courbet und Deutschland* (Hamburg: Kunsthalle, 1978), pp. 478–492.

31. He did, however, have ample time to finish it after it was shown in Paris. The work was not sold and was shown in its present form twice during Courbet's lifetime: in Bordeaux in 1865 and in Vienna in 1873 (*Courbet*, 1977, p. 243).

32. Charles Baudelaire, "The Salon of 1845" in *The Mirror of Art*, trans. J. Mayne (London: Phaidon, 1955), p. 29.

33. For the implications of the sketch and sketchiness in both modernist and more traditional practice, as well as the issue of the privileging of the personal touch of the artist over the illusionistic representation of subject or narrative, see my lecture "The Sketch, Sketchiness, and the Effect of the Aesthetic in Nineteenth-Century French Art," delivered at the National Academy of Design, New York, 1981.

34. *Courbet*, 1977, p. 247. This group is presided over by the tortured, lifeless and nude lay figure behind it, which in turn creates further

meanings, and extends the dark, "pessimistic" implications of this section as a whole.

35. Herding, "Das *Atelier des Malers*, p. 241 and note 81.

36. Not, it must be emphasized, within the context of art-historical "influence." I am not trying to posit a specific formal or inconographic "influence" relating Dürer's *Melencolia I* to Courbet's beggar-woman. Courbet scholars have, however, attempted to point out such a relationship between the figure of Proudhon in the *Portrait of Proudhon and His Family in 1853* and that of the Dürer engraving. See *Courbet und Deutschland*, p. 266 and fig. 262e.

37. Benjamin, *The Origin of German Tragic Drama*, p. 152.

38. Norman Bryson, *Word and Image: French Painting of the Ancien Régime* (Cambridge: Cambridge University Press, 1981), p. 71.

39. Eagleton, *Walter Benjamin*, p. 20 and Benjamin, *The Origin of German Tragic Drama*, p. 202.

40. Eagleton, *Walter Benjamin*, p. 20 and notes 35, 36 and 37, which give his references to Benjamin's work.

41. Frye, *The Anatomy of Criticism*, p. 89. Joel Fineman cites Frye in his discussion of this dimension of allegory in "The Structure of Allegorical Desire," *October*, 12 (Spring 1980), p. 49. Also see Frederic Jameson, who, in the preface to *The Political Unconscious* (Ithaca: Cornell University Press, 1981), p. 10, declares that "interpretation is here construed as an essentially allegorical act, which consists in rewriting a given text in terms of a particular interpretive master code." Probably no critic has done more to reinstate allegory as the primary figure of interpretation than the late Paul de Man, in whose seminal essay "The Rhetoric of Temporality," originally published in 1969 (republished in *Blindness and Insight: Essays in the Rhetoric of Contemporary Criticism* [Minneapolis: University of Minnesota Press, 2nd edition rev., 1983], pp. 187–228), symbol is disparaged as a mystification and allegory associated with an "authentic understanding of language and temporality" (Jonathan Culler, *On Deconstruction* [Ithaca: Cornell University Press, 1985], p. 185). Indeed, de Man's study of the nature of figural language in the work of Rousseau, Nietzsche, Rilke and Proust is entitled *Allegories of Reading* (New Haven: Yale University Press, 1979).

42. A Barthean *punctum*? Perhaps. But even a *punctum* can be unravelled. See Victor Burgin, "Diderot, Barthes, *Vertigo*," in *Formations of Fantasy*, eds. V. Burgin, J. Donald and C. Kaplan (London and New York: Methuen, 1986), esp. pp. 86–101, for an interesting attempt. Virginia Woolf has commented most appositely on the male display (what Lacan calls *parade*) embodied by Courbet in his striped trousers: "Your clothes in the first place make us gape with astonishment...every button, rosette and stripe seems to have some symbolical meaning." Virginia Woolf, *Three Guineas*, cited by Burgin in "Diderot, Barthes, *Vertigo*," p. 56.

43. Charles Baudelaire, "Puisque réalisme il y a" (1855) in *Œuvres complètes*, eds. Y.-G. Le Dantec and C. Pichois (Paris: Bibliothèque de la Pléiade, 1961), p. 637.

44. For the political implications of Courbet's image of Baudelaire in this painting, see the end of T. J. Clark's complex analysis locating the revolutionary context of Courbet's *Portrait of Baudelaire* (c. 1848), the image upon which that in *The Painter's Studio* is based. Of the portrait Clark says: "This is an image of privacy and self-absorption, a space where one man excludes the world of public statement." T. J. Clark, *Image of the People: Gustave Courbet and the 1848 Revolution* (Princeton: Princeton University Press, 1982 [orig. publ. 1973]), p. 75.

45. Charles Baudelaire, "Les Petites Vieilles" from *Tableaux Parisiens* in *Œuvres complètes*, pp. 85–86. ("Ces yeux mystérieux ont d'invincibles charmes/Pour celui que l'austère Infortune allaita!")

46. See Linda Nochlin, "Courbet's *L'Origine du monde*: The Origin without an Original," *October*, 37 (Summer 1986), pp. 76–86.

47. Or of ambiguously placed branches or "bisexual spindles," which Michael Fried, in his essay "Courbet's Femininity" in *Courbet Reconsidered*, eds. Sarah Faunce and Linda Nochlin (Brooklyn: The Brooklyn Museum, 1988), pp. 43–53, posits as signifiers of Courbet's feminine, or even proto-feminist, identification with his female subjects (more accurately, perhaps, defined as "objects").

48. The phrase "representing representation" of course refers to Michael Fried's article entitled "Representing Representation: The Central

Group in Courbet's 'Studio'," *Art in America* (September 1981), pp. 127–133.

49. For the relation of the ephebe, or youthful artist, to the master poet, see Harold Bloom, *The Anxiety of Influence: A Theory of Poetry* (London and New York: Oxford University Press, 1973), pp. 77–92.

50. Hélène Toussaint, and Klaus Herding following her, claim to see the portrait of Courbet's mother in the features of the nude model. See Herding, "Das *Atelier des Malers*," p. 309, note 13.

51. The female nude has been interpreted as an allegorical representation of Truth, Beauty, and/or Liberty by Margaret Ambrust Seibert, "A Political and a Pictorial Tradition Used in Gustave Courbet's *Real Allegory*," *Art Bulletin*, 65: 2 (June 1983), pp. 311–316. For a complex and suggestive iconographic reading of the nude and the central group as a whole in relation to an eighteenth-century allegorical print of The Rights of Man, see John F. Moffitt, "Art and Politics and Underlying Pictorial-Political Topos in Courbet's *Real Allegory*," *Artibus et Historiae*, 15: 8 (1987), pp. 183–193.

52. Klaus Theweleit, *Male Fantasies* (Minneapolis: University of Minnesota Press, 1987), vol. 1, p. 294. The italics are mine.

53. This youthful male figure can also, of course, be read as the Bloomean ephebe. See note 49 above.

54. Fried, "Courbet's Femininity," p. 45.

55. *Ibid., passim.*

56. He seems to have depicted himself as the post-coital lover in the 1844 version of this painting, in which he represented himself with his current mistress. He later painted her out and depicted himself wounded rather than relaxing.

57. For a good summary of the history of *The Wounded Man*, see *Courbet*, 1977, no. 35.

58. By the same token, one might postulate that Courbet was being proto-vegetarian in identifying, as I once suggested, with the dying trout in his poignant close-up painting, *The Trout*. What seems important to me is not whether or not the artist identifies with this or that figure or element in his painting, but what such identification means, how it is to be interpreted—and by whom.

59. Fried, "Courbet's Femininity," p. 46.

60. *Ibid.,* p. 47.

61. See Arthur Munby, *Munby: Man of Two Worlds* (Boston: Gambit, 1972) and *The Diaries of Hannah Culwick, Victorian Maidservant*, ed. Liz Stanley (New Brunswick: Rutgers University Press, 1984) for illustrations of the powerful working-class woman. A truly androgynous—and transgressive—imagery embodying muscular masculine arms and seductive feminine face had to wait for the twentieth century, most notably in the work of the woman collagist and member of Berlin Dada, Hannah Höch, in her provocative *Tamer* (1930).

62. For an important discussion of the theme of sleep in Courbet's work, viewed in the context of scientific and literary investigations of the theme during the mid-nineteenth century, see Aaron Sheon, "Courbet, French Realism and the Discovery of the Unconscious," *Arts*, 55 (February 1981), pp. 114–128.

63. Nor is the figure either fully awake or fully asleep, but rather in a state of languor associated with sexual availability or post-coital repleteness—again, a scandalous "intermediary" state.

64. Flora Tristan (Flore Célestine Thérèse Henriette Tristan y Moscozo), *Flora Tristan's London Journal: A Survey of London Life in the 1830s* (a translation of *Promenades dans Londres*), trans. D. Palmer and G. Pincetl (London: G. Prior, 1980), p. 78.

65. *Ibid.,* p. 78 and note 1. Horrifying as this image of transgression and degradation is, it becomes more so if we think of the "tossing of the liquids" as a euphemism for even worse—more basic acts of gendered desecration: men vomiting, urinating, or even defecating on the helpless bodies of women as a sign of ultimate contempt. Surely it is this ultimate transgressive befouling that the act—and Tristan's obsessive visual recounting of it—encodes. At the same time, the Tristan passages are interesting in the way that they seem to anticipate hostile critical reaction to the bold use of pigment characteristic of Manet and the Impressionists. This critical vocabulary constantly equates synoptic brushwork with "dirt," unmodulated passages of light and dark tones as "filthy," etc.

66. The presence of the male hat and gloves in the boat in the background of Courbet's painting also signals a certain attempt at moral narrative here. Holman Hunt's repentant fallen woman in the *Awakening Conscience* is also wearing white lingerie—a night-dress—as a token of her moral lapse.

67. This tract was published after its author's death in 1865. See P.-J. Proudhon, *La Pornocratie, ou Les Femmes dans les temps modernes* in *Œuvres complètes de Proudhon,* eds. C. Bougle and H. Moysset (Paris: M. Rivière, 1939), pp. 303–412.

68. P.-J. Proudhon, *Du Principe de l'art et de sa destination sociale,* in *Œuvres complètes de Proudhon,* eds. C. Bougle and H. Moysset (Paris: M. Rivière, 1939), pp. 1–301.

69. *Ibid.,* p. 199.

70. *Ibid.,* p. 201.

71. Susan Sontag, "The Pornographic Imagination," in *Styles of Radical Will* (New York: Delta, 1981), p. 45.

72. Of course, such practices within the realm of art need to be examined within the context of the nineteenth-century production of sexual discourses analyzed by Michel Foucault in the *History of Sexuality* (New York: Vintage Books, 1980). For the classic article on the differences constituted by reading vanguard practices in twentieth-century representation from a feminist perspective, see Carol Duncan, "Virility and Domination in Early Twentieth-Century Vanguard Painting," in *Feminism and Art History: Questioning the Litany,* eds. N. Broude and M. D. Garrard (New York: Harper and Row, 1982, orig. publ. 1973), pp. 293–313.

73. Susan Rubin Suleiman, "Pornography, Transgression and the Avant-Garde: Bataille's *Story of the Eye,"* in *The Poetics of Gender,* ed. Nancy K. Miller (New York: Columbia University Press, 1986), pp. 117–136.

74. I have attempted to stay as close to Suleiman's original text as possible in my transposition. Here is Suleiman, discussing Bataille as a prime example of the notion of discursive transgression in pornographic texts: "What we see here is the transfer...of the notion of transgression from the realm of experience—whose equivalent, in fiction, is representation—to the realm of words, with a corresponding shift in the roles and importance accorded to the signifier and the signified. The signified becomes the vehicle of the metaphor, whose tenor...is the signifier: the sexually scandalous scenes of *Histoire de l'œil* are there to 'signify' Bataille's linguistically scandalous verbal combinations, not vice versa." *Ibid.,* p. 120.

75. For the complex issue of women's viewing positions as set forth in recent feminist film theory, see Laura Mulvey, "Visual Pleasure and Narrative Cinema," *Screen,* 16: 3 (Autumn 1975), pp. 6–18; Mary Ann Doane, "Film and Masquerade: Theorizing the Female Spectator," *Screen* 23: 3–4 (September–October 1982), pp. 74–88; Alice de Lauretis, "Desire in Narrative" in *Alice Doesn't: Feminism, Semiotics, Cinema* (Bloomington: Indiana University Press, 1984), pp. 103–157; E. Ann Kaplan, "Is the Gaze Male?" in *Women and Film: Both Sides of the Cinema* (New York: Methuen, 1983), ch. 1; Annette Kuhn, *Women's Pictures: Feminism and Cinema* (London: Routledge and Kegan Paul, 1982), *passim*; and especially Mary Ann Doane, "The Desire to Desire" in *The Desire to Desire: The Woman's Film of the 1940s* (Bloomington: Indiana University Press, 1987), pp. 1–37.

76. This shifty and ambiguous viewing position must be differentiated from what has been termed "oscillation" and constitutes a pleasurable subject-position for women constituted in relation to an androgynous object of the gaze. I am grateful to Maud Lavin for bringing this distinction to my attention. See her *Cut with the Kitchen Knife: The Weimar Photomontages of Hannah Höch* (New Haven: Yale University Press, 1993). But this pleasurable oscillation is not possible in representations which position women as closed, replete, finished, perfect, natural objects; only in viewing those which position "her" as a construct of disparate fragments, as in the Dada photomontages of Höch, the present-day work of Barbara Kruger or the work of certain vanguard feminist film-makers.

77. Suleiman, "Pornography, Transgression and the Avant-Garde," p. 132. The author continues: "What does appear to me certain is that there will be no renewal, either in a poetics or in a politics of gender, as long as every drama, whether textual or sexual, continues to be envisaged—as in Bataille's pornography and in Harold Bloom's theory of poetry—in terms of a confrontation between an all-powerful father and a traumatized son, a confrontation staged across and over the body of the mother."

78. Heterosexual of course, and middle-aged, and above all, used to wearing clothes, having names and being in authority.

79. Proudhon, *La Pornocratie,* pp. 309–412. Proudhon firmly believed that women had the choice of being either housewives or harlots: nothing else. His book is the most consistent

anti-feminist tract of its time, and perhaps, any other, and as such is worthy of careful study. Certainly, it raises all the main issues about woman's position in society and her sexuality with a paranoid intensity unmatched in any other text.

80. I have borrowed the words, which seem appropriate to the occasion, of Julia Kristeva in "Motherhood According to Bellini" evoking the experience of *jouissance*. Julia Kristeva, "Motherhood According to Bellini," *Desire in Language*, ed. Leon Roudiez, trans. T. Gora, et al. (New York: Columbia University Press, 1980), p. 248. The women's laughter I have borrowed from the courtroom scene in Marlene Goris's film, *A Question of Silence*. Elaine Showalter, more briefly, imagines such role reversal in her dream of a feminist literary conference at the end of "Critical Cross-Dressing: Male Feminists and the Woman of the Year," in *Men in Feminism*, ed. A. Jardine and P. Smith (New York and London: Methuen, 1987), p. 132. (Showalter's article was originally published in *Raritan* [Fall 1983].)

81. Nevertheless, my utopian vision belongs to a well-established tradition, going back to the Middle Ages, that of the "world upside down." For a discussion of such role-reversing practices in early modern Europe and their relation to gender, see Natalie Zemon Davis, "Woman on Top," in *Society and Culture in Early Modern France* (Stanford, California: Stanford University Press, 1975), pp. 124–151. The classic investigation of carnivalesque practices, including that of role reversal, is Mikhail Bakhtin's *Rabelais and His World*, trans. H. Iswolsky (Bloomington: Indiana University Press, 1984). For the theme of utopian inversion in relation to Marxism, see Gerard Raulet, "Critique of Religion and Religion as Critique: The Secularized Hope of Ernst Bloch," trans. D. Parent, ed. T. Luke, *New German Critique*, 9 (Fall 1976), pp. 76–77.

82. Carnival, as Michael Holquist points out in his Prologue to Bakhtin's *Rabelais and His World*, must not, of course, be "confused...with self-serving festivals fostered by governments, secular or theocratic" (xviii). Our analogy between the traditional carnival and the Universal Exposition can only go so far. Nevertheless, Courbet made of it what he could: in a sense, he transformed, for his own productive purposes, a "self-serving festival"

into an irreverent carnival. The theme of the ruler paying homage to the artist had certain vogue in the earlier nineteenth century, in works created earlier in the century like Ingres's *Death of Leonardo da Vinci*, in which the artist expires in the arms of François I; or Joseph-Nicolas Robert-Fleury's *Charles V Picking Up Titian's Paint Brush*. See my "Gustave Courbet's *Meeting*: A Portrait of the Artist as a Wandering Jew," *Art Bulletin*, 49: 3 (November 1967), esp. pp. 218–219 and Francis Haskell, "The Old Masters in Nineteenth-Century French Painting," *Art Quarterly*, 34: 1 (Spring 1971), pp. 55–80.

83. For a detailed examination of hidden political references, often of a rather "basic" or "popular" nature, in two of Courbet's paintings of the 1850s—*La Mère Grégoire* and *Firemen Going to a Fire*—see Hélène Toussaint, "Le Réalisme de Courbet au service de la satire politique et de la propagande gouvernementale," Les Amis de Gustave Courbet, *Bulletin*, 67 (1982), pp. 5–27.

84. Fletcher, *Allegory*, p. 328. Fletcher further defines the political grounding of allegory as follows: "The art of subterfuge *par excellence*, it needs to be justified as an art proper to those moments when nothing but subterfuge will work, as in a political state where dictatorial censorship prevails" (p. 345). Also see Fineman, "The Structure of Allegorical Desire," p. 48: "...We can note that allegory seems regularly to surface in critical or polemical atmospheres, when for political or metaphysical reasons there is something that cannot be said."

85. See especially Thomas Crow, "Modernism and Mass Culture in the Visual Arts" in *Modernism and Modernity: The Vancouver Conference Papers* (Halifax, Nova Scotia: Nova Scotia College of Art and Design, 1983), pp. 215–264.

86. *Ibid.*, p. 224. For T. J. Clark on the *Burial at Ornans*, see his *Image of the People*, pp. 140–149 and 153–156.

87. For information about the Emperor's involvement in the Universal Exposition, see Herding, "Das *Atelier des Malers*," p. 238. For the most recent detailed examination of the art-politics of the 1855 Exposition, see Patricia Mainardi, *Art and Politics of the Second Empire* (London and New Haven: Yale University Press, 1987), pp. 32–120.

88. *Courbet*, 1977, p. 262.

89. See especially the letter from Courbet to his patron, Alfred Bruyas, describing his fateful luncheon with Nieuwerkerque, during the course of which the latter asked Courbet to do a painting for the Exposition of 1855 which would have to be submitted to two committees for approval. Courbet proudly rejected the offer, declaring to the Superintendent that he also was a Government and that he defied the Superintendent's to do anything for his (Courbet's) that he could accept. *Lettres de Gustave Courbet à Alfred Bruyas*, ed. P. Borel (Geneva: Pierre Cailler, 1951), p. 68.

90. Herding, "Das *Atelier des Malers*," p. 22.

91. Of course, it is important to remember that Courbet by no means renounced official acceptance. He showed eleven paintings—no small number for a relatively young man of thirty-six—at the government-sponsored exhibition in the Palais des Beaux-Arts.

92. For information about the fate of the painting between the time that Courbet exhibited it in 1855 and that of its purchase for the Louvre, see "En 1920, 'L'Atelier' de Courbet entrait au Louvre," Les Amis de Gustave Courbet, *Bulletin*, 29 (1961), pp. 1–13 and note 1, p. 2.

93. For a discussion of the depoliticization of Courbet and his work in the early years of the Third Republic, see my article, "The De-Politicization of Gustave Courbet: Transformation and Rehabilitation under the Third Republic," *October*, 22 (Fall 1982), pp. 65–77. Although there were always a few people, like Jules Vallès, who saw Courbet's life and his painting as primarily political in their meaning, the re-politicization of the artist's work was not achieved until 1941 when Meyer Schapiro published his remarkable article, "Courbet and Popular Imagery: An Essay on Realism and Naiveté," *Journal of the Warburg and Courtauld Institutes* (April–June 1941), pp. 164–191, in which the author insisted on the social and political meaning of Courbet's choice of language and the impact of 1848 on the formation of his style. This reading was the springboard for my own investigation of Courbet, in both my doctoral dissertation *Gustave Courbet: A Study of Style and Society* (New York: Garland, 1976, originally a Ph.D dissertation, New York University, 1963) and articles like "Gustave Courbet's *Meeting*: A Portrait of the Artist as a Wandering Jew" (see note 82 for reference). A full-scale revisionist reading of Courbet from the vantage point of a social history of art had to wait until T. J. Clark's *Image of the People* in 1973.

94. For a differentiation between *The Painter's Studio*, Courbet's work in general, and the project of modernism, see my "The Invention of the Avant-Garde: France, 1830–80" (see note 10 for reference).

95. The compulsive syndrome is, as Angus Fletcher astutely points out, the proper psychoanalytic analogue to allegory. See Fletcher, *Allegory*, p. 286. Compulsive behavior is, as Fletcher points out, like allegory, highly orderly and above all, supersystematic (p. 291); such compulsive systematization also marks to a high degree the utopian theories of Charles Fourier as well as the theories and practices of his followers: the utopian vegetarian, l'apôthe Jupille, for instance, who proselytized for socialist salvation through a non-carnivorous diet; or the Fourierist dramatist Rose-Marius Sardat, author of a bizarre didactic drama entitled "La Loi d'union, ou Nouvelle organisation sociale," in sixteen acts and a prologue, with a cast of 296 ranging in age from four to seventy, set in a "Temple de Bonheur" and setting forth the hopes, duties, pleasures and daily life in a phalanstery of eighty families in a rhetorical structure which might well be called, for lack of a better term, a "real allegory." Courbet's allegory must, of course, be distinguished from the wilder excesses of these utopian eccentrics described by Champfleury in *Les Excentriques*, 2nd edition (Paris: 1877, first publ. 1852), pp. 77–82, 149–151 and 155, but there is enough of that tradition of eccentric extremism remaining in *The Painter's Studio* to remove it from the realm of the simple, down-to-earth critique and elevate it to that of eschatological transformation. For the impact of Fourierist ideas on the iconography of *Studio*, see my "The Invention of the Avant-Garde," esp. pp. 18–19.

96. Ernst Bloch, cited in Raulet, "Critique of Religion and Religion as Critique."

Chapter Five
Notes to pages 152–179

1. Richard Thomson, for example, in his article "'Les Quat' Pattes': The Image of the Dog in Late Nineteenth-Century French Art," *Art*

History, 5: 3 (September 1982), p. 327, mentions the fact that Degas "included dogs in his portraits on several occasions" but does not mention the one in *The Bellelli Family*. He focuses on the more prominent pedigree hound represented in the artist's *Place de la Concorde* (now destroyed), and on other Degas works.

2. For the history of the portrait, its exhibition, and the identification of its subject, see the excellent analysis in the exhibition catalogue, *Degas*, eds. Jean Sutherland Boggs, et al. (Paris: Grand Palais; Ottawa: National Gallery of Canada; New York: The Metropolitan Museum of Art, 1988–89), cat. no. 20; hereafter cited as *Degas*, 1988–89. The painting is dated there 1858–67. For the classic analysis of the painting and Degas's relation to the family see Jean Sutherland Boggs, "Edgar Degas and the Bellellis," *Art Bulletin*, 37: 2 (June 1955), pp. 127–136. Also see the revision of that article in *Degas og familien Bellelli/Degas et la famille Bellelli*, ed. H. Finsen (Copenhagen: Ordrupgaard, 1983), pp. 14–19.

3. The ambiguity of the concept of the family at the time Degas painted the Bellellis is indicated by the fact that, during the 1860s, the "interior of the middle-class home became the prevailing metaphor for a refuge where authentic feelings could be safely acted out"; yet at the same time, "strained relations between the sexes—within marriage and without—provided the theme for countless novels, plays, illustrations and paintings of this period." For a discussion of both of these aspects in the representation of the family interior, especially in the visual arts, see Susan J. Sidlauskas, "A 'Perspective of Feeling': The Expressive Interior in Nineteenth-Century Realist Painting," Ph.D Dissertation, University of Pennsylvania, 1989, pp. 80–81 and 101. For a consideration of the theatrical representation of the theme of dissension within the "modern" family, see Charles Edward Young, "The Marriage Question in Modern French Drama," *University of Wisconsin Bulletin*, 5: 4 (1912), n.p. I will be dealing with the problems of the family and its representation in considerable detail below.

4. Roy McMullen, *Degas: His Life, Times, and Work* (Boston: Houghton Mifflin, 1984), p. 52.

5. *Degas*, 1988–89, pp. 81–82.

6. McMullen, *Degas*, p. 53.

7. *Ibid.*, p. 66.

8. For information and further interpretation of this painting, see *Degas*, 1988–89, cat. no. 146.

9. Compare, for example, Degas's *Giovanna and Giulia Bellelli* with Morisot's *Two Seated Women* (c. 1869, also known as *The Sisters*) or Degas's *Viscount Lepic and His Daughters* (1871) with Morisot's *Julie Manet and Her Father* to see the difference. The same point might be made in the case of the representation of fathers and sons by comparing Mary Cassatt's *Alexander Cassatt and His Son* (1884) with Degas's *Henri Rouart and His Son Alexis* (1895–98).

10. The term "uneasy" applied to Degas's images must inevitably recall Eunice Lipton's memorable study, *Looking into Degas: Uneasy Images of Women and Modern Life* (Berkeley/Los Angeles: University of California Press, 1986).

11. Henri Joseph Baudrillart, *La Famille et l'éducation en France dans leurs rapports avec l'état de la société* (Paris: Didier et cie, 1874).

12. Translated into English as Jacques Donzelot, *The Policing of Families*, trans. R. Hurley (New York: Pantheon Books, 1979).

13. Mark Poster, *Critical Theory of the Family* (New York: Seabury Press, 1978). The bourgeois family model differs significantly from earlier aristocratic and peasant ones, coming into being only with the rise of capitalism.

14. *Ibid.*, pp. 169–178, *passim*.

15. For an excellent analysis of the Habermasian schema and a critique of his social theorization of the family in terms of his neglect of the importance of gender roles in both the private sphere and within the economic world, see Nancy Fraser, *Unruly Practices: Power, Discourse and Gender in Contemporary Social Theory* (Minneapolis: University of Minnesota Press, 1989), pp. 113–143. As Fraser points out, "Habermas's account offers an important corrective to the standard dualistic approaches to the separation of public and private in capitalist societies. He conceptualizes the problem as a relation among four terms: family, (official) economy, state, and public sphere. His view suggests that in classical capitalism there are actually two distinct but interrelated public/private separations. One public/private separation operates at the level of 'systems,' namely, the separation of the state or public system, from

the (official) capitalist economy, or private system. The other public/private separation operates at the level of the 'lifeworld,' namely, the separation of the family, or private lifeworld sphere from the space of political opinion formation and participation, or public lifeworld sphere. Moreover, each of these public/private separations is coordinated with the other. One axis of exchange runs between private system and private lifeworld sphere, that is, between (official) capitalist economy and modern restricted nuclear family...The roles of worker and consumer link the (official) private economy and the private family, while the roles of citizen and (later) client link the public state and the public opinion institutions" (pp. 124–125).

16. Still further contradictions are offered by the fact that the older modes of conceiving of the family in some way coincided quite well with capitalist aims of cementing Gemeinschaft with Gesellschaft and making the family work together with larger public and capitalist institutions to further the objectives of productivity, i.e. the notion that stable, well-disciplined family units "worked" better. And yet such coherence goes against another notion of the family, familiar especially to readers of English social history of the mid-nineteenth century, as the very opposite, a redemption of the cold, impersonal, competitive public arena of money-making, an oasis of privacy, run by the "angel of the house" as an antidote to the harsh market-place which constituted the public, masculine world.

17. I borrow heavily here from the excellent analysis of the novel by Demetra Palmari, "The Shark Who Swallowed His Epoch: Family, Nature and Society in the Novels of Emile Zola," published in the collection of essays entitled *Changing Images of the Family*, eds. V. Tufte and B. Myerhoff (New Haven and London: Yale University Press, 1979), pp. 155–172.

18. *Ibid.*, p. 164. Palmari focuses on a single family represented in the novel, the Josserands, who, in their obsession with obtaining a good *parti* for their daughters, echo the situation recounted of Laura in the Bellelli chronicles. Says Palmari of the Zola's Josserands: "The daughters must be married, and the search for husbands is the mother's obsession, for marriage is the basis of their

moral system and world view. In truth, marriage is itself a mask of morality, for it is usually a façade for adulterous intrigues.

The Josserands are prepared to do anything to marry off their daughters, and the girls care little about the choice of husbands, for their paramount concern is to be married. Berthe's mother lies about her daughter's dowry and steals a small inheritance from her retarded son in order to enlarge the sum. Pushed into an extreme position—the mother admits she would go so far as to commit murder to get her daughter properly married—she reveals herself as a victim crippled by society who in turn victimizes and oppresses her daughter...The plot is a maze of illicit liaisons for which marriage and family are a thinly respectable façade. It ends with a final allegorization of the servants' court. 'When it thawed, the walls dripped with damp, and a stench arose from the little dark quadrangle. All the secret rottenness of each floor seemed fused in this stinking drain'" (pp. 164–165).

19. She continues: "It is a code so rigid and hostile to all that is natural—all that is spontaneous in humanity—that it is completely unenforceable. In creating such rigid moral standards society becomes not a protector but an enemy of life, love and honesty. Ideally, it is the family that provides order against external chaos, but to do so it must be allowed a degree of flexibility and naturalness. Too great rigidity in this...itself engenders chaos. Love and spontaneity reappear because these aspects of life cannot be eliminated, but they are garbed in their dark manifestations—as exploitative sexuality, brutal confrontations, violent outbursts—more disruptive, disorderly, and threatening to the social order than they would have been if allowed a proper place to begin with." *Ibid.*, pp. 165–166, *passim*.

20. The Goncourts, for instance, are obsessed with this issue. See T. J. Clark, *The Painting of Modern Life: Paris in the Art of Manet and His Followers* (New York: Knopf, 1985); Alain Corbin, *Les Filles de noce: Misère sexuelle et prostitution aux 19ᵉ et 20ᵉ siècles* (Paris: Aubier Montaigne, 1978); Hollis Clayson, "*Avant-Garde* and *Pompier* Images of Nineteenth-Century French Prostitution: The Matter of Modernism, Modernity and Social Ideology" in *Modernism and Modernity: The Vancouver Conference Papers* (Halifax, Nova

Scotia: Nova Scotia College of Art and Design, 1983), pp. 43–64; and most recently, Charles Bernheimer, *Figures of Ill Repute: Representing Prostitution in Nineteenth-Century France* (Cambridge, Mass., Harvard University Press, 1989), for important discussions of the discourse of prostitution. Clark and others have seen the confusion between respectability and prostitution as central to the construction of the social problems of later nineteenth-century France.

21. See, for example, their anecdote of the adorable and apparently respectable middle-class mother and daughter glimpsed in the park—the very models of domestic and filial virtue—whom they later find out are notorious whores specializing in serial fellatio, first mother, then daughter performing the act in the comfort of the client's own home. (I regret to say I can no longer locate the exact reference to this incident which I read many years ago in the complete edition of the Goncourt Journals: *Journal: Mémoires de la vie littéraire*, 1851–61, 1892–95, ed. Académie Goncourt [Paris: Flammarion, 1935–36], 9 vols. Attempts to track the story down in abridged versions of the *Journals* have been fruitless.)

22. For the complex publishing history of both the *Cardinal* stories and Degas's relationship to this publication, see "Degas, Halévy, and the Cardinals," in *Degas*, 1988–89, cat. nos. 167–169.

23. McMullen, *Degas*, p. 353.

24. Ludovic Halévy, "Pauline Cardinal," in *La Famille Cardinal* (Paris: Calmann Lévy, 1883), pp. 62–63.

25. Ludovic Halévy, "Madame Cardinal," in *ibid.*, pp. 19–20.

26. *Ibid.*, p. 32.

27. Edward D. Sullivan, *Maupassant: The Short Stories* (London: Arnold, 1962), p. 43.

28. Guy de Maupassant, *La Maison Tellier*, in *Œuvres complètes*, vol. 6 (Paris: Louis Conard, 1908), pp. 1–2. Indeed, as Emily Apter has pointed out, "the *maison close* (literally 'closed house') [is]...a subversive catachresis, yoking the bourgeois notion of 'home' to the morally tainted connotations of 'closet' sexuality," Emily Apter, "Cabinet Secrets: Fetishism, Prostitution, and the Fin-de-Siècle Interior," *Assemblage*, 9 [June 1989], p. 8.

29. Victor Koshkin-Youritzin, "The Irony of Degas," *Gazette des Beaux-Arts*, 87 (1976), p. 36.

30. For the series of brothel scenes, dated to *c.* 1876–85, see *Degas*, 1988–89, cat. nos. 180–188. Also see Eugenia Parry Janis, *Degas Monotypes*, (Cambridge, Mass.: Fogg Art Museum, 1968). Individual examples from the series will be referred to in terms of Janis's catalogue numbers, as "J."

31. I am, however, wary of exonerating Degas's complicity in the scopophilic practices of his time on the basis of the self-revelation of the medium constituted by these prints, as have, to some degree, Carol Armstrong and to a lesser one, Charles Bernheimer. See Carol Armstrong, "Edgar Degas and the Representation of the Female Body, in *The Female Body in Western Culture*, ed. S. R. Suleiman (Cambridge, Mass., Harvard University Press, 1985), pp. 223–242 and Charles Bernheimer, "Degas's Brothels: Voyeurism and Ideology," *Representations*, 20 (Fall 1987), pp. 158–186. I turn for the critique of this strategy of recuperation through formal practices to Constance Penley's negative assessment of structural materialist film practice and its attempt to subvert the identificatory modality of the apparatus by constantly revealing its presence, as a transgression which ultimately identifies with the Law. "The use of self-reflexive aesthetic strategies is, of course, almost the definition of avant-garde practice...[the use of] 'filmic material processes' as subject matter: celluloid scratches, splicing tape marks, processing stains, fingerprints, image slip, etc...But if we take Christian Metz's [the film theorist's] thesis that the primary identification is with the camera, then we must immediately question the 'objectivity' of the strategy of showing the spectator these 'prostheses' of his own body, of his own vision, because it is quite likely that this could *reinforce* the primary identification, which, as Metz argues, is the basis of the construction of a transcendental subject." Penley continues: "Side by side with the axiom of self-reflexivity is the emphasis on these films as epistemological enterprise." But, as she points out, "in its extreme form the desire to know slips from epistemology into epistemophilia, the perversion of the desire to know. This perversion involves the attempted mastery of knowledge and the demonstration of the all-powerfulness of

the subject." Constance Penley, "The Avant-Garde and its Imaginary, *The Future of an Illusion: Film, Feminism and Psychoanalysis* (Minneapolis: University of Minnesota, 1989), pp. 18–19. The same criticism could be offered of Degas's attempt to remove his work from the established codes of pornographic representation of his time through strategies of self-reflexivity. Both Armstrong and Bernheimer deal intelligently with the complex and, admittedly, ambiguous issues involved; I am not suggesting that there is an absolutely correct position on this issue: quite the contrary.

Chapter Six
Notes to pages 180–215

There are some discrepancies in the wording of titles and the dating of some of Mary Cassatt's work which will not be settled definitively until the *catalogue raisonné*, currently under preparation, is published. In a number of instances, the titles and dates in this essay vary from those given in *Mary Cassatt: Modern Woman*, the catalogue published in conjunction with the exhibition organized by the Art Institute of Chicago in collaboration with the Museum of Fine Arts, Boston, and the National Gallery of Art, Washington, D.C., 1998.

1. Griselda Pollock, "Modernity and the Spaces of Femininity," *Vision and Difference: Femininity, Feminism, and Histories of Art* (London and New York: Routledge, 1988), pp. 50–90.
2. Dorothy Richardson, *Pilgrimage* (New York: Alfred A. Knopf, 1967), vol. 3, p. 257.
3. *Ibid.*, p. 257–258.
4. *Ibid.*, p. 258.
5. Dorothy Richardson, "Some Notes on the Eternally Conflicting Demands of Humanity (*Not* 'Femininity'!) and Art," *Vanity Fair*, 24 (May 1925), p. 100.
6. Julia Kristeva, "Motherhood According to Bellini," *Desire in Language*, ed. Leon Roudiez, trans. T. Gora, et al. (New York: Columbia University Press, 1980).
7. Marie Christine Hamon, *Pourquoi les femmes aiment-elles les hommes? et non pas plutôt leur mère?* (Paris: Seuil, 1992).
8. Leo Steinberg, *The Sexuality of Christ in Renaissance Art and in Modern Oblivion* (New York: Pantheon Books, 1983).
9. For a discussion of Dodgson's photographs, see Susan H. Edwards, "Pretty Babies: Art, Erotica or Kiddies Porn?" *History of Photography*, 18: 1 (Spring 1994), esp. pp. 39–40.
10. Carolyn Kinder Carr and Sally Webster, "Mary Cassatt and Mary Fairchild MacMonnies: The Search for their 1893 Murals," *American Art*, 8 (Winter 1994), pp. 52–69.
11. Cassatt to Palmer in a letter of 11 October 1892. Cited by F. A. Sweet, *Miss Mary Cassatt, Impressionist from Pennsylvania* (Oklahoma: Norman, 1966), p. 131.
12. Judy Sund, "Columbus and Columbia in Chicago, 1893: Man of Genius Meets Generic Woman," *Art Bulletin*, 75: 3 (September 1993), pp. 443–466.
13. *Ibid.*, p. 464.
14. Cassatt to Palmer in a letter of 11 October 1892. Cited by Sweet, *Miss Mary Cassatt*, p. 130 and Sund, "Columbus and Columbia in Chicago, 1893," p. 462.
15. Nancy Mowll Mathews, *Mary Cassatt: A Life* (New York: Villard Books, 1994), p. 106.
16. Maud Howe Elliott, "The Building and Its Decoration," in *Art and Handicraft in the Woman's Building of the World's Columbian Exposition*, ed. M. H. Elliott (Paris and New York: Goupil and Company, 1893), p. 23.
17. Carol Zemel, *Van Gogh's Progress: Utopia, Modernity, and Late Nineteenth-Century Art* (Los Angeles and Berkeley: University of California Press, 1997), p. 235.
18. *Ibid.*, p. 237 and note 62, p. 280.
19. Cassatt to Palmer. Cited by Sweet, *Miss Mary Cassatt*, p. 131.
20. Laura Morowitz, *Consuming the Past: The Nabis and French Medieval Art*, Ph.D Dissertation, Institute of Fine Arts, New York, 1996, p. 1.
21. Cassatt to Palmer. Cited by Sweet, *Miss Mary Cassatt*, p. 131.
22. Cassatt to Hallowell. Cited in an 1864 letter from Hallowell to Palmer. See *Cassatt and Her Circle: Selected Letters*, ed. Nancy Mowll Mathews (New York: Abbeville Press, 1984), p. 254.
23. Louisine W. Havemeyer, "The Suffrage Torch, Memories of a Militant," *Scribner's Magazine*, 71 (May 1922), p. 528. Cited by Frances Weitzenhoffer, *The Havemeyers: Impressionism Comes to America* (New York: Harry N. Abrams, 1986), p. 205.
24. From Louisine Havemeyer's unpublished chapter on Mary Cassatt (intended for her

Memoirs), p. 33. Cited by Weitzenhoffer in *The Havemeyers*, p. 220.

25. Griselda Pollock, *Mary Cassatt* (London: Jupiter Books, 1980), p. 27.

Chapter Seven
Notes to pages 216–237

1. The smaller version, in the Berggruen Collection, on loan to the National Gallery, London, is painted in oil on canvas and measures $15^1/_2 \times 19^1/_4$ in. (39.5×49 cm). The large version in the collection of the Barnes Foundation, painted from 1886–88, measures about 7×10 feet ($81^3/_4 \times 121^1/_4$ in. or 207.6×308 cm). The relationship between the two versions is problematic, but I find convincing Françoise Cachin's suggestion that, rather than either being a preliminary sketch or a copy after the finished work, the smaller version may have been "an attempt to solve difficulties that Seurat encountered while he was painting the large version, probably in the summer of 1887." *Georges Seurat, 1859–1891*, ed. Robert L. Herbert (New York: The Metropolitan Museum of Art, 1991), p. 292; hereafter cited as *Seurat*, 1991.

2. For a fuller discussion of the issues at stake in the status of the male versus the female nude in the art practice of the late eighteenth and early nineteenth centuries, see Carol Ockman, "Profiling Homoeroticism: Ingres's *Achilles Receiving the Ambassadors of Agamemnon*," *Art Bulletin*, 75: 2 (June 1993), pp. 259–274 and Abigail Solomon-Godeau, "Male Trouble: A Crisis in Representation," *Art History*, 16: 2 (June 1993), pp. 286–312.

3. But see recent lectures by John Goodman, Whitney Davis and other scholars for a re-evaluation and reinterpretation of the role of both homophobia and (covert) homosexual desire in the emphasis on and construction of the male nude during the neoclassical period. On the other hand, the work of Jusepe de Ribera, who was the subject of an exhibition at New York's Metropolitan Museum in 1992, suggests that in certain cases the nude may not be the site of masculine desire at all, but rather that of suffering and martyrdom. In Ribera's painting the male nude constitutes the dominant theme of representation, while the female is completely absent. However, pain or incipient pain rather than sexual desire seems to be the emotion of choice in Ribera's *œuvre*, although the border between the two may, at times, be uncertain.

4. There is still another sense in which politics enters into the histories of both versions of the *Poseuses*: a politics of the possession of the actual paintings themselves rather than simply the bodies within them. In 1975 the conceptual artist Hans Haacke made the small version of the *Poseuses* the focus of a 14-panel installation questioning the commodification of so-called vanguard art and the increasing presence and power of corporate interests in the art market. The piece, however, was re-exhibited in the context of an exhibition featuring gender politics, a show called "Differences: On Representation and Sexuality" at the New Museum in New York in 1985. The late Craig Owen says of Hans Haacke's *Les Poseuses: Provenance of Small Version, 1888–1975*, that "Haacke's work has been included in a show dealing with gender difference presumably because its 'object' belongs to a long tradition of images of the female nude—images destined for a male viewer who supposedly accedes through the image to a position of imaginary control and possession" (Craig Owen, "Posing," in *Beyond Recognition: Representation, Power and Culture* [Berkeley: University of California Press, 1992], p. 202 [reprint of his essay in *Differences*]). Nor is this the only act of possession-dispossession suffered by the painting. In the case of the large version, the eccentric German collector Count Harry Kessler, urged on by Paul Signac who hoped that he would ultimately give it to the Berlin Museum, bought the work in 1898, had the margins cut, placed the painting on rollers and embedded it in the Art Nouveau decor of his house designed by Henry van de Velde, another arch-admirer of neo-Impressionism. See A. M. Hammacher, *Die Welt Henry van de Velde* (Antwerp: Mercator, 1967), p. 162, for a reproduction of the *Poseuses* as a feature of Kessler's decor. Says Hammacher of the *Poseuses* in this setting: "Two thirds of it was rolled up in a roller-frame (*Unrahmung*) which van de Velde expressly designed for that purpose, against his will under pressure from Kessler..." (p. 348). The painting was only released from architectural captivity in 1926 when Albert Barnes bought it, and deprived spectators of the opportunity to observe it

closely by placing it well above eye-level on a dimly lit wall in his mansion, where it remained, never available for other exhibitions, until the recent traveling show of "Great French Paintings from the Barnes Collection."

5. This was surely a subject that preoccupied Seurat. He treated it several times and from several vantage points throughout his career: in *Une Parade: Clowns et poney*, in which the audience is present; in *Le Chahut*, where it is suggested; and with most complexity, in *Circus*, where the audience assumes a dominating position.

6. See Billy Kluver, "A Short History of Modeling," *Art in America*, 79 (May 1991), pp. 156–168, 183.

7. See Gustave Kahn, *La Vie moderne*, 9 April 1887, p. 230. Cited in Henri Dorra and John Rewald, *Seurat: L'Œuvre peint, biographie et catalogue critique* (Paris: Les Beaux-Arts, 1955), p. 210.

8. Or perhaps, rather than the Three Graces, Seurat may have meant us to think of his *Poseuses* as an updated Judgment of Paris, with the artist, positioned outside the painting, as a latter-day Paris choosing which of the three models to hire. In any case, it is impossible to believe that Seurat took these traditional prototypes completely seriously. Not enough has been said about the role of humor and a kind of dry, acerbic caricature in Seurat's achievement as a whole, but it is an important factor in his expressive novelty: overt, of course, in the *Young Woman Powdering Herself*, less open in the figures in *Une Parade*; deft but definitely a factor in many of the Conté crayon drawings, which recall Daumier in their condensed satire of contemporary types and mores.

9. For an original and convincing analysis of these related visual phenomena in the nineteenth century, see Jonathan Crary, *Techniques of the Observer: On Vision and Modernity in the Nineteenth Century* (Cambridge, Mass., MIT Press, 1990).

10. See Françoise Cachin in *Seurat*, 1991, p. 278, for example, for reference to "the close grain of minute dots" that Seurat felt appropriate to the treatment of flesh in the large version of the *Poseuses*. I would like to thank Abigail Solomon-Godeau and Grant Rohmer of Eastman House, Rochester, for their help in finding and obtaining photographic material related to the *Poseuses*.

11. Richard Thomson, *Seurat* (Oxford: Phaidon, 1985), note 69, p. 231. Thomson himself rejects this suggestion in his excellent analysis of the *Poseuses* in this volume, p. 146.

12. Françoise Cachin in *Seurat*, 1991, p. 273.

13. Manet was perhaps the first painter to insist on the difference between the green of contemporaneity, green as an *artificial* color, and the green of nature. In works like *The Balcony* (1868–69), or *In the Conservatory* (1879), the green of the metalwork or of the bench on which a figure is sitting establishes the color as a blatantly synthetic and patently modern hue, as opposed to the more varied and subdued greens of leaves or foliage.

14. Cited in Dorra and Rewald, *Seurat*, p. 215.

15. This semi-hysterical intensification of decorative detail becomes even more pronounced in Seurat's unfinished final work, *Circus*, passages of which bear an unsettling resemblance to certain aspects of the art of the insane. This seemingly compulsive overworking is mainly in the foreground of the painting; the figures of the spectators in the background are quite differently, more calmly and descriptively treated. This variation leads one to think that Seurat's occasional decorative exaggeration is the product not of psychosis (there is no evidence that he suffered from one) but rather is the result of total—one might even say fanatical—adherence to a complex systematized method of pictorial expression. As Michael Zimmermann puts it: "Seurat's 'method' as he called it, was increasingly influenced by ideas about psycho-physics as transmitted by (Charles) Henry. He knew how he had to analyze the colors, what expressive effect the colors and lines would have, and how one went about isolating a picture as a harmonious unit from its surroundings. According to Teodor de Wyzewa, he even owned a catalogue in which a particular emotional effect was ascribed to every color" (Michael F. Zimmermann, *Seurat and the Art Theory of His Time*, Antwerp: Mercator, 1991). Zimmermann's book is invaluable for its detailed explication of Henry's psycho-mathematical aesthetic as well as for its examination of the impact of Henry's theories on Seurat. Zimmermann also takes seriously the social and political ambience of the artist, and devotes an entire chapter to Seurat and his anarchist friends (ch. 2, part VIII). In this

connection, one might look back to the rampant systematization and bizarre "methods" of certain political and social utopian movements. Fourierists, including Charles Fourier himself, were particularly prone to this obsession with system. For examples of such system-obsessed social saviors, see Champfleury, *Les Excentriques*, 2nd edition (Paris: 1877, first publ. 1852).

16. See Jonathan Crary, "Seurat's Modernity," in *Seurat at Gravelines: The Last Landscapes*, ed. Ellen Wardwell Lee (Indianapolis: Indianapolis Museum of Art in cooperation with Indiana University Press, 1990), pp. 61–69.

17. See Robert Herbert in *Seurat*, 1991, especially pp. 5–6, for a summary of the transformation of color from the "feminine" position of intuition to the "masculine" one of science in the theory and practice of Seurat and neo-Impressionism generally.

18. The most witty and reductive version of the central model is the standing *poseuse* in ink and graphite made to illustrate Paul Adam's article about Seurat in *La Vie moderne* in 1888. Here, Seurat suggests the rest of the painting by the most cursory fragments—part of the contour of an arm to the left and a curving back with the line of the buttocks just indicated to the right—and its technique, the *pointillisme* so associated with his style, by a sprinkling of dots. See *Seurat*, 1991, cat. no. 192, for a reproduction. The drawing was probably made after a small version of the *Poseuse de face*.

19. See *Seurat*, 1991, p. 286.

20. Carol Duncan, "Virility and Domination in Early Twentieth-Century Vanguard Painting," in *Feminism and Art History: Questioning the Litany*, eds. N. Broude and M. D. Garrard, (New York, Harper and Row, 1982, orig. publ. 1973), p. 300. More recently, the art historian James Herbert (not to be confused with Robert Herbert) has astutely pointed out in his discussion of the painting in a review of the recent Matisse literature: "The disinterestedness conveyed by modernist formal values provides the legitimating cover behind which the complex network of interests—sexual, financial, personal—between artist, model and viewer can play themselves out without revealing their interested character. Matisse's aesthetic makes the male gaze onto a nude woman appear as natural and above reproach as the process of arranging patches of pigment on canvas. Far from lifting art above the gender politics of its day," Herbert continues, "modernist formalism facilitated their silent operation by hiding them from view." James Herbert, *Art History*, 11: 2 (June 1988), p. 302.

21. See Thomson, *Seurat*, p. 146, for Seurat's identification with the models in the *Poseuses* in terms of being a wage-earner. "In February 1889 Octave Maus, who knew of an interested collector, wrote to ask the painting's price. Seurat replied that he would charge for a year's work at seven francs a day, by no means a high price for a large painting. Seurat could afford this with his private means...but he was charging much the same as a female model would earn a day...perhaps he saw his work as having much the same value as his models'."

List of Illustrations

Measurements are given in centimeters, then inches, height before width.

15.8 × 20.9 ($6\frac{1}{4}$ × $8\frac{1}{4}$). Collection of the Fundación Juan March, Madrid

25 HORACE VERNET *Scene of the French Campaign 1814*, 1826. Oil on canvas, 51 × 65 ($20\frac{1}{8}$ × $25\frac{7}{8}$). Private collection

26 HONORE DAUMIER *There's a Woman Who, in These Momentous Times, Is Content Merely to Play Stupidly with Her Children*, from the *Divorcees* series, 1848. Bibliothèque Nationale de France, Paris

27 HONORE DAUMIER *As Mother Is in the Throes of Creative Fervor, Baby Tumbles Head First into the Bathtub*, from the *Bluestockings* series, 1844. Bibliothèque Nationale de France, Paris

28 HONORE DAUMIER *The Laundress*, c. 1863. Oil on canvas, 49 × 33.5 ($19\frac{1}{4}$ × $13\frac{1}{8}$). Musée du Louvre, Paris. © Photo R.M.N.

29 THEODORE GERICAULT *The Raft of the Medusa* (detail), 1819: as **32**

30 THEODORE GERICAULT *Scene of Mutiny*, 1818. Brown ink over graphite on paper, 40.6 × 59.3 (16 × $23\frac{3}{8}$). Historisch Museum, Amsterdam

31 THEODORE GERICAULT *Family Group*, study for *Scene of Mutiny*, 1818. Brown ink over graphite on white modern laid paper, 20.3 × 29.9 (8 × $11\frac{3}{3}$). Courtesy of the Fogg Art Museum, Harvard University Art Museums. Bequest of Grenville L. Winthrop

32 THEODORE GERICAULT *The Raft of the Medusa*, 1819. Oil on canvas, 490.2 × 716.3 (16' 1 × 23' 6). Musée du Louvre, Paris

33 THEODORE GERICAULT *The Wounded Cuirassier*, 1814. Oil on canvas, 358 × 294 (11' 9 × 9' 8). Musée du Louvre, Paris

34 THEODORE GERICAULT *The Swiss Guard at the Louvre*, 1819. Lithograph, 39.5 × 33 ($15\frac{1}{2}$ × 13). Bibliothèque Nationale de France, Paris

35 THEODORE GERICAULT *Decapitated Heads*, 1818. Oil on canvas, 50 × 61 ($19\frac{5}{8}$ × 24). Nationalmuseum, Stockholm

36 THEODORE GERICAULT *Head of a White Horse*, c. 1816. Oil on canvas, 65.5 × 54.5 ($25\frac{7}{8}$ × 24). Musée du Louvre, Paris

37 THEODORE GERICAULT *Horses' Rumps and One Head*, 1813. Oil on canvas, 73.5 × 92.5 (29 × $36\frac{3}{8}$). Private collection

38 THEODORE GERICAULT *Portrait of Louise Vernet as a Child*, c. 1818. Oil on canvas, 60.5 × 50.5 ($23\frac{7}{8}$ × $19\frac{7}{8}$). Musée du Louvre, Paris

39 GUSTAVE COURBET *Portrait of Béatrice Bouvet*, 1864. Oil on canvas, 91.9 × 73.2 ($36\frac{1}{8}$ × $28\frac{7}{8}$). National Museum of Wales, Cardiff

40 BALTHUS *Young Girl with a Cat*, 1937. © ADAGP, Paris and DACS, London 1999. Oil on canvas, 88 × 78 ($34\frac{5}{8}$ × $30\frac{3}{4}$). Private collection. Photo: Pierre Matisse Gallery

41 THEODORE GERICAULT *Monomania of Envy*, 1822–23. Oil on canvas, 72 × 58 ($28\frac{3}{8}$ × $22\frac{7}{8}$). Musée des Beaux Arts, Lyon

42 THEODORE GERICAULT *Slave Trade*, 1823. Ink and pencil on paper, 30.6 × 43.7 ($12\frac{1}{8}$ × $17\frac{1}{4}$). Ecole National Superieure des Beaux-Arts, Paris

43 MARIE-GUILLEMINE BENOIST *Portrait of a Negress*, 1800. Oil on canvas, 81 × 65 (32 × $25\frac{1}{2}$). Musée du Louvre, Paris

44 THEODORE GERICAULT *Head of a Black Woman*, 1822–23. Oil on canvas, 40.5 × 32 (16 × $12\frac{5}{8}$). Musée Bonnat, Bayonne

45 THEODORE GERICAULT *A Pareleytic Woman*, 1821. Lithograph, 22.2 × 31.5 ($8\frac{3}{4}$ × $12\frac{1}{2}$). Bibliothèque Nationale de France, Paris

46 DANTE GABRIEL ROSSETTI *Found*, 1854. Oil on canvas, 36 × 31.5 ($14\frac{1}{8}$ × $12\frac{3}{8}$). Delaware Art Center, Wilmington, Delaware. Samuel and Mary R. Bancroft Collection

47 THEODORE GERICAULT *The Embrace*, c. 1817. Pencil, gouache and ink wash on paper, 13.5 × 21.3 ($5\frac{3}{8}$ × $8\frac{3}{8}$). Musée du Louvre, Paris

48 THEODORE GERICAULT *Nymph and Satyr*, 1817. Pencil, gouache and ink wash on paper, 18.7 × 23.7 ($7\frac{3}{8}$ × $9\frac{3}{8}$). Musée du Louvre, Paris

49 GUSTAVE COURBET *The Grain Sifters* (detail), 1855: as **50**

50 GUSTAVE COURBET *The Grain Sifters*, 1855. Oil on canvas, 131 × 167 ($51\frac{3}{4}$ × 66). Musée des Beaux Arts, Nantes

51 JEAN-FRANCOIS MILLET *The Gleaners*, 1857. Oil on canvas, 83.5 × 110 ($32\frac{7}{8}$ × $43\frac{1}{4}$). Musée du Louvre, Paris

52 GIOVANNI SEGANTINI *The Two Mothers*, 1889. Oil on canvas, 47 × 70.5 ($18\frac{1}{2}$ × $30\frac{3}{4}$). Galleria d'Arte Moderna, Milan. Photo Alinari

53 JEAN-FRANCOIS MILLET *Woman Feeding Her Child*, 1861. Oil on canvas, 114 × 99 ($44\frac{7}{8}$ × 39). Musée des Beaux Arts, Marseille

54 JULES BRETON *The Song of the Lark*, 1884. Oil on canvas, 110.6 × 85.8 ($43\frac{1}{2}$ × $33\frac{7}{8}$). Photograph © 1998 The Art Institute of Chicago. All Rights Reserved. Henry Field Memorial Collection, 1894.1033

55 JAN VERMEER *A Woman Asleep*, c. 1657. Oil on canvas, 87.6 × 76.5 ($34\frac{1}{2}$ × $30\frac{1}{8}$). The

86 GUSTAVE COURBET The Pavillon du Réalisme, drawing in an autograph letter, 1854. Musée Gustave Courbet, Ornans

87 EDGAR DEGAS *The Bellelli Family* (detail), *c.* 1858–60: as **88**

88 EDGAR DEGAS *The Bellelli Family, c.* 1858–60. Oil on canvas, 200 × 250 (78³/₄ × 98³/₈). Musée d'Orsay, Paris

89 EDGAR DEGAS *Young Spartans, c.* 1860–62, reworked until 1880. Oil on canvas, 109 × 155 (42⁷/₈ × 61). © National Gallery, London

90 EDGAR DEGAS *Interior, c.* 1868–69. Oil on canvas, 81 × 116 (31⁷/₈ × 45⁵/₈). Philadelphia Museum of Art. The Henry P. McIlhenny Collection. In memory of Frances P. McIlhenny

91 EDGAR DEGAS *The Duchessa di Montejasi with Her Daughters Elena and Camilla, c.* 1876. Oil on canvas, 66 × 98 (26 × 38¹/₂). Private collection

92 EDGAR DEGAS *Giovanna and Giulia Bellelli, c.* 1865–66. Oil on canvas, 92 × 73 (36¹/₄ × 28³/₄). Los Angeles County Museum of Art. Mr. and Mrs. George Gard De Sylva Collection

93 EDGAR DEGAS *Place de la Concorde,* 1876. Oil on canvas, 79 × 118 (31¹/₈ × 46¹/₂). Now destroyed. Photo Archives Durand-Ruel, Paris

94 EDGAR DEGAS *Ludovic Halévy Meeting Mme Cardinal Backstage,* from *La Famille Cardinal, c.* 1880. Black ink on white paper, 273 × 307 (10³/₄ × 12¹/₈). Private collection

95 EDGAR DEGAS *Dancers at Their Toilette, c.* 1879. Pastel and charcoal on gray, wove paper, 63.2 × 47.9 (24⁷/₈ × 18⁷/₈). Denver Art Museum

96 EDGAR DEGAS *The Name Day of the Madam,* 1876–77. Pastel over monotype, 26.7 × 29.5 (10¹/₂ × 11⁵/₈). Musée Picasso, Paris

97 EDGAR DEGAS *In the Salon, c.* 1876–85. Black ink on white paper, 15.9 × 21.6 (6¹/₄ × 8¹/₂). Private collection

98 EDGAR DEGAS *Two Women, c.* 1876–85. Black ink on light tan paper, 21.4 × 28.3 (8¹/₂ × 11¹/₈). Courtesy Museum of Fine Arts, Boston

99 EDGAR DEGAS *Waiting I, c.* 1876–85. Black ink on china paper, 21 × 15.9 (8¹/₄ × 6¹/₄). Private collection

100 EDGAR DEGAS *Two Girls in a Brothel, c.* 1876–85. Black ink on china paper, 16 × 12.1 (6³/₈ × 4³/₄). Private collection, Berlin

101 EDGAR DEGAS *Relaxation, c.* 1876–85. Black ink on china paper, 15.9 × 12.1 (6¹/₄ × 4³/₄). Private collection

102 EDGAR DEGAS *Siesta in the Salon, c.* 1876–85. Black ink on china paper, 15.9 × 21 (6¹/₄ × 8¹/₄). Private collection

103 EDGAR DEGAS *The Fireside, c.* 1876–77. Black ink on white paper, 42.5 × 58.6 (16³/₈ × 23). Private collection

104 EDGAR DEGAS *Brothel Scene, In the Salon, c.* 1876–85. Ink on china paper, 16.6 × 11.8 (6¹/₂ × 4³/₄). Private collection

105 EDGAR DEGAS *The Dancer with a Bouquet,* 1878. Pastel over monotype on paper, 40.3 × 50.5 (15⁷/₈ × 19⁷/₈). Rhode Island School of Design, Museum of Art

106 MARY CASSATT *Young Women Picking Fruit,* 1891. Oil on canvas, 130.8 × 90 (51¹/₂ × 35¹/₂). The Carnegie Museum of Art, Pittsburgh. Patrons of Art Fund

107 MARY CASSATT *Lady at a Tea Table,* 1883–85. Oil on canvas 73.4 × 61 (29 × 24). The Metropolitan Museum of Art, New York. Gift of the Artist, 1923

108 MARY CASSATT *The Cup of Tea,* 1880. Oil on canvas, 92.4 × 65.4 (36³/₈ × 25³/₄). The Metropolitan Museum of Art, New York. From the collection of James Stillman, Gift of Dr. Ernest G. Stillman, 1922

109 JOHN SINGER SARGENT *Lady Agnew,* 1892–93. Oil on canvas, 125.7 × 100.3 (49¹/₂ × 39¹/₂). National Gallery of Scotland, Edinburgh

110 NICOLAS POUSSIN *Self-Portrait,* 1650. Oil on canvas, 98 × 74 (38¹/₂ × 29¹/₄). Musée du Louvre, Paris

111 BERTHE MORISOT *Mme Pontillon,* 1871. Pastel on paper, 81 × 64.5 (32 × 25³/₈). Musée d'Orsay

112 MARY CASSATT *Miss Mary Ellison,* 1879. Oil on canvas, 85.5 × 65.1 (33³/₄ × 25⁵/₈). © 1998 Board of the Trustees of the National Gallery of Art, Washington D.C. Chester Dale Collection

113 MARY CASSATT *Emmie and Her Child,* 1889. Oil on canvas, 89.8 × 64.4 (35³/₈ × 25³/₈). Wichita Art Museum. The Rowland P. Murdoch Collection

114 MARY CASSATT *After the Bath,* 1901. Pastel on paper, 66 × 100 (26 × 39³/₈). © The Cleveland Museum of Art. Gift of J. H. Wade 1920

115 VINCENT VAN GOGH *Mme Roulin and Her Baby,* 1888. Oil on canvas, 92 × 73.5 (36¹/₄ × 28³/₄). The Philadelphia Museum of Art

116 MAX ERNST *Virgin Spanking Infant Jesus,* 1926. Oil on canvas 196 × 130 (77¹/₈ × 51¹/₈).

Private collection. © ADAGP, Paris and DACS, London 1999

117 PAULA MODERSOHN-BECKER *Mother and Child*, 1907. Oil on canvas, 82 × 124.7 (32¼ × 49⅛). Freie Hansestadt, Bremen

118 KATHE KOLLWITZ *Portraits of Misery IV*, c. 1903. Etching, 56.8 × 44.6 (22³/₈ × 17¹/₂). © DACS 1999

119 JAMES MCNEILL WHISTLER *Arrangement in Gray and Black: The Artist's Mother*, 1871. Oil on canvas, 144.3 × 162.5 (56⁷/₈ × 64). Musée du Louvre, Paris

120 MARY CASSATT *Reading "Le Figaro,"* 1877–78. Oil on canvas, 101.8 × 81.2 (39³/₄ × 32). Private collection, Washington D.C.

121 MARY CASSATT *Portrait of Katherine Kelso Cassatt*, 1889. Oil on canvas, 96.5 × 68.5 (38 × 27). The Fine Arts Museum of San Francisco

122 MARY CASSATT *Woman in Black at the Opera*, 1877–78. Oil on canvas, 80 × 64.8 (31¹/₂ × 25¹/₂). Courtesy Museum of Fine Arts, Boston. The Hayden Collection

123 MARY KELLY *Post Partum Document, Documentation VI*, 1978–79. Slate and resin, 18 units: 35.6 × 27.9 (14 × 11). Arts Council Collection, London

124 EDGAR DEGAS *The Tub*, c. 1886. Pastel on paper, 60 × 83 (23⁷/₈ × 32⁵/₈). Musée d'Orsay, Paris

125 MARY CASSATT *The Bath*, 1891–92. Oil on canvas, 100.3 × 66 (39¹/₂ × 26). The Art Institute of Chicago. Robert A. Waller Fund, 1910

126 KITAGAWA UTAMARO *Young Mother Bathing Her Baby* from *Customs of Women in the Twelve Hours* series, c. 1795. Print, 37.5 × 25 (14³/₄ × 9⁷/₈). The Metropolitan Museum of Art, New York. The H. O. Havemeyer Collection. Bequest of Mrs. H. O. Havemeyer

127 MARY CASSATT *The Bath*, 1890–91. Drypoint and aquatint, 29.5 × 21.8 (11⁵/₈ × 9³/₄). The Metropolitan Museum of Art, New York. Gift of Paul J. Sachs, 1917

128 MARY CASSATT *Little Girl in a Blue Armchair*, 1878. Oil on canvas, 89.5 × 129.8 (35¹/₄ × 51¹/₈). © 1998 Board of the Trustees of the National Gallery of Art, Washington D.C. Collection of Mr. and Mrs. Paul Mellon

129 MARY CASSATT *Baby's First Caress*, 1891. Pastel on paper, 76.2 × 61 (30 × 24). New Britain Museum of American Art. Harriet Russell Stanley Fund

130 MARY CASSATT *Mother and Child (The Oval Mirror)*, c. 1899. Oil on canvas, 81.6 × 65.7 (32¹/₈ × 25⁷/₈). The Metropolitan Museum of Art, New York. Bequest of H. O. Havemeyer, 1929. The H. O. Havemeyer Collection

131 MARY CASSATT *Mother and Child (Mother Wearing a Sunflower on Her Dress)*, 1905. Oil on canvas, 92.1 × 73.7 (36¹/₄ × 29). © 1998 Board of the Trustees of The National Gallery of Art, Washington D.C.

132 LEWIS CARROLL *Portrait of Evelyn Maud Hatch*, 1879. Rosenbach Museum and Library, Philadelphia

133 ROBERT MAPPLETHORPE *Jessie McBride*, 1976. Copyright © 1976 The Estate of Robert Mapplethorpe. Art + Commerce Anthology, New York

134 MARY CASSATT *Mother's Kiss*, 1890–91. Drypoint and aquatint, 43.5 × 30 (17¹/₈ × 11⁷/₈). Worcester Art Museum. Bequest of Mrs. Kingsmill Marrs, 1926

135 MARY CASSATT *The Fitting*, 1890–91. Drypoint and aquatint, 42.1 × 30.6 (16¹/₂ × 12¹/₈). Worcester Art Museum. Bequest of Mrs. Kingsmill Marrs, 1926

136 MARY CASSATT *The Coiffure*, 1890–91. Drypoint and aquatint, 43.2 × 30.5 (17 × 12). National Gallery of Art, Washington D.C. Rosenwald Collection

137 MARY CASSATT *The Letter*, 1890–91. Drypoint and aquatint, 34.7 × 22.8 (13³/₄ × 9). © 1998 Board of the Trustees of National Gallery of Art, Washington D.C. Chester Dale Collection

138 MARY CASSATT *The Lamp*, 1890–91. Drypoint and aquatint, 43.8 × 30.2 (17¹/₄ × 11⁷/₈). © 1998 Board of the Trustees of National Gallery of Art, Washington D.C. Chester Dale Collection

139 MARY CASSATT *The Omnibus*, 1890–91. Drypoint and aquatint, 45.7 × 31.4 (18 × 12³/₈). © 1998 Board of the Trustees of National Gallery of Art, Washington D.C. Chester Dale Collection

140 MARY CASSATT *Afternoon Tea Party*, 1890–91. Drypoint and aquatint, 42.5 × 31.1 (16³/₄ × 12¹/₄). © 1998 Board of the Trustees of National Gallery of Art, Washington D.C. Chester Dale Collection

141 MARY CASSATT *Modern Woman* mural for the south tympanum of the Hall of Honor, Woman's Building, World's Columbian Exposition, Chicago, 1893. Photo Chicago Historical Society

142 MARY FAIRCHILD MACMONNIES *Primitive Woman* mural for the north tympanum of the Hall of Honor, Woman's Building, World's Columbian Exposition, Chicago, 1893. Photo Chicago Historical Society

143 MARY CASSATT *Young Woman Picking Fruit*, 1892. Oil on canvas, 59.7 × 73 (23¹/₂ × 28³/₄). Private collection

144 MARY CASSATT Central panel of *Modern Woman* (detail), 1893: as **141**

145 CAMILLE PISSARRO *Apple Picking at Eragny-sur-Epte*, 1888. Oil on canvas, 60 × 73 (25⁵/₈ × 28¹/₄). Museum of Fine Arts, Dallas. Munger Fund Purchase

146 PAUL SIGNAC *Au Temps d'Harmonie*, 1895. Oil on canvas, 300 × 400 (118¹/₈ × 157¹/₂). Mairie de Montreuil

147 GEORGES SEURAT *Poseuses* (detail), 1886–88: as **149**

148 GEORGES SEURAT *Poseuses*, 1888. Oil on canvas, 39.5 × 49 (15¹/₂ × 19¹/₄). Berggruen Collection, Switzerland

149 GEORGES SEURAT *Poseuses*, 1886–88. Oil on canvas, 207.6 × 308 (81³/₄ × 121¹/₄) Photograph © Reproduced with the Permission of The Barnes Foundation™. All Rights Reserved

150 PIERRE-AUGUSTE RENOIR *The Large Bathers*, 1887. Oil on canvas, 115 × 170 (45¹/₄ × 67). Philadelphia Museum of Art. Mr. and Mrs. Carroll S. Tyson Collection

151 PIERRE PUVIS DE CHAVANNES *Autumn*, 1865. Oil on canvas, 106 × 100 (41³/₄ × 39³/₈). Wallraf-Richartz Museum, Cologne. Photo Rheinisches Bildarchiv, Cologne

152 WILLIAM BOUGUEREAU *The Nymphaeum*, 1878. Oil on canvas, 144.8 × 209.6 (57 × 82¹/₂). The Haggin Museum, Stockton, Calif.

153 J. E. DANTAN *The Model's Lunch*, 1881. Photo courtesy the author

154 JEAN-LEON GEROME *The Artist and His Model*, c. 1890–93. Oil on canvas, 51.4 × 38.7 (20¹/₄ × 15¹/₄). The Haggin Museum, Stockton, Calif.

155 JEAN-JACQUES PRADIER *The Three Graces*, 1831. Marble, height 172 (67³/₄). Musée du Louvre, Paris © Photo R.M.N.

156 J. MOULINS *The Three Graces*, c. 1855. Photo courtesy the author

157 A. CABARAS Sheet of Nude Studies, c. 1895. Photo courtesy the author

158 J. E. LECADRE *Profile Model Kneeling in the Clouds*, c. 1890. Photo courtesy the author

159 GEORGES SEURAT *A Sunday Afternoon on the Island of La Grande Jatte*, 1884–86. Oil on canvas, 207.6 × 307.9 (81³/₄ × 121¹/₄). The Art Institute of Chicago. Helen Birch Bartlett Memorial Collection

160 GEORGES SEURAT *Bathers at Asnières*, 1883–84. Oil on canvas, 200.9 × 299.7 (6' 6 × 9' 10). © National Gallery, London

161 GEORGES SEURAT *Still Life with Hat, Umbrella and Clothes on Chair*, study for *Poseuses*, c. 1887. Conté crayon, 31.1 × 23 .2 (12¹/₄ × 9¹/₈). The Metropolitan Museum of Art, New York. Bequest of Robert C. Baker, 1971

162 GEORGES SEURAT Drawing of a Bustle, study for *A Sunday Afternoon on the Island of La Grande Jatte*, 1885. Conté crayon, 30 × 17 (11³/₄ × 6³/₄). Musée Picasso, Paris. © Photo R.M.N./J. G. Berizzi

163 GEORGES SEURAT *Young Woman Powdering Herself*, 1890. Oil on canvas, 70.4 × 86.6 (27³/₄ × 34¹/₈). Courtauld Institute Galleries, London

164 GEORGES SEURAT *Le Chahut*, 1889. Oil on canvas, 168.9 × 140.9 (66³/₈ × 55¹/₂). Kröller-Müller Museum, Otterlo

165 JEAN-AUGUSTE-DOMINIQUE INGRES *Valpinçon Bather*, 1808. Oil on canvas, 146 × 98 (57¹/₂ × 38¹/₂) Musée du Louvre, Paris. Photo © R.M.N.

166 GEORGES SEURAT *Knitting Woman*, study for *A Sunday Afternoon on the Island of La Grande Jatte*, 1885. Conté crayon. Private collection

167 GEORGES SEURAT Back View of a *Poseuse*, study for *Poseuses*, 1886. Oil on panel, 24.5 × 15.6 (9⁵/₈ × 6¹/₈). Musée d'Orsay, Paris

168 GEORGES SEURAT *Poseuse de face*, study for *Poseuses*, 1886. Conté crayon, 29.9 × 24.1 (11³/₄ × 9¹/₂). The Metropolitan Museum of Art. Robert Lehman Collection, 1975

169 EDGAR DEGAS *Little Dancer Aged Fourteen*, 1880. Bronze, height 98.4 (38³/₄). Copyright Tate Gallery, London

170 HENRI MATISSE *Carmelina*, 1903–04. Oil on canvas, 81.3 × 59 (32 × 23¹/₂). Courtesy Museum of Fine Arts, Boston. Tompkins Collection. © Succession H. Matisse/DACS 1999

Index